بسم الله الرحمن الرحيم

In the Name of Allah
Most Merciful
and Compassionate

Port in a Storm

قَدْ نَرَىٰ تَقَلُّبَ وَجْهِكَ فِى السَّمَاءِ
فَلَنُوَلِّيَنَّكَ قِبْلَةً تَرْضَىٰهَا
فَوَلِّ وَجْهَكَ شَطْرَ الْمَسْجِدِ الْحَرَامِ
وَحَيْثُ مَا كُنتُمْ فَوَلُّوا وُجُوهَكُمْ شَطْرَهُ

We certainly see your face turning about the sky
Now We will surely turn you to a direction that shall please you
So turn your face towards the Holy Mosque
And wherever you all may be, turn your faces towards it

QUR'AN 2:144

Port in a Storm

A FIQH SOLUTION TO THE QIBLA
OF NORTH AMERICA

NUH HA MIM KELLER

WAKEEL BOOKS

AMMAN

© NUH HA MIM KELLER 2001

Published by
WAKEEL BOOKS, P.O. BOX 962660
AMMAN 11196, JORDAN
WWW.WAKEELBOOKS.COM

ISBN 9957-23-004-2 *paper*
ISBN 9957-23-014-X *cloth*

Library of Congress Control Number: 2001092401

*The Basmala calligraphy of the opening
page is in Persian Ta'liq script done by the late
Iraqi master Hashim al-Baghdadi. The other Arabic
calligraphy of the present volume is in Ijaza
script done by the contemporary master
Mehmet Özçay of Istanbul.*

Printed in England

Contents

List of Illustrations

Preface

NORTHEAST is the direction that the mihrabs of almost all mosques in North America have faced since the 1960s and 1970s. Exceptions to the present consensus have been previously confined to a few groups clearly far from the beaten path. But in the past year, some visiting mainstream Islamic scholars have also indicated, by word or deed, that the northeast qibla the majority pray to should be changed towards the east, or according to the second of the visitors, to the southeast.

The writer began the present work after being asked by a student in Los Angeles about the *fiqh* or "jurisprudence" position that a Muslim of the Maliki school finding his own direction for prayer far from Mecca may only face one of the four cardinal directions, north, south, east, or west, depending on which is closest to the actual physical direction of Mecca. The young man wondered whether as a Maliki under these circumstances it was obligatory for him to face towards the east when he prayed, or whether he could face towards the northeast. He was told at the time to simply pray towards the northeast, but when the author thought over the question afterwards, it seemed that a more comprehensive answer should be written, for a couple of reasons.

One is that the young man's belief that facing east is a Maliki position indicated that the issue might be understood as a fiqh difference; that just as one may choose one's school of jurisprudence, whether Hanafi, Maliki, Shafi'i, or Hanbali, one may also choose the qibla that corresponds to one's school, or to one's preference for some other reason. As the coming pages shall document in the fullest detail, drawn from both the schools themselves and from physical reality, this is not a fiqh difference. In reality, the Kaaba is one, and the qibla is one. Allah has created only one physical direction to Mecca from any particular place, termed the *samt* or "exact physical line direction" in the fiqh literature, while the schools only disagree as to how much of a margin of unintentional error or divergence from the exact direction is permitted to someone figuring out the qibla for himself, a margin comprised in what is termed the *jiha* or "approximate direction." The one qibla that all Muslims pray to, in the author's view the greatest symbol of Islamic unity, should not be compromised by a misunderstanding of this distinction.

Secondly, the arguments for facing east do not make the issue a "difference of ijtihad" in which the ordinary Muslim may choose as he will, because their premises are subtly but fundamentally flawed in ways that make them physically inapplicable to the real world in which alone the Sacred Law applies. This book's purpose is to lay these out for the reader's consideration in the simplest possible terms, while completing an authentic, knowledge-based fiqh understanding of what it means to face Mecca from North America.

The Need for This Book

A number of those who read the present work in manuscript asked the author searching questions. Was there a storm in the first place, that necessitated a port to put into? What need for this book, when most North American Muslims already pray to the northeast qibla? Why not just conduct a weekend seminar for the scholars concerned, present the points, and reach a private agreement that they could then convey to their students and followers?

The reasons are plain to whoever meets and speaks with these scholars, as the author has had the privilege to.

The first is that they are fuqaha who have taken a fiqh position, and fiqh positions are subject to discussion and refinement, acceptance and rebuttal, particularly when they affect numbers of Muslims. The traditional forum in Islam for such discussion has been fiqh treatises, which the present work, within its limited capacities, strives to emulate. In the author's view, the real danger is that the widespread incomprehension in North America today of the value of traditional Islamic knowledge will be aggravated by presenting as "fiqh" and "ijtihad" a qibla that most Muslims apprehend is a mistake. Although the east or southeast qibla is perhaps unlikely to ever win broad acceptance, the reputation of traditional knowledge is likely to suffer if no clarification is made. For many minds, a mistake labelled as fiqh could well label fiqh itself as a mistake.

Another is that the talent and hard work of the scholars concerned have made them well known in North America. They are sincere and intelligent; the eastern (or southeastern) qibla is not something that they have simply fallen for, but the result of considered thought and deliberation. If it has convinced people like them in the present, it will continue to convince people like them in the future, unless a knowledge-based answer is furnished today.

A third reason is that because the direction of the qibla concerns mosques across the continent, and mosques contain people, if unsettled it has the potential to become a divisive social issue among Muslims.

A fourth is that there are mental capacities which, while unrelated to other kinds of intelligence, Allah has given each of us in widely varying measures. The author, for example, routinely confuses right and left when they are mentioned about things in front of him. Other people apparently have the same difficulty, which doubtless has a technical name in the literature of human cognition.

Similarly, in discussions with people about the qibla, the author has discovered that many, while quite intelligent, have little ability to picture three-dimensional, concrete models to themselves, or to turn such images over and look at them from several sides in their mind's eye, or to draw accurate physical conclusions from them. Some have a "misplaced concreteness" of purely verbal terms in the discussion—like the names north, south, east, and west—that makes it very difficult for them to see just "what is wrong with a flat map." As books are written for people, it is important to realize that while many Muslims involved in the discussion of the qibla today can easily see in their minds the physical reasons for the northeast qibla from the fact of the sphericality of the earth, others cannot—unless, perhaps, they see them illustrated or in print. Most of us, of course, fall between the two extremes, and a work like the present is intended for all.

A fifth reason is that when someone prays towards a certain qibla five times every day for weeks, months, and years, a considerable psychic momentum builds up to persist therein, come what may. The initial belief that Mecca is in a certain direction becomes like an actual perception, born not out of stubbornness or self-consequence, but rather from the collective impetus of daily religious practice in someone who strongly identifies with this practice. Moreover, having followers (to say nothing of being a follower) can make it even harder, socially as well as psychologically, to reconsider.

Yet this is what the scholars of the Muslims used to do.

Imam al-'Izz ibn 'Abd al-Salam (d. 660/1262), for example, once gave a fatwa to a questioner but when the man left realized he had made a mistake. Because the questioner was unknown to him, he personally went around Cairo calling out, "Whoever Ibn 'Abd al-Salam has given the fatwa that such and such is the case should not act upon it, because it is a mistake"—so the man might hear and not go astray (al-Suyuti: *Husn al-muhadara* (e88), 1.315–16).[1]

Far from unique, such stories are related about Islamic scholars in many biographical works, such as Taj al-Subki's *Tabaqat al-Shafi'iyya,* and Imam Dhahabi's *Siyar a'lam al-nubala'.* This kind of candidness was a traditional measure of scholarly greatness, and it certainly befits everyone in the present discussion. A claim to "the right to make ijtihad" here only leads us to the nature of ijtihad, which should not be misunderstood as a judgement permissible to remain with after facts have become plain that contradict it, but rather is expending all of one's effort to know Allah's judgement about a matter. The present work accordingly deals not only with the question of the qibla, but with the nature of ijtihad itself, both in determining the direction of Mecca, and in the context of the Sacred Law as a whole.

On the Authority of Whom?

The present work is not a one-man effort. It represents the fiqh of both traditional Islamic legal works and well-known contemporary Muslim ulema. The fatwa promulgated by this book is that of the Egyptian

---

[1] All citations in the present work are indicated, as here, by in-text references giving the work's title, volume and page number, together with its number in bibliographical appendix E of the present work (e.g. "e88"), where full publication data is given.

Fatwa Authority (Dar al-Ifta' al-Misriyya), presented and expounded in 1998 by the Islamic Research Academy of al-Azhar, which at the instance of the late Sheikh al-Azhar Jad al-Haqq (Allah have mercy on him) made a study of the entire previous literature on the North American qibla and produced its fatwa after an interdisciplinary, consultative effort involving both scientific and religious bodies over a period of three years. This is the first time it has been published, in English or Arabic.

Other scholars who wrote substantive legal opinions (fatawa) for the present work include: the Mufti of Damascus Dr. 'Abd al-Fattah al-Bizm (Hanafi); the head of the fiqh department at the University of Damascus Dr. Wahbeh al-Zuhayli (Shafi'i); Dr. Muhammad Sa'id Ramadan al-Buti (Shafi'i), Sheikh Hassan al-Hindi (Hanafi), and Dr. Muhammad Hisham al-Burhani (Hanafi), all of Damascus; the late Hanafi Mufti of Aleppo Sheikh Muhammad Khalil al-Karmi (Allah have mercy on him); the mufti and teacher of Hanbali fiqh in Duma, Syria, Sheikh Isma'il Badran; the former Chief Justice of the Islamic Judiciary in Jordan Dr. Nuh 'Ali Salman al-Qudah (Shafi'i); the Dean of the Faculty of Islamic Sciences at the University of Baghdad Dr. Muhammad Ramadan (Shafi'i); the associate professor of fiqh there Dr. Ahmad Muhammad al-Balisani (Hanafi); the mufti of Ramadi, Iraq, and fiqh professor emeritus of the University of Baghdad Dr. 'Abd al-Malik al-Sa'di (Hanafi); the six Shafi'i muftis of the Fatwa Council of Tarim, Hadramawt, Yemen: al-Habib 'Umar ibn Ahmad al-Mashhur, Sheikh Muhammad 'Ali Faraj Ba-'Udan, al-Habib al-Sayyid Hasan ibn Mihsin al-Hamid al-Shaykh Abu Bakr, Sheikh Muhammad 'Ali al-Khatib, al-Habib 'Abdullah ibn Muhammad ibn Shihab, and al-Habib 'Ali Mashhur ibn Muhammad ibn Salem ibn Hafiz; the Mauritanian Maliki sheikh and professor of fiqh at the Shari'a College in Tarim, Hadramawt, 'Abdullah al-'Alawi al-Shinqiti; the Maliki scholar Muhammad al-'Amrawi of Fez, Morocco; the professor of Maliki fiqh and the methodological bases of fiqh Dr. Muhammad al-Tawil of the Qarawiyyin Mosque in Fez; the Maliki Mufti of Fez Dr. Muhammad al-Rugi, who also teaches at the Qarawiyyin; and Sheikh Idris Muhammad al-'Alami (Maliki), professor of the chair of qibla and prayer-time determination (tawqit) at the

Qarawiyyin. The cooperation of all these men well bore out the words of Imam Shafi'i: "Learning, among the virtuous and intelligent, is a strong family tie" (Ghazali: *Ihya' 'ulum al-din* (e26), 1.41).

The author would like to give special thanks to Sohail Nakhooda, who produced the author's illustrations and typeset everything connected with the book, as well as to Dr. S. Kamal Abdali of the National Science Foundation in Washington, D.C., and to Hamid Abugideiri for their technical assistance. Many other travellers, correspondents, and reviewers helped with factual matters presented here, and the reward of all is with Allah.

May Allah guide us to the straight path, and He is our sufficiency and the best to rely on.

PART ONE

Fact, Fiqh, and the Qibla

I

A Question of Fact

===

PLAINLY speaking, the visiting scholars who suggested the qibla be changed to the east or to the southeast were wide of the mark, for the very good reason that if one went in either of the directions they suggest, turning neither right nor left, one would never reach Mecca. One would not come even close. Though they are notable scholars, this should not particularly astonish us, because the direction of some particular thing on the surface of this earth is not a question of fiqh, their area of special competence, but a question of fact. One could be the greatest Islamic scholar alive, yet not know a particular point of geography in the physical world. Or be the greatest authority on a particular physical question, but not know the fiqh ruling on it. It is thus fitter to look first at the fact, the physical direction of Mecca, before we turn to the *fiqh,* the positions of living scholars on the qibla in North America, and the books of the four Sunni schools of jurisprudence, Maliki, Hanafi, Shafi'i, and Hanbali, on the qibla in general. Part of the disagreement must certainly stem from the words of the debate themselves, especially from the all-important term "direction," with which we will begin.

What Is Meant by the "Direction" of Something

The shortest distance between two points is a straight line. The exact direction described by it is also what we normally mean in ordinary language by "the direction" of something. If one were in sight of a mountain, for example, and were asked what direction the mountain is, one would point at it and say, "Right there." In ordinary language, there is only a single direction that it lies from one; namely, the straight line that if one were to travel upon "as the crow flies" without turning left or right one would reach it. If someone were to point to the left of the mountain and say, "What about that direction?" it is obvious

3

one can go over that way and then curve back towards the mountain, but this is not what is meant by its specific direction.

If one were now transported ten miles to the rear in a straight line directly away from the mountain, one would probably be unable to see its base, which would be hidden by the curvature of the earth, which is round, though the mountain would be still there, and its direction would be unchanged. Another fifty miles in the same direction, and perhaps only the top of the mountain would be visible on the horizon, though it would be still there. Yet another fifty, and the mountaintop itself would disappear from view, but the direction of the mountain would be the same, namely, the direction in which if you travelled in a straight line, veering neither left nor right, you would reach it. This is the way human beings use the word "direction" for anything on the face of the earth. Ask someone what direction something is, and he will point and say, "It's that way," and if he is telling the truth, what everyone will understand is that if one were to go in the direction he has indicated one would sooner or later come to it. Nobody disagrees with this, and several important points emerge from it:

First, the exact direction from oneself to anything is but one. Other directions can be pointed out, but they are not its specific direction, for which reason they are termed "other directions."

Second, the one exact direction is a straight line of travel, in the sense of curving neither left nor right.

Third, this straight line is the shortest possible travel distance between oneself and that thing. Roundabout, alternative routes have nothing to do with something's direction.

Fourth, while the earth is a planet, shaped more or less like a ball, and its surface curvature "makes things disappear in the distance" when one gets farther from them than the horizon, this does not affect the way we talk about their direction at all. The above-mentioned mountain remains "in that direction" and no other even after its top can no longer be seen, and even if continents and oceans intervene.

The present writer takes these four points to be the irreducible minimum entailed by the "facing the direction of something" that constitutes the human cognitive context of the word of Allah in Sura al-Baqara:

"We certainly see your face [O Muhammad] turning about the sky; now We will surely turn you to a direction that shall please you. So turn your face towards the Holy Mosque, and wherever you all may be, turn your faces towards it" (Qur'an 2:144);

namely, the context of human directionality itself. Their significance for the present discussion can be summarized in three cardinal axioms:

(i) The direction (samt) of anything is but one.

(ii) A line that curves to the left or right is not straight, so cannot be considered the direction of anything.

(iii) Only a line that curves neither left nor right but goes straight, curving only with the curvature of the earth, can be the direction of anything.

The reader who examines these carefully for any mistake, any ambiguity, or any counterexample will find they are plain and true, and rigorously correspond to how we talk about directions in the real world.[1]

We have relied here upon ordinary human experience to illustrate the most primitive components of the concept of "direction" and to produce its fundamental axioms not only because it conforms to common sense and ordinary language, but also because the two different meanings of "direction" in Islamic law mentioned in the preface in reality return to the more fundamental of the two, which is the concept of exact direction (samt) we have developed here. As mentioned in the preface, the approximate direction (jiha) by which three of the four Sunni schools of fiqh define the qibla is based upon this exact direction (samt), for if one wants to know whether one is facing the approximate

---

[1] As for the antipode, the point on the opposite side of the earth from any place, the directions from it to that place are innumerable. The directions, for example, that lead to the South Pole when standing at the North Pole consist in *every* direction. But if antipodes furnish a counterexample to axiom (i) above that is true, it is trivially true; not only because from every other point on the earth the direction is but one, but also because our context is the direction of the Kaaba, whose antipode is located far beyond all points of land out in the Pacific Ocean, where a boat would have difficulty staying in the same place, and as soon as it was the slightest bit off, the direction would revert to being one. It is thus not an objection, but a triviality.

direction (jiha), there is no way to answer the question except by reference to the exact direction (samt): if one diverges from the object's exact direction more than a certain amount, one is no longer facing the approximate direction; otherwise, one is facing it.

Although we shall return to the fiqh of this in chapter 11, it suffices here to note that, in quantifiable terms, this permissible divergence amounts to about 90 degrees on either side of the exact line direction (samt) for the Maliki school (Malik: *al-Mudawwana* (e55), 1.92), 45 degrees for the Hanafi school (al-Ramli: *al-Fatawa al-Khayriyya* (e73), 1.18), a "slight divergence" for the Hanbali school (al-Buhuti: *Kashshaf al-qina'* (e17), 1.305); while for the Shafi'i school one must be "straight in line with the exact direction, though by conventional rather than absolute standards ('urfan la haqiqatan)" (al-Haytami: *Tuhfa al-muhtaj* (e33), 1.484). Because the exact direction (samt) is the physical basis and defining criterion for the approximate direction (jiha), it forms the basis of our investigation.

The Direction to Mecca

Among others, navigators are interested in what direction they must go, for if they go the wrong way, they will not reach their destination. Whenever possible, they like to travel straight, neither left nor right, because anything else wastes valuable time and fuel. In the real world, one can see what this means on every single air flight, for example, from Chicago to Cairo, which is broadly speaking the same direction as the North American qibla to Mecca.

It must be an unceasing marvel to those who consciously or unconsciously believe that the earth corresponds to the flat maps we find in the flight magazines on these planes that a commercial airline should waste its money on a flight route that curves up in a great northerly arc towards Greenland before it descends southeast across Europe and the Mediterranean to Cairo. Why would anyone who knows that fuel costs money go hundreds of miles out of their way for nothing?

The mystery disappears if one takes a world globe and puts a flexible plastic draftsman's ruler on it—whose edge is perfectly straight and will not turn right or left, though the ruler's flexibility allows it to follow the curvature of the globe. Here, if one puts one end of its straight

Figure 1. The world globe, with the northeast qibla's direction indicated
on it by a solid line and the southeast qibla's by a dashed line

edge on Chicago and the other on Cairo, or better still Mecca, holding
its edge tightly to the surface of the globe, then turns the globe so
that one is looking at the line from directly above, one will see one is
looking at a *straight line* of travel, and that the northerly waters off
Greenland that appear to be the plane's great detour on the flat map
are at the middle of this line. It is straight, it is the direction of the
qibla, and it is a palpable, ocular demonstration that can be grasped by
anyone who does it. Its validity is a direct consequence of the validity
of our three axioms.

There is a hitch—otherwise there would be no need to write this—
not with the facts or proof, but with what, as noted in the preface, the
author has come to realize is the natural inability of some of us to follow
three-dimensional evidence in our minds, often accompanied by a pow-
erful if unwitting conviction that the physical directions of the earth

should correspond to the familiar "Mercator projection map" found in textbooks and on classroom walls everywhere in North America.

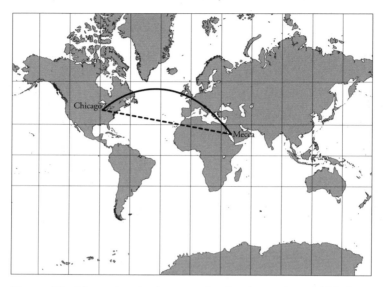

Figure 2. The Mercator projection map, showing the northeast qibla's direction as a solid line and the southeast qibla's direction as a dashed one. In the real world, the northeast qibla's direction is straight and the southeast qibla's is curved; while on a Mercator projection, the northeast qibla's is erroneously shown as if curved and the southeast's as if straight. The specific distortions engendered by the Mercator projection, as we shall discuss in detail on pages 55–66, are there by the navigational design of its inventor Gerardus Mercator (d. 1594), not by accident.

Direction Names

This conviction certainly lies deep within the words that in many human languages denote directions: *north* is towards the top edge of the map, *east* is towards the right edge of the map, *south* is towards the bottom edge, and *west* is towards the left. Early Muslim geographers had what the modern day would perhaps call "upside-down" maps, but the principle was the same: the world was viewed as a flat plane, and the four cardinal directions denoted the four sides of it.

No one can deny the usefulness of these direction words inherited from the past, or their applicability and adequacy for laying out plots of land, planning villages and towns, travelling from one locality to another, and finding the qibla and accomplishing many other useful functions at a local and even regional level. Indeed, the books of fiqh or Islamic jurisprudence were written in an age when these direction names were "as good as absolute," meaning that the relative closeness of the Islamic countries to Mecca for most of Islamic history made any other terms of discourse unnecessary. But this historical fact does not render either the direction names or the discourse sacred, for that would require evidence that Allah intended them as such, and there isn't any. Rather, Allah commands us in the Qur'an to simply face the direction of the Kaaba.

In the real world, direction names are not absolute, such that a straight line along one of them, say north, or southwest, or northeast will always remain "that direction," that is, retain its particular direction name. Why? Because the world we live on is a sphere, while north, south, east, and west are direction concepts and words inherited from a previous age in which they applied absolutely only to the world men conceived they lived in: a flat world which extended out in the four cardinal directions, north, south, east, and west, together with the directions between these that derived their names from them. As far as any man knew, a straight line in any of these directions, north for example, would remain north indefinitely, or until one reached the edge of the world, wherever that might lie.

In the discussion of the North American qibla, flat maps come at length to cast their shadows. Today we know that direction names are not absolute, and that in the real world, one and the same exact physical line direction (samt) if extended indefinitely can and generally does change its direction name, because the properties of the spherical planet we live on differ from the properties of the flat world our ancestors believed they inhabited.

Examples

The two following examples demonstrate the relative nature of these direction names on a spherical earth. Although they are found at the North Pole, a geographical location chosen because it throws some features of the discussion into high relief within a small physical scale, they apply in ways we shall see below to all latitudes north of the equator.

9

A. In the first example, let one imagine oneself standing at the North Pole, the precise location of which is marked by a spot in the snow ten feet in front of one. One's back is roughly towards Russia, and North America lies to one's right. Here, if one walks from point (1) of the illustration in a straight line right over the spot that marks the Pole and then walks the same distance beyond it to point (2), the first steps one takes are of course "north," as one is proceeding towards the North Pole, but one's first steps beyond the marker along one and the same straight line are called "south" and nothing besides, because they are now taking one directly away from the North Pole.

The twenty-foot line described here is straight, going neither left nor right, and so it can be the exact physical direction (samt) from point (1) where it begins to point (2) where it ends, as attested to by axiom (ii) on page 5 above. If we consider the example carefully, several conclusions emerge.

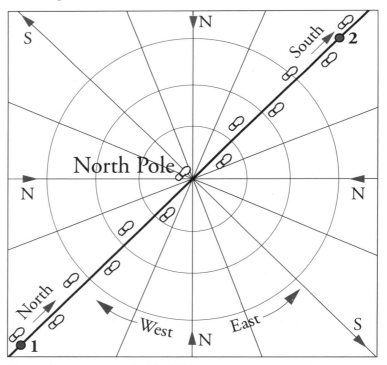

Figure 3. Footsteps across the North Pole

(1) One and the same exact physical direction (samt) need not be identified with a single direction name, for this one has two.

(2) Direction names are therefore not *absolute,* such that a straight line along one of them will always remain "that direction," retaining its particular direction name, in this case "north." Were they absolute, this counterexample (and as we shall see, many others) could not exist.

(3) Therefore, exact physical directions are distinct from and not to be confused with direction names. Sometimes the two coincide and sometimes they do not.

(4) Because the *jiha* or "approximate direction"—characterized in the preface above as the permissible "margin of error" or divergence from the exact physical direction (samt)—is logically derived from the exact direction, the previous conclusion (3) holds for it as well. That is, sometimes the approximate direction will coincide with a direction name and sometimes, particularly when extended to great distances, it will not. The fact that the two are distinct is highly material to any meaningful discussion about qibla issues because the word *jiha* in Arabic, confusingly, may be used for either, and if one wishes to avoid equivocation (and confusion), one must specify which sense one means.

To summarize, a twenty-foot straight line that can change at midpoint from "north" to "south" clearly shows us that these direction names are conventional and location-relative. Describing exact physical directions on the face of the earth in terms of direction names like north, south, east, and west is a circumstance of language inherited from a previous age of human understanding, which, if still useful and applicable on a local and regional scale, does not permit its generalization everywhere.

B. Our second example is a little more complex, but necessary to understand why the qibla in North America, which is a straight line of travel upon the earth towards Mecca, appears on flat maps of the world—or more precisely, the Mercator projection map—to be a northerly rising *arc* which subsequently descends southward towards Mecca. In this example, one retraces one's steps at the North Pole, and facing it as before, now moves to the right of the previous starting

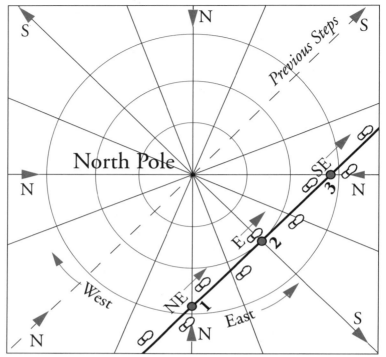

Figure 4. Footsteps beside the North Pole

point, and walks upon a line parallel to the first, but five feet to the right of it.

Here, to understand what direction names (north, south, east, west) one goes through as one walks along this second, parallel line in the same direction, it is useful, as before, to look at a diagram of it from above (figure 4), showing lines of *longitude*—those imaginary lines which radiate out from the North Pole and run north and south on the globe to ultimately coalesce again at the South Pole—and secondly, lines of *latitude,* which "parallel" the equator as horizontal lines on most flat maps, but in reality are concentric *circles* on planes parallel to the plane on which the equator lies, diminishing in their

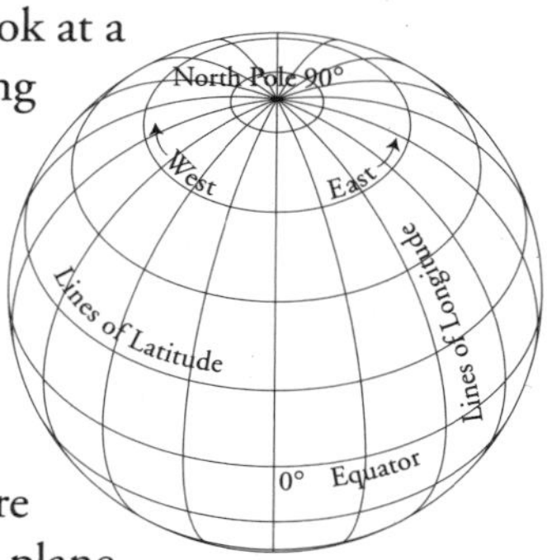

Figure 5. "Lines" of latitude are really circles.

circumference the farther to the north (or south) one goes, seen on the flat map as great rungs of a ladder climbing northward from the equator, but which conceptually exhibit themselves at the North or South Poles as the circles they really are.[1] If one follows one of these circles or "lines of latitude" around the globe in a clockwise direction in relation to the North Pole, one is going "west." If one follows one of them around in a counterclockwise direction, one is going "east." That is, they are lines that curve to the left or right, not straight. Reflect on this for a moment, as we shall have occasion to return to it.

Figure 4 on the left, "Footsteps beside the Pole," represents an area of no more than twenty by twenty feet. It shows one's footsteps at three different places or points on a "cartographic grid" of longitude and latitude lines, drawn here to show the four compass directions as they would appear at the North Pole. At the beginning of one's walk, which is parallel to one's first line of travel in the previous example, one is going "northeast" at point (1). Then, as one directly passes the Pole to one's left and touches for a moment tangentially on point (2) of the "line" of latitude (actually a circle around the Pole), one is going precisely "east." Then, proceeding straight ahead, one ends up going "southeast" at point (3)—all in a single, twenty-foot straight line. This example, like the previous one, discloses a number of salient conclusions:

(1) One and the same exact physical direction (samt) need not be identified with a single direction name, for this one changes its direction name from "northeast" to "east" to "southeast" within a distance of twenty feet (as do exact physical direction lines of greater lengths at lower latitudes).

(2) Direction names are therefore not *absolute* such that a straight line that begins along one of them will always retain its particular direction name. Rather, they are conventional and location-relative.

(3) Both the exact physical direction (samt) and the approximate direction (jiha) which logically derives from it are distinct from direction

---

[1] Geographers generally term lines of longitude "meridians" and lines of latitude "parallels." The present work uses "lines of longitude" and "lines of latitude" throughout because they are more familiar to most readers.

times they do not, as here, for example, when they take a number of successive direction names.

(4) Although not yet mentioned, it is noteworthy that a flat Mercator projection map at its upper "northern" edge would depict the twenty-foot-long straight line just described (if it showed it) precisely as a northerly ascending *arc* that then descends to the southeast. It would incidentally appear to stretch almost half the entire length of the map, from east to west, illustrating the tremendous distortion of distances and physical features that such maps are prey to, the farther one gets from the equator.[1]

(5) The changes undergone by the direction names of this line are those undergone by the line of the exact physical direction (samt) of the North American qibla without any difference whatsoever (as shown in figure 6 on the facing page). In other words, this example is analogous to the northeast qibla in every respect.

To confirm the latter, one but has to take a globe, put a flexible ruler on one's position in North America with the other end on Mecca, holding it fast to the globe, and take a look. The Kaaba is that direction, it is a straight line of travel, and it begins facing northeast. It is the plainest proof of the North American qibla that there is.

---

[1] This is because lines of longitude, which in the real world come together at a single point at the North Pole and South Pole, are pictured on the Mercator projection map as if they were parallel in all places. Moreover, we use the words "if it showed it" above because as we shall see in chapter 4, the Mercator expands degrees of latitude by continually increasing the drawn distance between them the farther north or south one gets from the equator, until they expand at the Poles to infinity, which the Mercator obviously cannot depict, for which reason it simply cuts off the top and bottom of the map well below the Poles, generally at around 80° north. Our thought experiment here of drawing on a Mercator the line just walked beside the Pole, which would be depicted as extending in a great arc from east to west, is nevertheless valid and in principle possible because it is some fraction of a degree of latitude south of the ninety degrees of the Pole that a Mercator cannot show. Other peculiarities of the Mercator projection map are detailed, as previously noted, in chapter 4 from page 55 to 66.

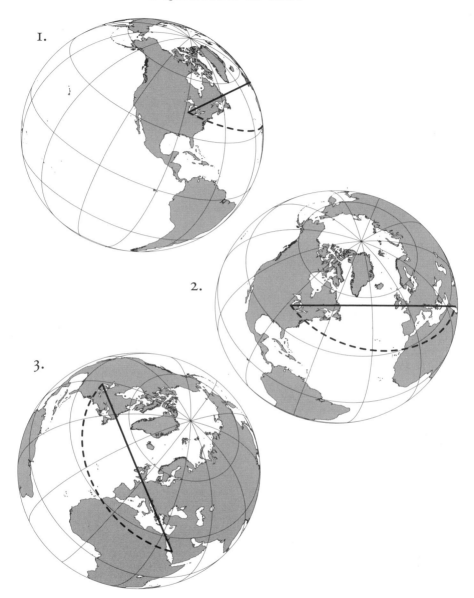

Figure 6. Three views of the globe, each showing both the northeast qibla (as a solid line) and the southeast qibla (as a dashed line). The northeast qibla begins its course to Mecca towards the "northeast" (1), proceeds "due east" (2), and ends towards the "southeast" (3).

Concentric Rows Around the Kaaba

Almost as plain is a second proof, the "proof of concentric circles," which is based on the rows of people praying facing the Kaaba who normally stand in circles around it. Everyone who has prayed at the Kaaba in Mecca—or seen photographs of it taken from above when Muslims are at prayer around it—has seen these concentrically expanding rings of people praying towards it. No matter how far away they can be imagined, such circles will remain centered on Mecca as long as the people are facing the Kaaba itself, even if lands and seas come beween. If one were to enlarge these circles on the face of the globe larger and larger until they reached North America, those standing in them would be facing northeast, proving the Kaaba is in that direction alone.

One can demonstrate this to oneself by taking a world globe in one's hands and placing a bowl, rim down, upon the globe's surface with the center of the bowl directly over Mecca. The rim of the bowl will show the direction of a row of worshippers facing the Kaaba from any number of places in Europe and Asia. If one now repeats the procedure with a large pot whose rim approximates the diameter of the globe, centering it on Mecca as before, and then looking where the rim touches North America (or comes closest to it), one will see that a row of worshippers there would face to the northeast and no other direction. Like our previous proof of the flexible ruler on the globe, the proof of concentric rows of worshippers around the Kaaba is as evident as the word of Allah Most High

> "Turn your face towards the Holy Mosque, and wherever you all may be, turn your faces towards it" (Qur'an 2:144).

The ease with which these proofs may be grasped, their basis in human sense perception, and their correspondence with physical reality appear to have won widespread acceptance for them among Muslims. According to Sayyid Muhammad Syeed, the executive director of the Islamic Society of North America, there are some 3000 mosques today in the United States and Canada. Less than half of 1 percent of these face any other direction than northeast.

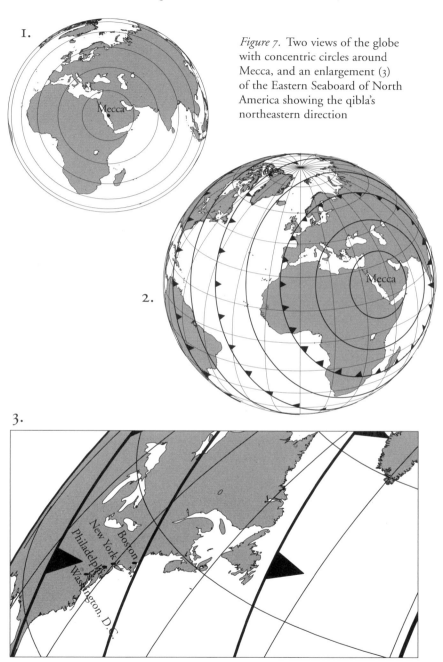

Figure 7. Two views of the globe with concentric circles around Mecca, and an enlargement (3) of the Eastern Seaboard of North America showing the qibla's northeastern direction

The Great Circle

The same consensus exists among Muslim astronomers and geographers today in North America who have investigated the question and are in virtually unanimous agreement that the qibla is to the northeast. A list of their articles about it in print would be long. The present writer has avoided citing them because they deal with mathematical proofs of spherical trigonometry not readily comprehensible to non-specialists, and because the above-mentioned evidences on the world globe are equally convincing and equally correct.

In general, their methods are in conformity with those Muslim mathematicians and scientists who knew that the earth was round centuries before Columbus discovered America and who wrote on how to scientifically determine the qibla, scholars such as Ibn al-Haytham (d. 433/1040), Abu al-Rayhan al-Biruni (d. 440/1048), and Nasir al-Din al-Tusi (d. 673/1274).

An example will clarify the method they used to find the unique direction Allah has created between the Kaaba and any place in the world. Here, let one imagine oneself in a room, looking at another person. The direction he lies is plain: the straight line from oneself to him which if it were continued beyond him, would go on and on, following the surface of the earth around the globe and eventually coming right to the back of one's head, thereby circumscribing the globe and dividing it into two equal halves.

The huge circle thus described is central to the concept of true directionality between two things on the face of the earth. If one were to now look at something else in the room and draw another straight line to it, this line would also conceptually continue beyond it and go right around the world and return to the back of one's head, circumscribing the globe and dividing it into two equal halves. And so it is with every conceivable straight line direction between oneself and anything on the face of the earth: reflection reveals that it can only be part of such a "great circle": the greatest circle possible on a globe because it divides it into two halves. It is an imaginary construct, to be sure, but of singular importance in determining the real direction between two geographical points on earth because it makes the line between them firstly *unambiguous*—in keeping with its physical uniqueness in the real world—and secondly *calculable* in a mathematically precise way.

This was the central methodological insight of Ibn al-Haytham, al-Biruni, al-Tusi, and other ancient Muslims scientists who determined the qibla. They called this the *da'ira 'udhma* or "great circle," and by means of it, for example, al-Biruni more than nine hundred years ago calculated with nearly perfect accuracy the qibla for Ghazna (al-Biruni: *Tahdid nihayat al-amakin* (e15), 272–74), where the great Friday mosque was built by his patron Sultan Mahmud of Ghazna some 1,933 miles from Mecca in present-day Afghanistan. It was a Muslim discovery that has been the basis for scientific calculation of the qibla for nearly a thousand years.

In other words, they discovered that the true *direction* from anything to anything else on the face of the earth is in fact the shortest distance along such a great circle. They called it a "circle" because, although it is a straight line of travel curving neither left nor right on the surface of the earth, it follows the earth completely around and comes back to itself. They termed it "great" because it is the largest circle possible on a sphere; namely the one that divides the sphere into two equal halves. To picture it, one has but to think of the equator, which is the most familiar example of a great circle. Other examples are our previous illustrations on pages 8 and 15 of the northeast qibla direction drawn as a straight black line between North America and Mecca on the world globe, each line of which is actually a segment of a great circle.

The validity of the great circle is a physical consequence of the fact that the world is round, in reality a mere application of our previous three axioms to the earth on which we live. Consideration of it yields the two last axioms of this work:

(iv) A straight line between any two points on the surface of the earth will always be found to be a segment of a "great circle," meaning the girth that goes all the way around the globe and comes back to itself, incidentally bisecting the earth.

(v) The exact physical direction (samt) of anything on earth can only be the shortest line segment of such a "great circle" between oneself and that thing, since the "long way around" cannot be a direction.

These two axioms, agreed upon for a thousand years by Muslim geometers, are indispensable to finding a qibla direction from North America to Mecca that is both unambiguous and calculable.[1] Hence the importance of the great circle to our discussion.

---

[1] Al-Biruni actually discovered four different ways to calculate the direction of the qibla, which he defined in terms of the great circle. Because he found it difficult to mathematically prove that the shortest path between two points on a sphere is along the great circle between them (the consequence of our axioms (iv) and (v) above, which we have established by ordinary human intuition and common sense rather than mathematics), al-Biruni resorted to several spatial constructs to mathematically define the direction of the qibla from the person praying.

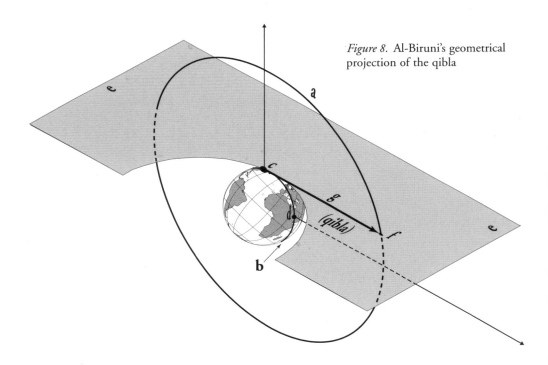

Figure 8. Al-Biruni's geometrical projection of the qibla

He first imagined a *celestial* or "sky" great circle ((a) in the diagram), circling the earth in the sky above, exactly paralleling the *terrestrial* or "earth" great circle (b) going around the earth below it. This celestial great circle, naturally having the same altitude everywhere in its course around the earth, would be intersected at two points,

A Tower Rising High Above Mecca

Among the qualities of the great circle is that from any point within a large portion of the earth's surface, if a huge tower were built into the sky above one's destination point, the tower's top would only appear on the horizon in the direction of the great circle. Unsurprisingly, the top of the tower would appear only in the direction that the thing under it actually *is*.

To see what this means for our discussion, one but has to take a six-inch diameter world globe, hold it in front of one so that, say, Boston, Massachusetts, is on the top of the middle of it, and then put a long car antenna or other rod on it standing straight out from the position of Mecca. The top of the rod will appear on Boston's horizon in the northeast, and in the northeast alone, because the Kaaba is in that

---

by two vertical lines of equal length, the first rising straight up from the person praying (c), and the second straight up from the Kaaba (d).

He then imagined a tangential or "touching" plane (e), perfectly flat and touching the spherical earth at one point alone: the exact place where the person is praying (c). (In the diagram the plane is partially "cut away" to show the earth under it.) This plane (e) would be under the person's feet, extending forward into space, not following the curvature of the earth, while the celestial great circle (a) would be directly above such a person, and arching forward and down from overhead to the horizon, straight towards the space above Mecca (d), parallel to the terrestrial great circle (b) underfoot. The celestial great circle (a) will intersect the surface of the plane at a point (f), directly ahead of the person.

Al-Biruni defined the direction of the qibla as a line (g) drawn upon such a plane between the point where the person is praying (c) and the point (f) where the celestial great circle overhead would intersect the plane, in its arching course down to the horizon in front of the person on its way around the globe towards the space above Mecca (parallel to the terrestrial great circle to Mecca). That such a line would be in the same direction as the terrestrial great circle is obvious, and al-Biruni only resorted to it because of the mathematical ease with which he could prove the shortest direction on a *plane* as opposed to on a spherical earth.

From these considerations, which al-Biruni details on page 137 of his *Kitab al-tafhim* (e14), it is plain how misconstrued is the assertion, made by one proponent of the southeast qibla, that "al-Biruni actually knew the earth was round, and yet in his calculations for the qibla he used a spherical sky and a flat earth projection." A tangential plane touching a spherical earth at one point is not a "flat earth projection," or indeed any kind of earth projection; nor would a celestial great circle parallel to the terrestrial great circle have any meaning without a spherical earth: there would simply be no celestial great circle to calculate with.

physical direction and no other. Anyone who tries this can see the direction of the Kaaba from North America before his very eyes.

This proof, like the previous two proofs of placing a flexible ruler on the globe between Mecca and North America, and concentric circles around the Kaaba, is a palpable, physical demonstration that vindicates the northeast qibla direction. It is not as comprehensive as the previous proofs, however, because of the physical limitation that such a tower, no matter how tall, could only be seen from half the surface of the earth, the half or "hemisphere" that has Mecca as its center point. The reason for this is that the line of vision of an observer standing on the earth at the perimeter of such a circle would be *parallel* to the tower's height, so the line of his vision could not intersect the line of the tower, which would be unmet by his gaze. Likewise the angle of the line of vision of someone beyond this perimeter would be wider than parallel to that of the tower, so he would never see it.

We say the proof is "not as comprehensive" as those mentioned previously, because the perimeter of such a circle, if one were to draw it in a precise way on a globe, would enclose only the northeastern corner of the United States, describing a great circumference line stretching northwest roughly from Boston to Montreal and to points beyond the two cities on either side. That is, the circle of the half of the earth with Mecca as its center point would only enclose the states of Maine, New Hampshire, and some of Massachusetts. The rest of the United States would be outside of it, though the position of Mecca from them would of course be unaffected, remaining in the same general direction.

Sighting the Kaaba from North America

As theoretical as all this may sound, it finds a very practical consequence in another ancient way of finding the qibla especially favored in Muslim lands far from Mecca, which is to wait until the sun is directly over the top of the Kaaba, as it is at two times every year, and simply take a look at the sun. This is the exact equivalent of building a tower above the Kaaba, and is as accurate as one's clock.

Nasir al-Din al-Tusi (d. 672/1274) explains the process in his *Kitab al-tadhkira fi 'ilm al-hay'a* [Memorandum on astronomy], which describes the position of the sun on the ecliptic—the great circle of the celestial sphere which is the apparent path of the sun among the stars—at the two times every year, namely when it reaches the eighth degree of Gemini (al-Jawza') and when it reaches the twenty-third degree of Cancer (al-Saratan), in modern terms on May 28 and July 16, when the sun's declination at the time of its zenith (highest point in the noon sky that day) is at the latitude of Mecca (+21° 25' 24" N, and of course at Mecca's *longitude* by the mere fact of being at its zenith), and is consequently above the Kaaba at that moment. Al-Tusi writes at the end of the twelfth section of chapter 3 of his work:

> There are many ways to know the exact direction (samt) of Mecca, it being inappropriate to mention [all of] them here, so we will confine ourselves to an easy one; namely, that the sun passes exactly over Mecca when in the eighth degree of Gemini and the twenty-third of Cancer at the time of midday there. The difference between its midday and the midday of all other places [where one wants to determine the qibla by sighting the sun above Mecca at that time] is commensurate with the difference between the two [places'] longitudes. So let the difference between the two be found, and one hour be figured for each fifteen degrees [of longitude], and four minutes [added] for each [additional] degree. The resulting total is the interval in hours from midday [that the sighting will occur in that place]. We wait on that day for that time—before midday if Mecca is east or after it if to the west of one. The direction of the shadow at that moment is the direction of the qibla (*Kitab al-tadhkira* (e94), 272).

In this more than seven-century-old text, the author tells how to calculate the time at one's location to ensure that one's seeing the sun is actually simultaneous with its being vertically above the Kaaba. The method appears to have been used from al-Tusi's day down to the times of such latter-day scholars as the Meccan sheikh 'Alawi ibn Ahmad al-Saqqaf (d. 1335/1916), who details the same procedure in his Shafi'i fiqh commentary on al-Mallibari's *Fath al-Mu'in* in the section of prayer conditions on how to face the qibla (*Tarshih al-mustafidin* (e79), 50). In our day, accurate clocks can take the place of having to make calculations for simultaneity. Anyone within the half of the earth from which the sun is visible when directly over the Kaaba who has a good watch and knows how many time zones away Mecca is can see the direction of the Kaaba from his location by merely looking at the sun at the right time.

The sun's verticality above the Kaaba is physically observable every year in Mecca at these two times. The former head of astronomy at the Muslim World League Habib 'Alawi Ibn al-Shaykh Abu Bakr ibn Salem, who lives in Mecca, says,

> On May 28 and July 16 of any year, we find that the declination of the sun from the north equals the latitude of Noble Mecca, so the sun is exactly[1] overhead at noon, and is above the horizon towards Noble Mecca [from other vantage points]: on either of the two above-mentioned dates, were we to stand a vertical stick upright on the surface of the earth at the time of high noon in Noble Mecca, then draw a line along the stick's shadow, the opposite direction to that of the shadow would indicate the direction of the Noble Kaaba (*Ta'yin ittijahat al-Ka'ba* (e45), 1–2).

The former date was announced in Saudi newspapers in 1421/2000, the year of the present writing, so that people in the kingdom outside of Mecca could see and check the accuracy of their qibla. As we shall presently describe, Mahmoud Jastaniah travelled from Jordan to the Meccan Haram and witnessed the sun's zenith there on July 16.

Determining the qibla by sighting the sun directly above the Kaaba is valid from a fiqh standpoint because the majority of Sunni legal schools hold that the space directly above the Kaaba is legally considered part of it. That is, to see the sun at either of these two times each year when the sun *occupies* this space is legally seeing the Kaaba itself. Imam Ibn 'Abidin, the foremost fatwa resource of the late Hanafi school, conveys,

---

[1] The sun is said to "exactly" occupy the space vertically above the Kaaba at these two moments, though in point of absolute precision, the center of the sun is a few tenths of one degree (of 360 degrees) from the actual latitude of the center of the Kaaba, which means that the vertical column of space just beside or partially sharing the sun's space in the sky is actually the celestial axis of the Kaaba. This is of little practical significance for the validity of sighting it, because the juxtaposition is negligible, and it is physically impossible to look at the one without seeing the other. Whoever sees the sun at such a moment is of an absolute certainty seeing the axis of the Kaaba, and this is its Islamic legal significance.

The criterion for the qibla is the area occupied [by the Kaaba] ('arsa), not its physical structure (bina'), it extending from the deepest depths of the earth [lit. "seventh earth"][1] to the very Throne above (*Radd al-muhtar* (e37), 1.290).

Imam Mansur al-Buhuti of the Hanbali school says,

The prayer is valid towards the space above it [the Kaaba]—and likewise if one were to dig a pit below the level of its structure [and pray towards the space under the Kaaba] it would be valid to pray towards its space—because as previously mentioned the criterion is its space (buq'a), not its walls (*Kashshaf al-qina'* (e17), 1.301).

And Imam Ibn Hajar al-Haytami of the Shafi'i school conveys that

the meaning of the "Kaaba itself" (al-'ayn) [which is obligatory to face according to the Shafi'i school] is not its walls, but rather something agreed upon by convention; namely, the exact direction (samt) of the Kaaba, and the space above it up to the sky and below it to the deepest earth (*Tuhfa al-muhtaj* (e33), 1.484).

The Hanafi, Hanbali, and Shafi'i schools thus explicitly state that the space directly above the Kaaba is considered exactly like the Kaaba, as high as it may go. The works of the Maliki school speak instead of the Kaaba's "approximate direction" (jiha) which, because seeing the direction of the sun in such an event means seeing the direction of the Kaaba that lies exactly below it, has the same fiqh consequences as the other schools. Seeing the sun from North America at the two times of the

---

[1] One should note here that "seventh earth" in the Arabic idiom means the deepest depth of the earth, which it is impossible to go deeper than. This of course terminates at the center of the earth, past which one is no longer going deeper, but rather shallower and shallower, towards the opposite surface of the globe. That the "Kaaba" in this sense does not extend past the earth's center is also plain from the fact that if it extended past this, it would ultimately reach the opposite surface, while the Kaaba's location on the face of the earth being one and not two is necessarily known of the religion of Islam (ma'lum min al-din bi al-darura)—one of those things that any Muslim, even a child, would know if asked, and the denial of which is to deny the religion itself. So the idea of an axis extending down from Mecca past the center of the earth and then out the other side of the globe as a sort of "second Kaaba" on the earth's surface is false from a religious standpoint as well.

year when it is over the Kaaba is thus from a legal point of view a visual *sighting* of the Kaaba from North America according to the Hanafi, Hanbali, and Shafi'i schools, and of the Kaaba's direction (jiha) according to the Maliki school.

This year, 1421/2000, as in other years, these times fell on May 28 at 12:18 PM local Saudi time (midday), and on July 16 at 12:27 PM Saudi local time. The former time in May corresponded in Boston, Massachusetts, and Montreal, Canada, to 5:18 AM, about 8 minutes after sunrise in Boston and 9 minutes after sunrise in Montreal. The latter time in July corresponded in both cities to 5:27 AM, some 7 minutes after sunrise in Boston and 6 minutes after it in Montreal. The author contacted Islamic bodies in the United States and Canada, asking them to send delegations to these cities to observe this event.

At the first of these two times, midday on May 28 at 12:18 PM Saudi and Jordanian local time, the author was on the roof of his house in Amman, Jordan, marking with a pencil and ruler the direction of the shadow of a vertical pipe on the top of the cement wall the pipe was set in. Upon compass measurement and allowing for magnetic declination, the line drawn was found to point towards 161.33° south-southeast, exactly the direction calculable for Mecca from Amman by spherical trigonometry.

At the same moment on Revere Beach at the northern outskirts of Boston, Massachusetts, Imad al-Din Abu Hijleh was standing looking east across the Atlantic Ocean just after sunrise with a group of nine men from four Islamic organizations in the Boston area, together with the representative of a surveying firm Imad al-Din had hired to determine the direction of the sun with professional surveying equipment. It was overcast, and they did not see the sun at the precise moment hoped. The cloud cover lifted eleven minutes later, when the sun had appreciably risen and inclined almost one degree to the south. The surveyor reported:

> The measured bearing was obtained utilizing a Berger Transit located at Revere Beach, Massachusetts, USA approximately at latitude 42° 25' North, longitude 70° 59' West. Based on these co-ordinates, the Canadian Geomagnetic Reference Field Web Site calculates the magnetic declination on May 28, 2000 as 15° 49' West.

Adjusting the observed bearing for the magnetic declination results in a bearing of the sun's position relative to true North, on May 28, 2000 at 5:29 AM EST at Revere Beach, Massachusetts, USA at N 61° 23' 45'' E (*Report* (e100), 28 May 2000, 1).

In decimal terms, the sun was seen and measured at 61.3958° to the northeast by east, while the mathematically exact direction calculable for Mecca from Revere Beach by spherical trigonometry is 60.48°. This showed beyond a reasonable doubt what direction Mecca was from North America, but from an Islamic legal point of view did not qualify as a physical sighting of the Kaaba because the timing was not exact.

The author therefore contacted Imad al-Din again a few days before the second time, July 16, and asked him to repeat the operation, and also contacted a group of Muslims in Toronto led by Sheikh Talal al-Ahdab, who were to travel to Montreal to try to observe the sun there at the right time.

When the second of the two times came, the sun was above the Kaaba in Mecca, where the Hanafi student Mahmoud Jastaniah had travelled by bus a few days earlier from Amman, Jordan. He said:

On 15 Rabi' II 1421 / 16 July 2000, in order to see whether the sun was directly vertical above Mecca at noon, I took a large size empty Pepsi bottle, put some sand in the bottom of it, took it to the Meccan Haram, and set it there on a flat surface. I did this reasoning that if the sun was exactly above it, it would shine down through the open top of the bottle and cast a circle of light on the middle of the sand. When the adhan came, which was at 12:27 PM according to local prayer time calendars, I looked at the sand at the bottom of the bottle and saw the circle of the sun's light was in the middle of it (*Letter* (e49), 23 July 2000, 1).

At the same time in Amman, the author was on the roof of his house, where the shadow from the pipe fell exactly on the pencil mark left there on May 28.

In Boston Imad al-Din was observing, but no one else. Rain, clouds, and fog prevented anything from being seen.

In Montreal, the group led by Sheikh Talal prayed the dawn prayer and waited under cloudy skies until a few minutes after sunrise, when the sun came out and was seen by them at precisely the right moment,

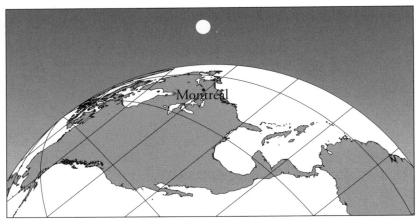

Figure 9. The sun above Mecca seen from Montreal

above the horizon at 58° northeast by east, a virtually exact confirma-tion of the direction of the qibla from Montreal calculable by spherical trigonometry. When they returned to Toronto, they wrote:

In the Name of Allah, Most Merciful and Compassionate

15 Rabi' II 1421 /16 July 2000
Toronto, Canada

Praise be to Allah, Lord of the Worlds. Allah bless our master Muhammad, his folk, his Companions, and give them peace.

To commence: We the undersigned traveled from Toronto to Mon-treal, Canada, and at 5:27 AM in Montreal this morning, Sunday 16 July 2000, six minutes after sunrise, we observed the sun to the northeast by east. We measured its direction with four compasses and found the mean compass bearing of its direction was 58 degrees from true north.

And praise be to Allah, Lord of the Worlds.

TALAL AL-AHDAB [signed];
AHSON AHMAD [signed];
MOSTAFA AZZAM [signed].

(*Letter* (e4), 16 July 2000, 1)

28

With this, the Kaaba had been legally sighted from North America to the northeast by a group of upright Muslim witnesses, whose testimony necessitates acceptance and lifts the question from the level of ijtihad to that of observed fact. And with it, our discussion of the "question of fact" of the North American qibla comes to a close.

CONCLUSIONS

We have distinguished above between the *fact* of the qibla—the exact physical line direction (samt) towards Mecca created by Allah uniquely to every place on the globe—and the *fiqh* of the qibla, defining the approximate direction (jiha) by which Islamic jurists have specified the limits of unintentional divergence from this exact direction permissible to the person figuring out the qibla on his own. This approximate direction, as a specific variance from the exact direction, is physically defined by the exact direction and logically derived from it.

This means that if the followers of one school of jurisprudence are praying to one direction and the followers of another school are praying to another, it is not because their schools of jurisprudence differ, but because one of them is geographically mistaken about the exact direction (samt). Since there is such a difference of opinion in North America, we have sought first to understand the meaning of "exact direction" through concrete examples in the real world, which brought to light five axioms we believe central to the discussion:

(i) The direction (samt) of anything is but one.

(ii) A line that curves to the left or right is not straight, so cannot be considered the direction of anything.

(iii) Only a line that curves neither left nor right but goes straight, curving only with the curvature of the earth, can be the direction of anything.

(iv) A straight line between any two points on the surface of the earth will always be found to be a segment of a "great circle," meaning the girth that goes all the way around the globe and comes back to itself, incidentally bisecting the earth.

(v) The exact physical direction (samt) of anything on earth can only be the shortest line segment of such a "great circle" between oneself and that thing, since the "long way around" cannot be a direction.

The validity of these axioms in turn attested the validity of our three visible proofs using the world globe that the exact physical direction (samt) of Mecca from North America is towards the northeast. We followed these by the fourth proof, of the sun actually having been physically seen when it was above the Kaaba earlier this year in the northeast direction by observers in North America, which we fully documented and presented with the fiqh texts that clarify its legally decisive character.

We have summarized the argument so far in order to introduce the terms of discourse used by the *fatwa* or "formal legal opinion" of al-Azhar that is the subject of the next chapter, to which we now turn.

2

The Azhar Fatwa

INTRODUCTION

THE following is probably unique among fatwas that have appeared about the North American qibla not only for the number of scholars involved, the time spent on it, and its detail, but for the integrity and courage of the man responsible for it, the late Sheikh of al-Azhar Jad al-Haqq, in ordering the reinvestigation of a previous fatwa issued by his office when it became apparent that he might have made a mistake.

The first fatwa, dated 7 February 1994 and signed by Muhammad Yusuf 'Afifi, President of the Central Management of the Office of the Sheikh of al-Azhar, was based on the opinion of a single consultant, Mahmud Jum'a, and asserted that the correct direction of the qibla in North America was to the southeast. This fatwa is familiar to North American Muslims because of the wide circulation it has enjoyed in a pamphlet published in Philadelphia in 1994 by the Lebanese-based Association of Islamic Charitable Projects.

After the fatwa appeared, the Islamic Fiqh Academy in Jedda, as well as scholars from Damascus and elsewhere in the Arab world who had actually been to North America and prayed there, contacted Sheikh Jad al-Haqq and raised the issue of its factual accuracy. He responded in 1995 by reopening the investigation, which he assigned to the forty-member Body of Major Scholars at the Islamic Research Academy of al-Azhar, in conjunction with engineers, geographers, and astronomers whose expertise was deemed needed.

THE TEXT

As mentioned in the preface, since its completion in 1998, this is the first time the full text has been published in English or Arabic. A facsimile of the original appears in appendix B. It reads in English as follows:

In the Name of Allah, Most Merciful and Compassionate

al-Azhar
The Islamic Research Academy
Directorate of Committees and Quarters

THE OPINION OF THE ISLAMIC RESEARCH
ACADEMY ON FACING THE KAABA DURING
THE PRAYER IN NORTH AMERICA

Praise be to Allah, and blessings and peace upon our liegelord the Messenger of Allah, and his folk and Companions.

His Excellency the Supreme Imam, the Sheikh of al-Azhar [Jad al-Haqq] received a letter from the administration of the Fiqh Academy of the General Secretariat of the Islamic World League in Mecca the Noble, numbered 10/10188 on 3 Shawwal 1415 [5 March 1995] containing the question of the General Secretary and Vice President of the Islamic Fiqh Academy session Dr. Ahmad Muhammad 'Ali concerning the correct direction of the qibla in North America. His Excellency referred the question to the Islamic Research Academy, and convened a committee of scholars of Sacred Law and experts in engineering and astronomy to investigate the matter, after having made an exhaustive study and examination of all inquiries and studies received from various quarters, including the Research Center for the Application of Islamic Shari'ah, the Fiqh Council of North America, the Islamic Society of Orange County California, the Islamic Association of Arab Alumni of Canada, the Association of Islamic Charitable Projects of North America, and Dr. Kamal al-Din Husayn, Dr. Tawfiq Muhammad Shahin, Mr. [Muhammad] Amin al-'Awwam, and Mr. Muhammad Hammadi of Montreal, Canada.

Because facing the qibla is among the conditions of the validity of the prayer, as Allah Most High says, "Turn your face towards the Holy Mosque; and wherever you all may be, turn your faces towards it" (Sura al-Baqara, verse 144); and because Muslim has related in his *Sahih* that the Messenger of Allah (Allah bless him and give him peace) said, "When you stand to pray, make a thorough ablution, face the qibla, and say 'Allahu akbar'" [*Muslim* (e62), 1.298: 397(2). S];[1] and because Muslims unanimously agree that it is obligatory to face the qibla to pray: the majority of scholars have ruled that someone praying who can see the Kaaba must face the Kaaba itself, though if far from it, it is sufficient to face the direction of the Kaaba, and one need not face the Kaaba itself, since the condition is that a portion of the face must be towards the direction of the Kaaba.

What follows is the fatwa of the Egyptian Fatwa Authority (Dar al-Ifta' al-Misriyya) concerning this matter:

> Facing the qibla in the prayer is one of its integrals, because of the word of Allah Most High:
>
> "We certainly see your face [O Muhammad] turning about the sky; now We will surely turn you to a direction that shall please you. So turn your face towards the Holy Mosque; and wherever you all may be, turn your faces towards it" (Sura al-Baqara, verse 144).
>
> As for determining the direction of the qibla in respect to anywhere in the world, those responsible for it are the distinguished experts: the engineers, the scholarly bodies of surveying and astronomy, the scholars of geography, and other experts in the field. The Egyptian Fatwa Authority calls upon Muslims living in North America to follow the scientific bodies specialized in this matter, and to avoid differences that harm, not help. The Egyptian Fatwa Authority agrees with defining the direction of the qibla for North American Muslims according to what experts on the matter say, in obedience to the word of Allah Most High, "Ask those who know well, if you know not" (Sura al-Anbiya', verse 7).
>
> "Those who know well," in the question of defining the qibla are the engineers and the experts who assist them such as scholars of astronomy, geography, and others.
>
> And after this defining of the direction of the qibla by experts, we must remember the word of Allah Most High 'To Allah the

---

[1] All hadiths in the present work (with the exception of a single spurious hadith we shall draw attention to in chapter 8) are either rigorously authenticated (sahih), indicated at the end of each hadith reference, as here, by the capital letter S, or else well authenticated (hasan), indicated by the capital letter H.

east and west belong: wheresoever you turn, there is the countenance of Allah; verily Allah is all-encompassing, all-knowing'
(Sura al-Baqara, verse 115)."[1]

The experts here with us in Egypt when we asked them about this matter informed us that the qibla in all parts of North America is to the
northeast, the angle varying from one locality to the next according to
the longitude and latitude without departing from the [general] direction of the northeast.

There is the opinion of one individual [Mahmud Jum'a] who con-
tradicted the consensus of the Islamic Research Academy and said that
the direction of the qibla in respect to North America is to the southeast, although the absolute majority of the Islamic Research Academy
are of the former opinion, that it is to the northeast in North America
and Canada.

(There is appended [following the signatures below] an explana-
tory copy of what experts from Egypt and elsewhere have written.)

The experts brought together by the Islamic Research Academy agree
upon the following points:

(1) The general direction of the qibla in the regions of North
America is the northeast, the angle varying from one location to another with the longitude and latitude, as experts have determined.

Someone facing towards the southeast in these regions is so far off
that he is in danger of not facing the direction of the Kaaba, and he
does not fulfill the legal condition of facing the qibla.

(2) The mihrabs intended for new mosques must face the direction
of northeast, while allowing for the variance in angle with the longitude and latitude from one location to another, and those now standing should be corrected towards this direction.

The prayer of whoever prayed towards any other direction out
of personal reasoning in the past before [learning of] this fatwa is
legally valid.

---

[1] Al-Tabari reports from the early Qur'anic exegete Mujahid ibn Jabr (d. 102/719)
that the verse "wheresoever you turn, there is the countenance of Allah" means "the
qibla of Allah, so wherever you are, east or west, face it" (*Jami' al-bayan* (e89), 1.505).

(3) An exception to what has been said [about the northeast] is the far easterly North American continent, for the direction of the qibla in the middle of Greenland is due east, to the east of which it is valid to face southeast. As for the far westerly North American continent, in the city of Dawson [Yukon Territory] in western Canada, the direction of the qibla is due north.

As for to the west of that area, namely the region of Alaska, the direction of the qibla in it is towards the northwest.

(4) All Muslims must cease discord and disagreement among themselves, and accept what scholars have finally agreed upon in this matter as mandatory and not permissible to contravene under any circumstances whatsoever.

The Islamic Research Academy holds that the qibla in one city should face one direction, to obviate disagreement and encourage the unity which Muslims are obliged to live under.

And Allah is the Giver of Success.

[drafted by] 'IZZ AL-'ARAB

Written on 28/10/1418 AH; 25/2/1998 AD

Secretary General of the Islamic Research Academy
SAMI MUHAMMAD MUTAWALLI AL-SHA'RAWI [signed]
5/3/98

Seal of AL-AZHAR [stamped]
General Secretariat of the Islamic Research Academy

[typed by] RAMADAN
Duplicate of the Original
MUSTAFA ABU AL-SU'UD WAHDAN [signed]
12/2/2000
AL-AZHAR: THE ISLAMIC RESEARCH ACADEMY [stamped]

(*Fatwa* (e47), 25 February 1998, 1–3).

[Enclosure:]

In order to determine the direction of the qibla on the surface of the earth, it is obligatory to accept the following facts:

(1) The earth is round, not flat, so one must deal with it according to the laws of spherical trigonometry, not the laws of plane geometry.

(2) Using flat maps leads to mistakes in defining the direction of the qibla, since on maps, especially Mercator projection maps, the direction to the north is parallel in all places, while it should come together at one point, namely the Pole, as it actually does on the surface of the sphere of the earth.

THE METHOD OF DETERMINING THE DIRECTION OF THE QIBLA ANYWHERE ON THE FACE OF THE EARTH

It is necessary in order to define the direction of the qibla in any place that a vertical plane pass through three points: the place of the person praying, Mecca, and the center of the earth. This plane determines the direction of the qibla from the location of the person praying, and it cuts the surface of the earth in a circle known as the "great circle," half of whose diameter equals half of the diameter of the earth. The straight line from the person praying to Mecca the Noble is that which [on this vertical plane] is tangential to [touches] this great circle at the point where the person is praying.

It is then necessary to identify the direction of true north from the place of the person praying, so he may refer to it to know the angle [of the compass direction] of the qibla. The direction of north in any place is the direction of the North Pole, which is one of the signs that legally define the qibla [sic], so [if one does not know true north, but must find it,] another vertical plane must pass through the location of the person praying, the North Pole, and center of the earth, this plane cutting the surface of the earth in a great circle known as the "longitude" of the place of the person praying. The angle between the two above-mentioned planes at the place the person is praying defines the angle the qibla inclines from true north.

Based on the foregoing, the correct direction for the qibla in all parts of North America is to the northeast, the angle varying with the longitude and latitude from one location to another without departing from the northeasterly direction.

And likewise, by applying the foregoing in Australia, it is found that the direction of the qibla throughout lies towards the northwest, with some variance in the angle with the longitude and latitude from one place to another, without departing from the northwesterly direction.

From a thorough acquaintance with the articles and studies that have reached the secretary of the Islamic Research Academy regarding this topic, it is apparent that the overwhelming majority support the direction of [the qibla in North America being towards] the northeast with scientific fact and computation, among them, not exclusively, but only by way of example:

—The late Dr. Husayn Kamal al-Din (professor emeritus of the Academies of Engineering in Egypt, and of the Islamic University of Muhammad ibn Sa'ud and the University of Riyadh in Saudi Arabia);
—Dr. Olav Slaymaker (professor of geography at the University of British Columbia, [Vancouver,] Canada);
—Dr. Jon Kimerling (professor of geography at Oregon State University);
—Dr. Muhammad Salih al-Sawi (director of Islamic Legal Research at the Islamic Academy for Scientific Research);
—Admiral Muhammad 'Abd al-'Aziz Sallam (Arab University for Maritime Navigation);
—Dr. 'Arafat al-'Ashi (director of the Islamic World League in Canada);
—Dr. Ahmad Muhammad 'Ali (general secretary of the World Islamic League and vice president of the Islamic Fiqh Council).

This then, and Allah alone gives success. "Our Lord, cause not our hearts to swerve after having been guided, but show us mercy from You; verily You are the Ever-bestowing" [Qur'an 3:8]. And peace be upon you and the mercy and blessings of Allah.

The Members of the Committee:

[Chairman] PROFESSOR DR. AHMAD ISMA'IL KHALIFA (signed);
PROFESSOR DR. ANAS IBRAHIM 'UTHMAN (signed);
DR. 'ABD AL-'AZIZ 'AKRI (signed);
Engineer MAHMUD MUS'AD IBRAHIM;
Engineer HAMDI AL-SHA'RAWI (signed);

(Ibid., 4–5).

CONCLUSIONS

The above is the fatwa of the Islamic Research Academy of al-Azhar, the most material of its features to our discussion being five points:

(1) It is not the solution of a single person, but the result of a consultative effort involving experts of both Sacred Law and physical science, perhaps the most acceptable way in our times to achieve a knowledge-based answer to fiqh problems involving many-sided issues.

(2) It has studied the scholarly arguments for and against previously offered solutions for determining the North American qibla, and it agrees with the opinion of the Egyptian Fatwa Authority (Dar al-Ifta' al-Misriyya) that those responsible for it "are the distinguished experts: the engineers, the scholarly bodies of surveying and astronomy, the scholars of geography, and other experts in the field."

(3) Its finding, based on the testimony of such experts, is that the physical direction (samt) of the qibla in North America is to the northeast, a result that conforms to the physical reality of our previous three visual proofs of the northeastern direction using the world globe and the fourth proof of visually sighting the sun above the Kaaba to the northeast from North America earlier this year (1421/2000).

(4) Although the fatwa states that someone praying towards the southeast "does not fulfill the legal condition of facing the qibla," it declares legally valid the prayer of whoever prayed towards any other direction out of personal reasoning (ijtihad) in the past before learning of it, so it is a mercy to people, who need not make up past prayers.

(5) It concludes that all Muslims must "accept what scholars have finally agreed upon in this matter as mandatory and not permissible to contravene under any circumstances whatsoever." Considering its credentials and the care with which it was arrived at, it does not seem farfetched that it should be just what it claims to be; namely, a binding legal text (nass) that obliges Muslims in North America to pray towards the northeast.[1]

---

[1] Chapter 14 below discusses this in light of the personal ijtihad on the qibla that some schools of fiqh hold to be obligatory.

This said, some conceptual difficulties about the northeast direction and its implications will doubtless remain in a few minds. But if the above fatwa corresponds to both physical reality and the ruling of Allah Most High, factual and convincing answers should be plain. To these we now turn, confining ourselves to issues actually raised to date by advocates of the east or southeast qibla. Their objections will be introduced in the following chapters by the subheading "Difficulty," and the answers to them by "Response."

PART TWO

Answers to Difficulties

3

The Qiblas of the Sahaba

===

DIFFICULTY

T HE Azhar Fatwa states that spherical trigonometry should be used to determine the qibla, while the prophetic Companions (Sahaba) did not use precision direction finding, but only used to face the approximate direction of the qibla, the evidence for which, as mentioned in Ghazali's *Ihya' 'ulum al-din* and elsewhere, is the rigorously authenticated (sahih) hadith that Ibn 'Umar (Allah be well pleased with him) said:

> While people were praying the dawn prayer at Quba' [near Medina], someone came and said, "Last night a revelation came to the Messenger of Allah (Allah bless him and give him peace) and he was commanded to face the Kaaba, so face it." Their faces were towards the north (al-Sham), so they turned around towards the Kaaba (*Muslim* (e62), 1.375: 526. S).

Imam Ghazali says the evidence in this is that

> they turned around in the midst of the prayer without seeking signs to guide them, and they were not censured for doing so—their mosque being called "that of the two qiblas"—whereas to know that one was facing the exact direction of the Kaaba itself from Medina to Mecca would require mathematical proofs lengthy to investigate, so how could it have been plain to them during the prayer, and in the darkness of night? It is also attested to by their building mosques around Mecca and in all Islamic cities without ever having had an engineer present when determining the mihrabs, while facing the exact direction of the Kaaba itself could not be determined without precise mathematical calculation (*Ihya' 'ulum al-din* (e26), 2.234).

Moreover, in another rigorously authenticated (sahih) hadith the

Prophet (Allah bless him and give him peace) told the people of Medina, "Everything between where the sun rises and sets is a qibla" (*Tirmidhi* (e93), 2.173: 344. S).

It is plain from these hadiths that precision direction-finding means like spherical trigonometry were not something the Companions used, though they understood the religion better than we do, and making such means the standard might even lead to declaring the ancient qiblas the Companions established to be mistaken.

RESPONSE

The best description of the Companions, and of every sincere Muslim, is the word of Allah Most High

"Be as godfearing as you are able to" (Qur'an 64:16).

The Companions went forth from Medina after the time of the Prophet (Allah bless him and give him peace) to spread the religion and they never came back, but died wherever they fell, having spent their time, efforts, and their very lifeblood for Islam. Whoever reads about them realizes that their efforts were limited only by human capacity.

Human capacity varies with the time, place, and person. Allah has commanded us to face the Kaaba when we pray, and the capacity of a traveller far from town, for example, to respond to this command is not the same as that of someone building a mosque in a city. Indeed, Imam Ghazali mentions the above hadiths in a chapter called "Tasks One Must Repeatedly Do Because of Travelling."

As soon as the people praying the dawn prayer at Quba' heard of the change in the qibla, in the words of Ibn 'Umar, "they turned around *towards the Kaaba*." Despite the lack of mathematics and engineers, there is no need to doubt the literal accuracy of this report, for Mecca lies almost exactly due south of Medina, the opposite direction of the North Star, which is visible in the night sky almost every night of the year in Medina, a fact known to its inhabitants, who travelled not infrequently between the two cities. The direction of the Kaaba would have been plain to everyone who knew from the daytime the direction the mosque faced, namely, north by west, towards Jerusalem.

The Mihrabs of the Companions

The second difficulty, that the Companions built their mosques without engineers, can best be answered by visiting those of their mosques preserved down to our times with their original mihrabs. The present writer has been able to check with accurate compasses the mihrabs of six mosques whose direction may be reasonably supposed to have been set by the ijtihad of the Companions.

The first is the mosque built by 'Amr ibn al-'As (Allah be well pleased with him) in Cairo, Egypt, in the presence of eighty Companions of the Messenger of Allah (Allah bless him and give him peace) (al-Sawi: *Bulgha al-salik* (e21), 1.292). Its compass bearing is 135 degrees southeast, which after compensating for magnetic declination is off absolute 100 percent accuracy by less than two degrees (out of the 360 degrees of the compass), an error factor hardly greater than one-half of 1 percent. If one were praying therein and wanted to turn slightly enough to compensate for this, one would be unable to do so.

Considering that 'Amr ibn al-'As arrived at this conclusion at a distance of about 810 miles over land and sea from Mecca, and five hundred years before the invention of the compass, it indicates no small concern for accuracy. Presumably something of the ancient geometrical knowledge of Egypt remained at that time, and it is not recorded whether he took advantage of it, but whatever else his results may prove, they do show he did his utmost to be precise; and none of the eighty other Companions present found anything to object to in this.[1]

---

[1] Some sources that mention this mosque say its qibla was initially "facing extremely easterly, and that [the governor of Egypt] Qurra ibn Sharik (d. 96/714) razed the mosque and rebuilt it in the time of [the Umayyad ruler] al-Walid ibn 'Abd al-Malik, turning it slightly to the right" (Ibn Duqmaq: *al-Intisar* (e38), 4.62). Of the fifteen historical works in Arabic the author has been able to find that mention the mosque's history, several refer to this story (in almost identical words, suggesting that they had it from each other), the oldest of which is the author cited here, Ibn Duqmaq, who died in 809/1407. Among the reasons why this cannot be considered substantiated is that all who mention it wrote at least seven and a half centuries after the supposed event, while none can name a historical source for it, but rather all introduce it with the words *qil* "it has been said," or *yuqal* "it is said," despite their manifest preference everywhere in their works to mention the historical authorities they report from. Moreover, their relating that the mosque was built far to the left

The second is the mosque of 'Ali ibn Abi Talib (Allah ennoble his countenance) at a distance of some 817 miles from Mecca in Kufa, Iraq, whose qibla 'Ali established in the presence of a great many Companions.[1] Its compass bearing is 195 degrees south by west, which after compensating for magnetic declination as before, turns out to be off absolute perfection by an error factor of about 1.02 percent. Here also, if one wanted to turn slightly at prayer to compensate for the error, one would find no way to do so.

The third is the Grand Friday Mosque of San'a, the first mosque in Yemen, built in the sixth year of the hijra by Wabr ibn Yuhannas al-Ansari (Allah be well pleased with him) (al-Hajri: *Masajid San'a'* (e30), 23).[2] It is comparable in accuracy to the others. San'a is set in the

---

and then rebuilt slightly to the right suggests that it remained facing well to the left of the qibla, which was not then the case. Imam al-Maqrizi (d. 845/ 1441), in a work devoted to ascertaining the accuracy of the qiblas of the mosques of Egypt, states: "If we were to posit a line extending from [each of] the actual mihrabs of Egypt placed there by the Sahaba, and going straight, without veering or turning aside, it would reach the Kaaba and directly touch it" (*al-Mawa'iz wa al-i'tibar* (e58), 2.263). And Ahmad ibn 'Ali al-Qalqashandi (d. 821/1418) in his chapter on the mosque of 'Amr ibn al-'As conveys that Imam Taqi al-Din al-Subki said, "I asked a scholar in qibla determination, and he told me that Sheikh Taqi al-Din Abu al-Tahir, the foremost authority of qibla and prayer time scholars ('ulama' al-miqat) of his day, used to say, 'Of the proofs of the correctness of our work in determining the qibla [by applied geometry] is that it agrees with the mihrab of the ancient mosque [of 'Amr ibn al-'As]'" (*Subh al-a'sha* (e65), 3.386). But perhaps the most telling confirmation comes from a contemporary author, the architectural historian Hasan 'Abd al-Wahhab, who in his two-volume work on the history of ancient mosques in Cairo, presents a series of six floor-plans of the successive enlargements of the mosque, pillar by pillar, showing that all were parallel to the original foundation (*Tarikh al-masajid al-athariyya* (e2), 1.24).

[1] Imam Taqi al-Din al-Subki says of this mihrab: "[The Shafi'i Imam] al-Ruyani [d. 402/1108] considered the qibla of ['Ali's mosque at] Kufa an objective certainty (yaqin), though not the qibla of Basra, meaning that it was permissible to use personal ijtihad whether to turn slightly right or left at Basra, but not at Kufa. This position has also been related from Ibn Yunus al-Qazwini, since 'Ali prayed at Kufa with most of the Sahaba, and there is no ijtihad alongside the consensus (ijma') of the Sahaba" (*Fatawa al-Subki* (e87) 1.161).

[2] Other Yemeni historians, while concurring that it was built by a Companion, mention that it may have been built by one of the other three Sahaba who successively governed Yemen after Wabr: Aban ibn Sa'id al-Umawi, Farwa ibn Musayk

mountains, some 510 miles from Mecca, over many mountains and valleys. A visitor to the mosque today, if he takes out a compass and looks, will find that the mihrab, which is so old that its Arabic inscription is in the ancient Himyaritic script, faces 332.5 degrees northwest by north. Correcting for magnetic north, as in the previous examples, the error factor from total accuracy is about 2.21 percent. In other words, like the others, it is of great accuracy.

The fourth mosque is at Janad, Yemen, near Ta'izz, about 608 miles from Mecca, and was first built by Mu'adh ibn Jabal (Allah be well pleased with him) at the instance of the Messenger of Allah (Allah bless him and give him peace) in his lifetime (al-Hajri: *Majmu' buldan al-Yaman* (e29), 1.148). Its compass direction is about 318 degrees northwest, which after compensating turns out to be off absolute perfection by an error factor of about 4.49 percent. Here, from a fiqh point of view, according to the Shafi'i school one must face the same direction but may adjust for the 4.49 percent by turning very slightly to the right (tayamun), while in the Maliki and Hanafi school there is no adjustment, and one must face the same direction because it was set by a prophetic Companion.

The fifth mosque is in Zabid, Yemen, about 553 miles from Mecca, and was built by the Arabs of Bani al-Ash'ar, among whom was the Companion Abu Musa al-Ash'ari (Allah be well pleased with him) and his companions (al-Hadrami: *Jami'a al-Asha'ir* (e28), 22). Its compass bearing is less than 1 degree north by east, off absolute perfection by about 6.79 percent, the above fiqh points applying to it as well.

The sixth is the Grand Mosque in the walled Old City in Kairouan, Tunisia, some 2047 miles from Mecca. The original mosque was built there by the Companion 'Uqba ibn Nafi' (Allah be well pleased with him) in 50/670, though the present is the fifth mosque on the same site, built more than 130 years later (*Britannica* (e23), 9.834). The

---

al-Muradi, or al-Muhajir ibn Abi Umayya, the brother of Umm Salama (Allah be well pleased with all of them), though these are less reliable positions, the strongest view being that Wabr built it (al-Maruni: *al-Wajiz* (e59), 30). In any case, it was the first mosque to be built, the Muslims prayed there, all of the above four were Companions, and no one has suggested it was built by anyone else.

author has been unable to learn if any adjustments in the qibla were made in the building of these, but the error factor itself, the greatest of any of the mosques measured, suggests that nothing was done to alter the earliest direction placed by this Companion, as indeed nothing should have according to the Hanafi and Maliki schools which successively governed the region in earliest times. The present mosque faces 148 degrees southeast by east, about 10.5 percent off perfect accuracy.

These mosques testify to the practice of the Sahaba and early Muslims in the matter of their qibla. While they represent only the ancient mosques of the Sahaba that the author is aware of, their remarkable achievement of an average of 95.69 percent of perfect accuracy in determining the direction of the Kaaba at an average distance of 890 miles gives little reason to suppose that the tremendous precision they represent as a group, especially for the time and place, came about by accident. Their builders were plainly striving for total accuracy. This is also borne out by the fact that the three cities of greatest accuracy, Cairo, San'a, and Kufa, represented not only greater numbers of the Companions, but were also urban centers with presumably more Muslims knowledgeable in geography and direction finding available for them to consult than would have been found in minor towns like Janad or Zabid, or the then frontier garrison of Kairouan. Allah says of the believers, "Their way is consultation between them" (Qur'an 42:38).

Between Where the Sun Rises and Sets Is a Qibla

As for the hadith "Everything between where the sun rises and sets is a qibla," there is no evidence in it against the preferability of determining the qibla for the mosques of North America by the most accurate means available, because the hadith refers to situations where *certainty of the direction does not exist.*

This is shown first by the agreement of all Imams of fiqh that when complete certainty is possible by actually being at and seeing the Kaaba, one must face it, and "everything between where the sun rises and sets is a qibla" is not applicable, because certainty has taken its place. As the Maliki Imam Ibn 'Abd al-Barr says:

The ulema are in unanimous agreement (ijma') that the qibla that Allah has ordered the Prophet (Allah bless him and give him peace) and His servants to face the direction of in their prayer is the Kaaba, the Sacred House in Mecca. Allah Mighty and Majestic says, "Turn your face [O Prophet] towards the Sacred Mosque; and wherever you all are, turn your faces towards it" (Qur'an 2:144). They unanimously agree that it is an obligation incumbent upon whoever sees it and beholds it to face the Kaaba itself, and that if one does not face it while seeing it, one has no prayer. And they unanimously agree that whoever is out of sight of it, be he far or near, must face towards it by every means in his power to discover its direction, whether through the stars, mountains, winds, or anything else (al-Istidhkar (e35), 7.215).

Secondly, this is shown by the ijtihad of Malik, Imam of the people of Medina, who draws the interesting conclusion below that the upper limit for unintentional error in one's qibla is, in modern terms, roughly 90 degrees from the exact direction (samt), meaning that one has a 180-degree sweep, in the middle of which is the actual physical direction (samt). Sahnun relates from Ibn al-Qasim in the *Mudawwana:*

> Malik said, regarding someone who prays with his back to the qibla or his right or left side towards it (sharraqa aw gharraba), thinking that that is the qibla, but who then realizes he is not facing the qibla: "he should stop what he is doing, then recommence his prayer." He said, "If he has finished his prayer, but then learns of it within its time, he must repeat it." He added, "But if the time is over, he is not obliged to repeat it." Malik also said, "If a man were to pray turned somewhat aside from the qibla (inharafa) without his right or left side being towards it [i.e. less than a right angle], and he learns of it before finishing his prayer, he should turn back towards the qibla, then finish his prayer without stopping" (al-Mudawwana (e55), 1.92).

Malik's words at the end of this passage plainly entail that one should not remain turned somewhat aside (inharafa) from the actual direction—let alone begin that way—when one knows it with certainty.

49

Indeed, as the famous Maliki fiqh text, the *Mukhtasar* of Imam Khalil ibn Ishaq al-Jundi (with the commentary of Sheikh Salih ibn ʿAbd al-Samiʿ al-Abi (A:)) explains:

> If the mistakenness (A: of the qibla one is facing) becomes plain during a prayer, one stops praying [in order to begin again facing the right direction], unless one is blind or is merely turned somewhat aside from the qibla (*munharif yasiran*, i.e. less than 90 degrees), in either of which cases one turns to face it (A: that is, face the qibla, and merely completes the rest of the prayer that one has begun facing away from it. If in either case one does not turn to face towards it, but merely completes the prayer facing the direction whose mistakenness has become plain, then the prayer is legally invalid for the blind person if he is turned greatly aside from the qibla (*munharif kathiran*, i.e. 90 degrees or more), while such a prayer is legally valid for someone merely turned somewhat aside from the qibla (*munharif yasiran*, i.e. less than 90 degrees), whether sighted or blind, though for either [sighted or blind] to do so is unlawful) (*Jawahir al-iklil* (e3), 1.45).

That is, Malik and other authorities of his school understand the dispensation in the hadith to apply to someone who believes he is facing the correct direction, not to someone who is certain that he is turned, even if only somewhat, away from it.[1] When certainty exists, it must be followed. The Mufti of Hadramawt ʿAbd al-Rahman Ba-ʿAlawi (d. 1251/1835) notes:

> The context of the approximate direction (jiha) being adequate, according to the position itself, is when one is without knowledge of the evidences that direct one towards the actual Kaaba. As for someone able to face the Kaaba itself, if possible through ijtihad, it is by no means adequate to face the approximate direction. Nothing induced the proponents of the approximate direction (jiha) to advocate this except their view that it was impossible to face the actual Kaaba itself through ijtihad, so the difference of opinion is merely verbal, Allah Most High willing, if one reflects upon their lines of evidence (*Bughya al-mustarshidin* (e9), 39–40).

---

[1] This point is further developed in chapter 13 on pages 153–54.

That is, the difference is merely verbal between advocates of the approximate direction (jiha), such as Ghazali, Abu Hanifa, and Malik, whom the author here explains really only permit this for someone without knowledge of the evidences directing one towards the actual Kaaba itself; and those on the other hand such as Shafi'i, who advocate the exact direction (samt), "though by conventional rather than absolute standards ('urfan la haqiqatan)" (al-Haytami: *Tuhfa al-muhtaj* (e33), 1.484)—so both return to a single criterion: to face the Kaaba as accurately as one can, given one's evidences and capacity for ijtihad, and nothing more than this is sought or expected by Sacred Law.

CONCLUSIONS

The two hadiths mentioned by Imam Ghazali in the *Ihya'* do attest to his position that it is obligatory for someone far from the Kaaba to face its approximate direction (jiha) rather than the exact direction (samt) that is considered obligatory in the Shafi'i school. Imam Ghazali, though a Shafi'i, is verbally at least contradicting his own school on this point, and his position is not weak, being the position of the other three schools of Sunni jurisprudence.

The two hadiths, however, give little support to the view that there is anything wrong or against the Islamic tradition in using the most accurate means available to establish the direction of the qibla for mosques built in North America or elsewhere. The fact that the six mosques examined above were within an average of 4.31 percent of perfect accuracy at an average distance of 890 miles from Mecca leaves little to add about their exactitude. Accuracy was the way of the Sahaba who built these mosques.

We also saw that the wide leniency expressed in the hadith of the Prophet (Allah bless him and give him peace) to the people of Medina that "everything between where the sun rises and sets is a qibla" has been understood by Islamic scholars as a dispensation for those who believe they are facing the correct direction, not those who are certain the Kaaba is in a particular exact direction but deliberately turn aside from it, even if only somewhat. When certainty of the direction of the Kaaba exists, this certainty must normally be acted upon, for Allah says, "Be as godfearing as you are able to" (Qur'an, 64:16).

4

Mecca and the Mercator Projection

===

DIFFICULTY

IF anyone in North America, young or old, is asked, "Which direction is Mecca?" they invariably say, "East." The direction of Mecca being east is therefore *mutawatir* or "reported by so many witnesses it is impossible that they should all have conspired to lie about it," and the *mutawatir*, as scholars concur, is a decisive proof, obviating the need for recourse to a globe or mathematical calculation.

RESPONSE

That the direction of Mecca is east is indeed what they say, and what we say, but is of no consequence as a proof for the qibla because of an equivocation imbedded in the word "direction" here. Equivocation is an error in reasoning that invalidates any proof it is found in, as for example when one says:

(1) My friend loves to run;

(2) when he came by this afternoon, he only had time to eat and run;

(3) therefore, he did something he loved.

In this example, even though (1) and (2) are each true in themselves, conclusion (3) is invalid because of the equivocation of using *run* in one sense in the first premise, namely the bodily exercise; and in a completely different sense in the second premise, namely leaving too soon after one has arrived. While we have outwardly used one and the same word in both, the conclusion does not follow because we have equivocated.

Similarly, the reasoning of the above difficulty may be expressed as:

(1) Muslims must turn towards the direction of Mecca for prayer;

(2) the direction of Mecca from North America, by consensus of everyone, is east;

(3) therefore, Muslims must face to the east for prayer.

Here, conclusion (3) is invalid because the word *direction* in premises (1) and (2) means two fundamentally different things.

In premise (1) "direction" means the "straight way towards Mecca" or exact direction (samt) which if one travelled along it going neither left nor right, one would reach the Kaaba. As we saw in chapter 1, the approximate direction (jiha) used to define the qibla in some schools of fiqh is merely an extension of this meaning, an allowable degree of unintentional divergence from it that as such is physically defined by it. We have also seen above that such a straight line of travel only occurs in the real world as a segment of a "great circle," which is not a circle in the sense of going left or right, but rather a straight line of travel which if followed all the way around the globe, would come back to itself, incidentally bisecting the earth into two equal halves.

In premise (2) a different sense of "direction" has been unwittingly substituted; namely, that of *compass direction name* (also confusingly called a *jiha* in Arabic, but with an obviously different meaning than "approximate direction" in the above fiqh sense), which in the case of "east," in the Northern Hemisphere at least, means a segment of a *circle* in the sense of its not being a straight line of travel, but one that rather continually curves towards the left as one proceeds along it. To say that "Mecca is to the east" broadly means it is fairly close to one's own latitude, but "lines" of latitude as we have seen above are *curved*, not straight, and in reality concentric circles on planes parallel to that of the equator, circles whose curvature is more patent the farther one gets from the equator, as they grow smaller and smaller.

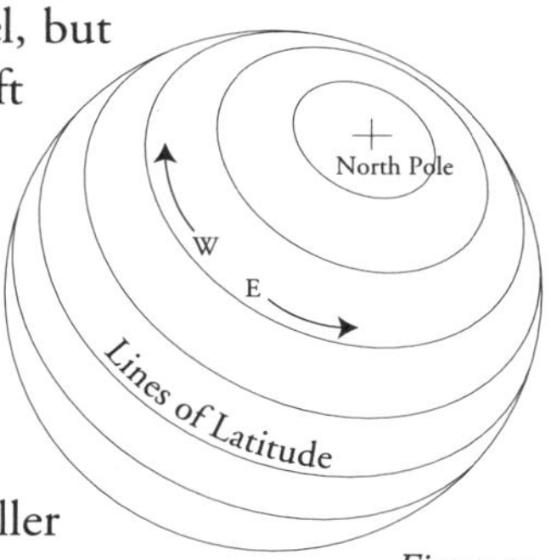

Figure 10

This is most obvious at the North Pole, where if one were to kneel beside the place of the Pole, draw a two-foot diameter circle around it, then move one's hand round and round this circle counter-clockwise, the "direction" one's hand would be going is precisely "east."

One can see what this means at lower latitudes when one takes a globe and puts a straight edge flexible ruler on it heading "due east" from North America or anywhere else in the Northern Hemisphere. One soon discovers that this is quite impossible, because the straight edge simply cannot conform to the curved "lines of latitude" running east and west that are not lines at all. Though "east" and "west" are names of compass directions, at anywhere besides the equator, this sense of the word "direction" is fundamentally different from what we mean by the *direction towards* something that we are *facing*, which, as we saw in the example of the mountain at the beginning of this work, can only be the *straight way* towards that thing.

To summarize, the direction we face towards Mecca cannot be a segment of a circle that curves to the left, as "east" is, but only the straight line of travel that leads directly to Mecca. The fact that everyone knows Mecca to be "to the east" of North America only means they acknowledge it to be along this curved line segment that bears continuously to the left. It is a "direction" at the distances we are talking about in this specific sense only,[1] namely the compass direction "east," but is not a "direction" in the sense used in premise (1) above, which means the way straight towards something that is the shortest possible distance to it.[2]

The difficulty is invalid because it confuses these two senses of "direction."

One does not have to look very far to see where the ambiguity comes from. These two separate senses of "direction" only seem to be alike on a flat map, on which "east" (or "east-southeast") from North America appears to be a straight line direction. The only thing for this is a reality check, by putting a world globe in front of one and a flat map, and deciding which of them one thinks is closer to the real world in which the rulings of the Sacred Law apply.

If this suffices as a general reply to the above difficulty, the question "Why?" may linger in some minds, and to answer it, we have to

---

[1] We shall examine more precisely what compass directions are on pages 56–66 below, "The Thinking Behind the Mercator."

[2] See the following chapter, "The Shortest Distance."

consider for a moment the nature of flat map projections in general, and the Mercator projection map in particular.

The Mercator Projection Map

The central fact of map projection is disclosed by the Arabic word for it, which is *tastih* or "flattening." The fundamental impossibility of faithfully representing the surface of a three-dimensional object on a flat piece of paper is plain from reflecting how one's own appearance might change if one were suddenly flattened. One would look very different.

The attempt to do this with the world has resulted in literally hundreds of different map projections, some 141 of them depicted, for example, in the U.S. Geological Survey's *An Album of Map Projections* (e83) alone, of which we present a few examples in appendix D at the back of the present work. These are not mere thought experiments, but rather each was devised to accomplish specific aims, in Islamic terms placing them in the realm of *fann* or "technique" rather than *'ilm* or "knowledge." As the map historian Peter Whitfield says:

> The project of representing the world on paper, of compressing three dimensions into two, has, by its very impossibility, provoked endless explorations of the problem. There is of course no one correct and valid projection, only projections with different properties and characteristics. Since Mercator's radical approach in the sixteenth century many projections have been mathematically devised for specific purposes (*The Image of the World* (e98), 134).

The "radical approach" referred to is the map drawn by the Flemish cartographer Gerardus Mercator in 1569, which he specifically designed to depict every compass direction or "rhumb line" (e.g. "south," "northeast," "south-southwest") as a straight line (*Britannica* (e23), 8.26). He accomplished this by drawing the north-south "lines of longitude" as parallel, and the east-west "lines of latitude" as parallel, spacing the latter farther apart as they neared the poles. With sacrifices in accuracy we shall enumerate below, he succeeded in producing a map that not only depicted compass directions as straight lines (which by no means all are), but for any particular geographical point in the cartographic grid, yielded the correct ratio of that point's numerical values of longitude and latitude.

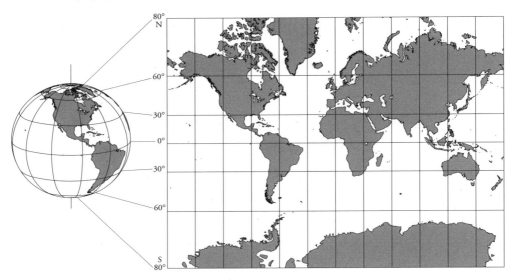

Figure 11. The Mercator projection map, showing the reason for the increasing distortion with increasing distance from the the equator

The Thinking Behind the Mercator

To understand why Mercator designed his map the way he did, we have to remember that the principal means of sea navigation in his day was by finding true north from the ship's compass, or the North Star on clear nights, from which one could infer the other compass directions. Other devices such as the astrolabe and later the sextant told the latitude, but one steered mainly by the compass. Now, one might suppose it would have been ideal for ships at sea to travel in a straight line, along the "great circle" direction that represents the shortest distance between two points. But before the age of computers, this was very difficult because at world distances the direction name or "compass bearing" of such a straight line of travel would continually change (as we have previously seen in figure 4 on page 12, for example), which would necessitate continuous recalculation of the compass bearing in order to proceed along such a line.

The reason why straight lines typically change their compass direction name in their path across the surface of the earth lies in the nature of what a compass direction is.

To see what this means, it is instructive to look at the circular "compass card" or face of a mariner's compass (below), which has thirty-two *rhumbs* or "points" and a circle divided into 360 degrees. The compass card is dominated by two perpendicular axes, a north-south axis and an east-west axis, which terminate in the four cardinal directions: *north* at 360 degrees, *south* at 180 degrees, *east* at 90 degrees, and *west* at 270 degrees. The compass point or "rhumb" of any line of travel, its "compass direction," whether expressed as a direction name or a numerical degree, is by definition its angle of relation to this central north-south axis. "East," for example, means that its relation to this axis is a 90-degree angle, "east-northeast" that its relation to this axis is a 68-degree angle, and "east-southeast" that its relation is a 113-degree angle, and so on.

Figure 12. The compass card

By agreed upon human convention, "north" and "south" anywhere on the face of the earth mean the straight direction lines called "lines of longitude" that lead to the North and South Poles located at the axis upon which the earth turns in its twenty-four-hour rotation.

By human convention also, the compass direction or "rhumb" of a line of travel is defined and agreed upon as its angle in relation to true north, meaning the angle at which it intersects each north-south "line of longitude" that it crosses in its *trajectory* or "path" across the surface of the earth. By convention also, we speak about compass directions analogically with the way we speak about the angle relation of the "rhumbs" or points of the compass card to their north-south axis. We say, for example, that we are going "east" when our trajectory crosses these north-south lines of longitude at a 90-degree angle, we are going "east-northeast" when our trajectory crosses the lines of longitude at a 68-degree angle, and we are going "east-southeast" when we cross them at a 113-degree angle, and so forth.

As long as our trajectory continues to cross every single line of longitude at the same angle, we are going "the same compass direction," and our trajectory has the same "rhumb" or direction name, whether "east," "east-northeast," "east-southeast," or other. Geographers term such a trajectory a "rhumb line." The southeast qibla's direction is a rhumb line, by definition retaining its constant compass direction and its same direction name throughout its trajectory.

Now, a rhumb line, with its constant angle of crossing the north-south lines of longitude, would be straight if and only if each successive line of longitude it crossed were parallel to all the others, as in figure 13 below, in which the straight line of travel, "east-southeast," crosses each of the parallel vertical lines at the same 100.75-degree angle, the southeast qibla's compass bearing from Chicago to Mecca.

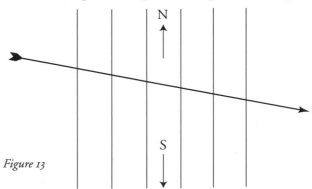

Figure 13

But in the real world, the north-south lines of longitude that a rhumb line crosses at the same angle are not parallel. Rather, they radiate out

like great spokes of a wheel from the North
and South Poles, which means that they are
not actually parallel anywhere on the face of
the earth, as in figure 14, which shows why the
radii emanating from a central point, as lines
of longitude do from the poles, can never, by
their very nature, be parallel to each other.

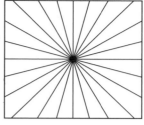

Figure 14

The question arises, What happens to a rhumb line, given that the
lines of longitude it intersects everywhere at the same angle—the very
meaning of its "constant compass direction"—are not parallel, but
radial? The answer, as strange as it may seem, is that its trajectory must
curve in order to intersect each radius at the same angle. There are
only two ways it can do this.

(1) The first is if the rhumb line's trajectory is
a circle, or segment of a circle, whose center
point is the center point of the radii it crosses,
as in figure 15. In such a case, it will cross each
radius at a 90-degree angle.

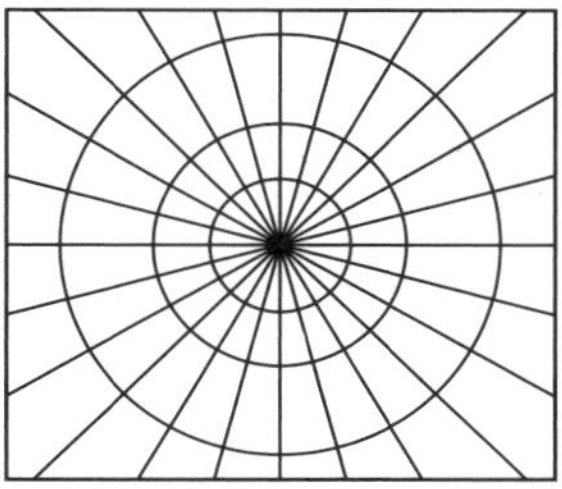

In the real world, a rhumb line that crosses

Figure 15

each north-south line of longitude at such a 90-degree angle will be
going either "due east" or "due west," following a line of latitude (in the
Northern Hemisphere) respectively either counterclockwise or clockwise in relation to the North Pole. Because "lines of latitude" are really

circles, as shown in figure 16,
all rhumb lines with a constant
compass direction of "due east"
or "due west" necessarily curve to
the left or right, with the sole
exception of the equator, which
as we have seen in chapter 1 is a
"great circle," and therefore has
a straight trajectory.

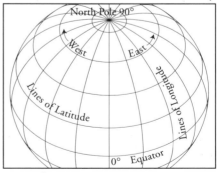

Figure 16

(2) The second, and only other, way that a trajectory can intersect
all the radii coming out from a central point at the same angle—as a
rhumb line, by its very definition as a constant compass direction, *must*

59

intersect the north-south lines of longitude radiating out from the poles—is if it is a *spiral*.

Figure 17 shows how a spiral trajectory intersects all the radii of a central point at a constant angle, here 120 degrees. If one reflects for a moment, it is plain that apart from (1) above, the spiral is the only conceivable trajectory that can intersect all radii at such a constant angle.

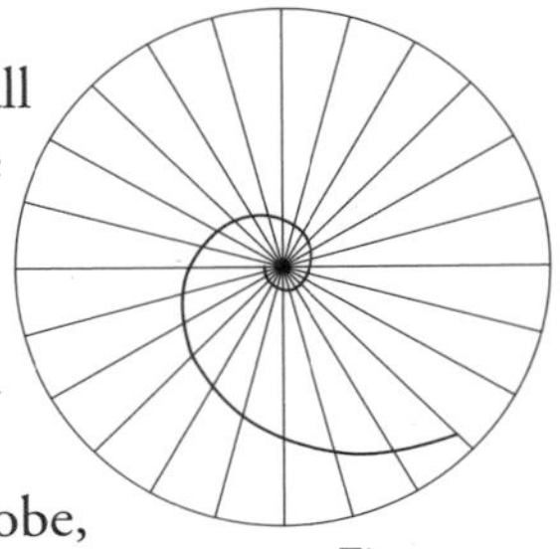

Figure 17

In the real world, which is a three-dimensional globe, the spiral trajectory which intersects at the same angle all lines of longitude radiating out from the North Pole is in fact a three-dimensional "helical spiral," winding down from the Pole like a great spring uncoiling itself. Aside from (1) above, such a trajectory is the only one that can cross every line of longitude at the same constant angle, meaning at the same compass direction, which is the definition of what a rhumb line is. Figure 18 shows the trajectory of the southeast qibla, which is a rhumb line with a constant compass direction. It shows how it intersects each line of longitude at a constant angle, which is what it means to have a unitary compass direction, and shows that to do so, it must continually curve in a helical spiral across the surface of the earth.

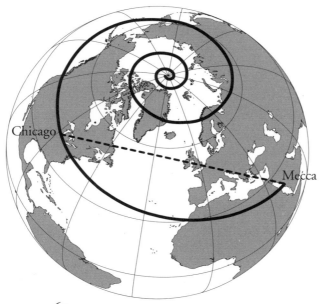

Figure 18. The southeast qibla direction, a "rhumb line," from Chicago to Mecca shown as a solid line, revealed on the world globe as the segment of a helical spiral that it actually is. The northeast qibla direction, a "great circle" line segment and therefore straight, is shown as a dashed line for comparison.

To summarize (1) and (2) above, all rhumb lines—which by definition have constant compass directions or "direction names" such as east-southeast—curve left or right, except those that follow either the equator or else a line of longitude, both of which are straight because they are also great circle directions. In every other case but the equator or longitudes, a constant compass direction or "rhumb line" will be curved, whether because it follows, as in (1) above, a line of latitude due east or west in a circle around the pole, crossing each longitude at a constant 90-degree angle; or whether because, as in (2) above, it is a segment of a helical spiral, crossing each line of longitude at a constant non-90-degree angle, as almost all rhumb lines in the real world do, including the southeast qibla. In either case, the curvature of a rhumb line of course disqualifies it from being the actual physical direction (samt) towards anything (as a qibla must be), because of our axiom (ii) that "a line that curves to the left or right is not straight, so cannot be considered the direction of anything."

Despite this curvature, rhumb lines to Mecca within the same hemisphere are generally accurate enough to ascertain the qibla, because the gradualness of their curvature at such distances allows them to approximate the straight trajectory of the great circle that is the exact direction (samt). Figure 19 below shows how closely a rhumb line between Tangier and Mecca conforms to the great circle direction, which is why flat maps "work" to find the qibla at such a scale, just as figure 18 to the left shows why from North America they do not.

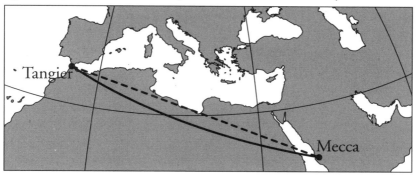

Figure 19. Detail from a globe, showing the qibla from Tangier to Mecca. The true qibla's great circle direction is shown as a dashed line and the rhumb line "flat map" qibla direction is shown as a solid line.

With this, we have penetrated to the heart of the mystery of the two qiblas in North America. It lies in the double meaning of the word *jiha* or "direction" with which this chapter began. Where on earth is a curved rhumb line, with its unchanging compass bearing and unitary direction name (jiha) (such as "northeast," "southwest," or "east-southeast"), virtually identical with the actual direction (also called "*jiha*") of the qibla that Muslims try to face in prayer? Only in the traditional Muslim heartlands, where the scholars who espouse the east and the southeast qibla come from.

These two senses of *jiha*, so obviously distinct in places far from the Muslim heartlands, become closer and closer in meaning the closer one draws to Mecca, where the practical significance of the distinction dwindles to almost nothing. Indeed, because something so lacking in fiqh consequences is not typically discussed or taught or known in traditional circles of learning, few Islamic ulema from these countries are probably even aware of the ambiguity. It simply does not matter there.

The question remains why their North American students have followed them in this, and to answer it we have to return to mapmaking for a moment.

Now, if lines of longitude were everywhere vertically parallel to each other in the real world (instead of radiating out from the poles, as they actually do), rhumb lines would be straight. Navigation would be immensely easier using a map of such a world because one could plot a course on it by simply drawing a straight line from one's position to one's destination, and it would be a rhumb line, by definition having a constant compass bearing, something easily followable with a compass, the main navigational aid of Mercator's day. This is why Mercator drew a projection of the world in which north-south lines of longitude were everywhere parallel, which of course straightened out every rhumb line on the new map. His great simplification of plotting courses that could be easily followed by compass was his lasting contribution to sea navigation.

Thereafter, to navigate a ship by compass, one merely had to draw a straight line on the chart to one's destination, find the compass bearing or "rhumb" of the line drawn, and pilot the ship according to it by using a ship's compass to stay steadily on that bearing. It was a simple procedure, and the charts worked, although when following a single compass bearing for days and weeks, the helmsman would actually be adjusting the ship's course through the water subtly to the left or the right in order to follow the "rhumb line" in its curved path across the spherical surface of the earth. So if the course of such a voyage at intercontinental distances was inevitably a curved trajectory, it was nonetheless easy to follow because one had only the single compass bearing, taken from the chart, that would eventually bring one round to one's destination. Though longer because of its curvature, such a course was more calculable and more followable with an ordinary compass, and hence more reliable for mariners of old.

So the "radical approach" of Mercator's map was not to faithfully portray the earth, but rather to permit plotting an effective navigational course at world distances. It has incidentally also proved its lasting worth in local maps for surveying, for highway travel, and for other functions at short enough distances to make the distortional effect of flattening the earth's sphericality negligible. Our sea charts and road maps to this day are Mercator projections.

As a world map, however, such functions have little to do with finding the qibla between continents, because a curved line, even if shown as straight on a map projection, cannot be the direction of anything. The uncritical use of the Mercator projection map in the discussion in North America as an "all-purpose map of the world" shows how many confusions this can engender. Some of the more important of them can be summarized under five headings.

(1) For many, it is *the* map of the world. With local road maps drawn according to the same principles and causing little distortion in their relative distances and directionality, most people unconsciously assume that the same principles extended to global distances will produce a relatively distortion-free map of the world. Many of the difficulties addressed by the present work stem from the strength of this impression, which seems "self-evident" to many people and renders basic facts of physical geography in the real world "counterintuitive" to them.

An example may best show why flat maps are inadequate to find the qibla at global distances while they work perfectly well locally.

If one were to draw a straight black line upon the surface of a basketball extending halfway around it, then cut a small, one-inch square out of its surface bearing a segment of the line drawn, and to lay this square flat upon the ground, the line segment drawn upon it would appear to be perfectly straight, and the square almost perfectly flat. But it is impossible to think of a way to cut and spread out the whole surface of the basketball in one large square that would depict the entire straight line from one side of the basketball to the other. The small square works, but the big one does not. The points on the line of the latter are simply too far apart on the spherical ball from which they come to ignore the very real difference between its round shape and the flatness of a square. This is why one can tour Spain for a month with a road map without getting lost, but cannot depend on such a map to accurately find a straight line direction between North America and Mecca.

(2) The Mercator projection map lays out the size and location of land masses, with their respective geometric relations, such as the direction of Mecca from North America, according to its own system of depicting latitudes and longitudes.

As explained above, "lines of longitude" (meridians) are drawn on a Mercator projection map as parallel and equally far apart at all places, north and south, while in reality they converge at the poles. One distortion this causes is that its horizontal "lines of latitude" (parallels) extend out farther and farther to the east and west the farther one gets from the equator. For example, the circumference of the circle we call the "line of latitude" of 80 degrees north, shown on the Mercator as parallel and equal to the 24,902-mile-long equator, is actually only 4,317 miles long. Were a human being to exaggerate this much, he would not inspire much confidence as a qibla authority.

Too, in order to achieve its navigational purposes, the Mercator must expand the degrees of latitude farther and farther apart as one gets farther and farther north or south of the equator, until they are expanded to infinity at the poles. That is, the Mercator must exponentially increase the distance between degrees of latitude the farther one goes north, so that the map would in principle extend to an infinite distance at the top or bottom if this were possible. Because it is not, the Mercator simply cuts off the northern and southern edges of the map at a latitude (generally at 80 degrees north) well below the 90 degrees north represented by the Pole.

(3) In consequence, landmasses are vastly distorted, not only in regard to the real direction (samt) between them, with its obvious consequences for finding the qibla, but also to their relative size. On a Mercator projection, for example, the landmass of Greenland appears to be greater than that of the continent of South America, whereas in actual area, Greenland is smaller than Saudi Arabia.

(4) The Mercator projection map generates an unconscious habit of regarding the polar regions as the "edge of the world," too remote to be the direction of anything, though in reality they are but part of a continuous surface, an exact direction line (samt) passing through polar regions being no different than one passing through anywhere else.

(5) As dealt with above in our discussion of the thinking behind it, the Mercator projection map's specific way of depicting the surface of the spherical earth as a flat surface was intentionally designed to make "rhumb lines" or constant compass directions such as "southeast," "northwest," and "east" appear as straight lines, whereas most such "directions," as we have seen, reveal themselves on a globe to be lines that curve to the left or right.

Conversely, except for the equator and the north-south lines of longitude, every single exact direction (samt)—which we have seen above is invariably a straight line of travel on the globe curving neither left nor right because it is a segment of a "great circle"—will be depicted on a Mercator projection map as a line curved to the left or right.

In other words, what most people by habit regard as "the map of the world" was specifically designed by Mercator to embody the very navigational features that have so confused those who pray towards the east or southeast from North America today. If navigationally expedient, such perceptions have no more validity than their degree of correspondence to the real world, for there is no proof that Allah intended

Muslims to disregard that world and adopt a map projection conceived and drawn by Gerardus Mercator in Flanders in 1569. As noted above, other map projections exist drawn on completely different principles, because the purposes for which they were drawn differ.

The Azimuthal Projection Map

Among them is the azimuthal projection map. The word "azimuth" in English derives from the Arabic *as-samt* or "exact direction line," and this is what an azimuthal projection map shows, although only for the geographical point that is at the center of the map. The azimuthal projection most familiar to readers is perhaps the "polar projection," shown in figure 20 here:

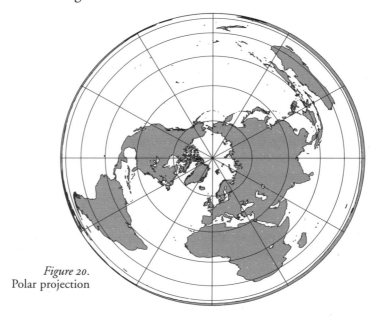

Figure 20.
Polar projection

This projection is used today in military and strategic studies because it correctly shows northern Europe and Asia as quite close to North America, in reality right across the North Pole from each other, whereas the Mercator projection map gives the impression that they are far apart. But the most important tasks of this or any other azimuthal projection map are:

66

(1) to show the exact direction (samt) between anywhere in the world and the center point as a straight line; and

(2) to show all points equally far on the surface of the earth from the central point as equally far from it on the map, for which reason it is sometimes termed an "azimuthal *equidistant* projection map."

Although it accomplishes these aims at an increasing sacrifice of accuracy in the shapes of land masses the farther one goes from the center, its usefulness for finding the qibla when *Mecca* is placed at the center of it cannot be lost on anyone. Indeed, the mathematical principles of azimuthal projections were first discovered by Muslim scientists, most probably al-Biruni, for this very purpose, and later perfected and drawn as maps on the brass qibla-finding instruments that furnish the subject of Professor David King's monumental *World Maps for Finding the Direction and Distance to Mecca* (e53), recently published in the Netherlands.

Figure 21, a modern version, shows the exact direction towards Mecca from any place in the world, relative to the cartographic grid.

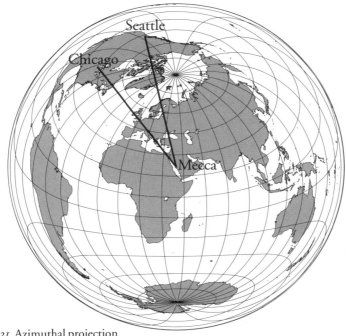

Figure 21. Azimuthal projection
map centered on Mecca

We are indebted to Dr. S. Kamal Abdali for this map, which has been adapted from his article entitled "The Correct Qibla" (e1) about scientific aspects of determining the qibla in North America. The map is a veritable traveller's friend, since anyone who carries a photocopy of it with him can see at a glance the exact geographical direction of Mecca from wherever in the world he may be.

In the modern day, azimuthal projection maps have been used extensively for air navigation, as they show the exact direction (samt) from all places to whatever point lies at the center of them. Two of them, centered respectively on Pearl Harbor and Delhi, appear in *The Image of the World* by Peter Whitfield, who says:

> The outstanding characteristic of these maps is that a straight line from the center, from Delhi or Pearl Harbor, is the direct route and the shortest distance to any point on the globe. Moreover, the scale along that line is constant. It will be seen at once that these properties would have great practical value in plotting air routes, and their principal use is in air navigation. They are the precise two-dimensional equivalent to drawing straight lines upon a globe. Their true directional properties relate only to the one central point, and a different map must be plotted for London, New York, Melbourne, or any other city. The entire earth is shown, but distortion away from the central point becomes extreme, so that the resulting map is alien and apparently nonsensical. In fact it is no nearer to or further from geographic reality than for example the Mercator projection, but the latter is visually less disturbing because it is sanctified by familiarity (*The Image of the World* (e98), 134–35).

CONCLUSIONS

Flat is not the only way maps lie. The fundamental difficulty with flat world maps is distortion, from which the specific features they are designed to show are the exception. They are not representations of the world, as a globe is, but rather devices for accomplishing various *aims*. These aims are extremely diverse, and hundreds of map projections exist, of which we have discussed but two in the present section.

The first was the Mercator projection map, which we saw was specifically designed by its inventor to make compass direction lines that are curved on the actual earth's surface seem straight, and it conversely makes exact direction (samt) lines that are straight on the earth's surface seem curved. By design rather than by accident, it produces the misconceptions it has come to engender in the minds of those who unreflectively rely on it to find the direction to Mecca at world distances, a function the Mercator does not do and was not designed to do.

The second was the azimuthal projection map, originally designed by Muslim scientists to determine the direction to Mecca, and which indicates the exact direction (samt) from all points on the map to the central point. The first example we saw was the polar projection, with the North Pole as its center point; while the second was the qibla projection drawn with Mecca at its center. The main feature of azimuthal projection maps is that, in Whitfield's words, "they are the precise two-dimensional equivalent of drawing straight lines upon a globe," which is precisely what is sought in determining the qibla. They work because they were designed to.

As for selecting the Mercator projection map for some other reason than function, such as its familiarity, in spite of its manifest inadequacy for global direction-finding, this is mere emotive preference, and emotive preference is not a measure of Sacred Law.

5

The Shortest Distance

DIFFICULTY

G RANTED that on a globe, the northeast direction is the shortest distance from North America to Mecca and the east is the longer route: there is no authoritative text in the books of fiqh to show that the "direction" of something means the shortest distance to it.

RESPONSE

That the direction of the Kaaba or anything else on the planet is the shortest distance to it is simply the meaning of the word "direction," both in ordinary speech and as used by scholars and books of fiqh that discuss qibla determination. This is the understanding we found with the fuqaha of the Hanafi, Maliki, and Shafiʻi schools of jurisprudence whom we asked about the question.

The Fuqaha

The Hanafi Mufti of Damascus Dr. ʻAbd al-Fattah al-Bizm in his fatwa ((e16), 21 August 2000, 1) quotes Imam Ibn ʻAbidin citing al-Kaki (d. 749/1348), author of *Miʻraj al-diraya,* who says:

> The meaning of the "direction" (jiha) of the Kaaba is the way which if one turned toward it, one would be facing (musamit) the Kaaba or the space above it, whether exactly or approximately—"exactly" meaning that if a *line* were imagined directly out from one's face at a right angle towards the horizon, it would reach the Kaaba or the space above it—and "approximately" meaning slightly turned (munharif) from it or the space above it while still somewhat facing it, such that part of the surface of one's face would still be *in direct line* with it or the space above it [italics the translator's] (*Radd al-muhtar* (e37), 1.287).

Here, the key word *musamit* or "facing something" lexically derives from the word *samt* or "exact line direction"—just as the physical fact of facing something derives from the exact direction—its being the shortest distance implicit in the term. As for an explicit statement of this from the books of the fuqaha, the Hanafi sheikh Hassan al-Hindi of Damascus says:

> It has not been explicitly mentioned in books of fiqh whether "direction" means the "shortest distance" or not, the fuqaha neither confirming nor denying it for two reasons:
>
> The first is that in none of the regions for which they specified the rules of the qibla did they imagine a division into two directions, one longer and the other shorter, but rather the direction in all the examples they mentioned was always the shortest distance, the fuqaha being in a small portion of the world, namely the lands around Mecca.
>
> The second reason is that the question does not require an explicit text because it is obvious. Had it been otherwise, the fuqaha would have had to explicitly say so, since it would have been the opposite of what comes to mind.
>
> This definition is self-evident and understood from the plain language of the Arabs. For when a questioner asks after the direction of a town, he means the shortest distance leading to it. Otherwise, it would be valid for someone face-to-face with the Kaaba to turn his back to it and say, "This is the [direction of the] Kaaba," adducing that the earth is a continuous surface extending around to the Kaaba from the other side, and we would be unable to condemn him for this (*Fatwa* (e34), 20 July 2000, 6–7).

The Maliki scholar Dr. Muhammad al-Tawil of the Qarawiyyin in Fez, Morocco, says:

> The meaning of "the approximate direction" (jiha), for those who say one must face it [the Hanafi, Maliki, and Hanbali schools], is the direction in which the Noble Kaaba is situated in relation to the person praying, such that his face is turned that way and that direction when he is at prayer. It might be to the east or the west or some other cardinal or derived direction, such as the southeast or northeast, as is borne out by the hadith "Everything between

where the sun rises and sets is a qibla," which Tirmidhi related and declared authentic.

So too, the criterion for what is considered to be the "direction" (jiha) is the shortest distance between the Kaaba and the face of the person praying, for this is "his direction" which he is facing. And if the texts of the fuqaha do not contain an explicit indication that the shortest distance or the farthest is the criterion, we find in their words that which plainly entails this; namely:

(1) Their agreement that the prayer of someone who turns his back on the qibla is legally invalid. This shows that what is intended is the closest direction, since whoever has his back to the qibla from the closest direction is *facing* it from the farthest direction because of the sphericality of the earth. So from this we may say that the shortest distance is the criterion, since if just any route were intended, they would not be in unanimous agreement that the prayer of whoever has his back toward it from the shortest distance is legally invalid.

(2) The hadith of turning around the qibla [from Jerusalem to Mecca], for if what it meant were [a free choice] to face the Kaaba from either the nearer or farther direction, Allah would not have ordered them to turn the qibla around; since when they were praying towards Jerusalem (Bayt al-Maqdis), they had their backs to it [the Kaaba] from the shortest distance but were facing it from the long way around, as someone [between the two places] facing Jerusalem has his back to the Kaaba, and vice versa, as Ibn Hajar [al-'Asqalani] has indicated in the *Fath* [al-Bari (e8)], 1.507.

Thus, whoever is facing Jerusalem from the nearest distance is necessarily facing the Kaaba from the farther distance because of the sphericality of the earth. So the command to turn the qibla around is proof that the criterion is the shortest distance, not the farthest.

Otherwise, it seems clear that this meaning of "direction" is the lexical sense, for "direction" (jiha) is derived from "facing something" (muwajaha). It is said, "I faced So-and-so," [meaning] "I turned my face to his face." It is plain that "facing towards him" can actually only come about by being in the nearest direction; for otherwise, if one were facing the long way around to him, one would be "facing something else" (*Fatwa* (e90), 10 March 2000, 1–2).

The six Shafiʻi muftis of the Fatwa Council of Tarim, Hadramawt, in Yemen, write:

> In respect to the question "Is the criterion in determining the qibla the shortest path to it or not?"; the answer is that the qibla is something physical, as mentioned in the *Tuhfa al-muhtaj* of Ibn Hajar [al-Haytami] (1.496)—and that the "physical" means the perceptible [al-mushahada], as is mentioned in the *Nihaya al-muhtaj* by the great scholar Muhammad al-Ramli (1.439). Therefore the criterion for determining the direction of the qibla is the shortest path to the Kaaba, for this is what is normally termed the "direction," as opposed to the longer way to something. This is implicit in the words of the great scholar Ahmad Bek al-Husayni in his book *Dalil al-musafir* (p. 68) . . . .
>
> The Mufti of Tarim, our sheikh the great scholar and faqih Sheikh Fadl ibn ʻAbd al-Rahman Ba-Fadl (Allah Most High have mercy on him), when asked this very question by one of his students, explicitly stated that the criterion to be relied upon for determining the direction of the qibla is the shortest and closest path. That was the answer he gave, and he made reference to the position of the great scholar Ahmad Bek al-Husayni from his book *Dalil al-musafir* (*Fatwa* (e54), 12 September 2000, 1–2).

Indeed, that the "direction" of anything is the shortest distance to it is shown by three separate proofs: from common sense, logic, and the Arabic language.

Common Sense

The proof from common sense is that the "direction" towards something is understood by everyone to be a straight line leading from one's position directly to that thing, not a line first going left or right and then returning back to it. Ask anyone precisely what direction something is, and he is expected to point straight at it.

If there were any doubt about this, we could make a simple experiment in a living room with a number of people. Let us choose an object in the room such as a wall clock, select a panel of judges, and pick someone and tell him that he will win a purse of a thousand dollars if he can correctly point to the direction of the clock. What is the normal expectation? If he were to point to the left of the clock or any other direction besides the shortest distance to it, we would normally wonder what got into him, or what cognitive dysfunction he suffers from, or how he could have misunderstood such simple instructions.

If he were then to explain to the judges that the direction to the left which he has pointed to is also correct, because a curved trajectory in that direction could come back and reach the clock, it is not easy to see how any of the judges would accept this. They would judge him wrong because human language judges him wrong. This is not the way the word "direction" is used by anyone who speaks. Usage dictates that the "direction" of something means the shortest distance to it, and that the roundabout way is completely irrelevant to what we mean by its "direction."

Logic

The second proof, from logic, is that the shortest possible distance defines what a direction is, and to negate it negates the very concept of directionality.

If we claim that the shortest distance—the straight line that we indicate when we point at something and say, "It's there"—is only one of a number of possible correct directions to that thing, and that a curved line of travel that goes obliquely out from one's position and then returns to the object in a roundabout way may also be called the correct direction, this means that every single direction in 360 degrees from one's position is also admissible as the correct direction, for there is no direction that cannot curve back and reach the object in some way or another.

Such a concept of "direction" of course ends up cancelling itself, for if something is simultaneously *all* directions, it is no particular direction whatsoever, and "its direction" becomes completely meaningless, because it gives no information about the thing's whereabouts at all. But since the concept is meaningful, it can refer to only one direction, which is the straight line that is the shortest possible distance to the thing. Its oneness entails its directness.

Arabic

The third proof, from Arabic, is the word of Allah Most High in Sura al-Baqara:

> "We certainly see your face [O Muhammad] turning about the sky; now We will surely turn you to a direction that shall please you. So turn your face towards the Holy Mosque; and wherever you all may be, turn your faces towards it (*shatra-hu*)" (Qur'an 2:144).

That "the shortest distance" is central to the concept of "direction" is borne out by nearly every synonym offered by the earliest scholars of Islam to explain the word *shatra-hu* or "towards it" in the above verse.

The first of the synonyms for *shatra-hu* (lit. "its half" or "its center"), given by Ibn 'Abbas, who personally met and knew the Prophet Muhammad (Allah bless him and give him peace), and by other ancient authorities, is *nahw,* which derives from *naha,* "to travel towards" or "go in the direction of" (*Lisan al-'Arab* (e42), 15.310)—which shows how closely "path of travel" is connoted by facing "towards" something in Arabic.

Mujahid ibn Jabr (d. 102/719), a student of Ibn 'Abbas and main Qur'anic exegete of the students of the Companions (tabi'in), also said, "*Shatra-hu* means *nahwa-hu*" (*Tafsir al-Imam Mujahid* (e61), 216), a meaning also related by al-Tabari (d. 310/922) directly from Ibn 'Abbas (*Jami' al-Bayan* (e89), 2.21), and related by Abu Ishaq al-Zajjaj (d. 311/923), one of the most celebrated early lexical specialists in Arabic, who said, "There is no disagreement among lexicologists (ahl al-lugha) that *shatr* means *nahw*" (*Ma'ani al-Qur'an* (e99), 1.222).

Ibn Manzur, author of the fifteen-volume *Lisan al-'Arab,* says that *nahw* is "a synonym for 'straight aim' (qasd) and for 'path' (tariq)" (*Lisan al-'Arab* (e42), 15.309). The word *qasd,* used here by Ibn Manzur as a synonym for *nahw* and by al-Tabari in his own exegesis of *shatra-hu* in the above Qur'anic verse (*Jami' al-Bayan* (e89), 2.20), is explained by no less a lexical authority than al-Raghib al-Isfahani to mean "straightness of path" (istiqama al-tariq) (*Mufradat* (e46), 672), an explicit statement from an expert in Qur'anic usage of the connotation of "shortest distance" in the idea of facing "towards" something, since *straightness of path* means nothing besides.

Al-Tabari (*Jami' al-Bayan* (e89), 2.21) also relates that the word *shatra-hu* was explained by Qatada (d. 118/736) as meaning *tilqa'a-hu,* a word which derives from *liqa'* or "to meet" and is explained by Ibn Manzur as meaning *hidha'a* or being "face to face" or "directly facing" (*Lisan al-'Arab* (e42), 15.254). Yahya ibn Ziyad al-Farra' (d. 207/822) also says of Allah's word *shatra-hu* in the above verse, "He means *nahwa-hu* (towards it) and *tilqa'a-hu* (directly facing it): it is the same as to say, 'Turn your face *shatra-hu* (towards it), or *tilqa'a-hu* (face to face with it), or *tujaha-hu* (facing towards it)'" (*Ma'ani al-Qur'an* (e24), 1.84). The word *tujaha-hu* is explained by Ibn Manzur as being "when one thing is directly across from (istaqbala) another thing" (*Lisan al-'Arab* (e42), 13.557). The derivation of these terms is instructive because it shows that the two proofs previously presented from common sense and logic apply with equal force to Arabic, for the good reason that we are not at the level of mere languages here, but of the "deep meaning" imbedded in all languages, common to all of them precisely because they map out human experience at its most fundamental level.

Each of the terms used above by the earliest Muslim exegetes to explain Allah's command to face the qibla denotes a particular unique physical relation between the person who faces and the thing being faced; namely, the direct path to it. And the direct path between two points is nothing besides the shortest possible distance between them.

CONCLUSIONS

Our examples from fiqh, common sense, logic, and the Arabic language all show that the "direction" of something is normally understood to mean the shortest distance to it.

As for not expressly finding this definition in the classical books of the schools, neither does one find in their books that the nose, for example, is generally in the middle of the face; not because the fuqaha are divided about the issue, but because it is not their job to state the obvious. Rather, the question to ask is "Where is there a text that shows that the fuqaha (or anyone else) ever considered the long way around to be the direction to anything?"

6

A Tunnel Through the Earth

DIFFICULTY

JUST as the fuqaha permit to the person praying a margin of "horizontal divergence" to the left or right from the exact direction (samt) of the Kaaba, namely the *jiha* or approximate direction; so too, they permit a margin of "vertical divergence" above and below, in that they have said that the space above and below the Kaaba is like part of it. So from a fiqh point of view, it is valid to pray in the direction of an imaginary tunnel going straight southeast through the earth's crust from North America to Mecca, as this is also a "shortest distance."

RESPONSE

Several points are inferable from this description.

(1) The tunnel described here as "going straight southeast" is straight, not curving left, right, up, or down.

(2) It therefore runs under the ground in a straight line.

(3) A line drawn directly above the tunnel on the surface of the earth, like the tunnel, would not curve to the left or right.

(4) "Facing the direction" of such a tunnel means standing on the surface of the earth facing the direction of this line. This is the point of mentioning a permissible "vertical divergence," which merely means that the line drawn on the earth towards Mecca that the person is praying upon would be unaffected by the tunnel's depth. That the person facing the tunnel's direction is standing on the earth is also plain from the fact that most places in North America are more than a quarter of the circumference of the globe away from Mecca, and in consequence

such a tunnel would plunge downward into the earth at a slope steeper than 45 degrees. As it is impossible for someone to stand (or pray) facing down such a decline, praying "in the direction of" such a tunnel can only mean standing upon the line drawn on the surface of the earth directly above it.

(5) The suggested evidence therein is that such a line would go towards the southeast direction from North America, which is thus valid to pray towards as one's qibla.

The reply to this is that such a line would not go towards the southeast from North America. It would go only to the northeast, the great circle direction, because the tunnel is what in geometry is termed a *secant,* a line that connects two points (Mecca and North America) on the circumference of a circle which in this case lies on the plane (vertical with the person standing) running through the center of the earth, dividing the earth in half, as shown in figure 22 below. That is, a line drawn directly above such a tunnel on the surface of the earth would go only in the great circle direction, because the tunnel, together with the line drawn on the surface of the earth above it and the great circle,

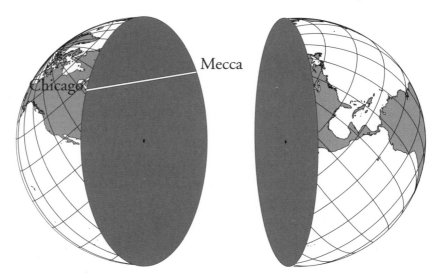

Figure 22. Cross section of the tunnel

would all be on one and the same plane—the vertical plane that is perpendicular to the chest and face of the person praying to the northeast from North America.

The only stipulation we have added to the above description to lead to this conclusion is the obvious one that the line drawn on the earth's surface be *directly above* the tunnel, that is, directly vertically in line with both the tunnel and the center of the earth. Such a line is where a vertical plane running the length of the tunnel would intersect the earth's surface.

Any other plane angle than vertical would be absurd, because it would generate a line on the surface of the earth not straight but *curved* to the left or right. If, for example, the axis of the plane extending the length of the tunnel were not vertical but tilted at a slant from the left of the tunnel's floor to the right of the its ceiling, it would intersect the surface of the earth at a curved trajectory, initially towards the southeast but inexorably curving back to the left to rejoin the tunnel's exit. This is inadmissible, first, because a line that curves left or right cannot be the direction of anything, and second, because it nullifies the whole evidentiary basis of the example, which is the tunnel's *straightness.*

CONCLUSIONS

As long as the tunnel from North America to Mecca is straight, it provides little rationale for the southeast direction. For if we mean by its "direction" facing the direction of a line drawn directly above it on the surface of the earth, this adds nothing new to the exact direction (samt) of Mecca calculable by other means; that is, it lies to the northeast. And if we mean by it facing the direction of the tunnel itself, in most of North America it would entail praying steeply down into the earth, which no faqih has ever suggested. And farther west, in Hawaii, for example, the tunnel would go straight down into the earth, and a person would have to devise a way to stand on the wall praying straight towards the floor. Whatever the merits of such a prayer, it would be unlikely to be free of distraction.

7

Considering the Earth Legally Flat

———

DIFFICULTY

OUTWARD rulings of Sacred Law are derived from people's direct sensory perception of reality. The earth is experienced by sense perception "as if" flat, even though, as we all know, it is not flat. Islamic legal rulings are interpreted according to the *'urf* or "what is commonly acknowledged" by ordinary human usage and convention, so for legal purposes the Qur'anic command to face the qibla should be understood within this perceptual context.

This is also borne out by the fact that there is no text of fiqh that says knowing the earth is round is obligatory for someone finding the qibla. If this were obligatory to know for something so common as finding the qibla, the fuqaha would have explained it, and they have not.

The direction of the qibla should thus be legally determined according to the *'urf* or "common acknowledgment" of considering Mecca to lie to the east or southeast of North America as it is on the flat map, regardless of any geographic or geometric considerations.

RESPONSE

The points of this difficulty need to be examined one by one, after perhaps giving the short answer, which is that a flat world is an imaginary place, the rulings of Allah apply exclusively to the real world, and the real world is round.

The Word of Allah

In essence, the difficulty opposes a "fiqh world," which in conformity with human experience is flat, to a real world which is round. This fiqh world is claimed to take precedence over the real world in determining the qibla because of the alleged legal primacy of human sense perception and common acknowledgement ('urf) over other knowledge.

To evaluate this claim, it is useful to consider how the methodology of fiqh approaches primary texts that contain commands such as "Wherever you all may be, turn your faces towards it" (Qur'an 2:144), in which words like "wherever," according to scholars, may be either intended by Allah in their original primary sense (asl) or in some transferred sense (naql).

The Arabic lexicographer Majd al-Din al-Fayruzabadi (d. 817/1415) notes that *haythu* or "wherever" in its original primary sense is "a word denoting the *place* (makan), just as *hina* (when) does with the time (zaman)" (*al-Qamus* (e25), 168). What sort of place? The only sort of place that would come to the minds of those to whom the verse was first revealed, namely a place that can in principle *exist,* such that they could *be* in it. Such places lie only in the physical world beneath our two feet.

As for interpreting the word *haythu* or "wherever" as applying to a hypothetical world, the "as if" world of the flat map, this is a figurative departure that represents a transfer (naql) of the meaning from its original primary sense of "some actual place in the real world" to a figurative understanding of "some place in a flat-map world." This transfer of meaning, which the above difficulty characterizes as sanctioned by sense perception or common acknowledgement ('urf), is unacceptable because it contradicts the methodological bases of Islamic fiqh (usul) by which scholars understand the texts of the Qur'an and sunna. Imam Ghazali says,

> If a word [in a scriptural text] may be used in both a literal and figurative sense, the word is taken in its literal sense until some proof indicates that the figurative sense is intended (*al-Mustasfa* (e27), 1.359).

Taj al-Subki (with Jalal al-Din al-Mahalli's commentary (M:)) says,

> It (M: i.e. the figurative) and the transferred sense (naql) [away from the original primary meaning] are exceptions to the rule (khilaf al-asl) (M: so that if a word may [1] be taken in either a literal or a figurative sense, or [2] be taken in either an original or transferred sense, the rule, meaning that which outweighs its alternative, is that the word [in the case of (1)] be taken in its literal sense, for

the literal meaning requires nothing else to prove it, or [in the case of (2)] in its primary original meaning, because of the ongoing presumption that it retains its fundamental sense that it had in the first place) (*Jam' al-jawami'* (e84), 1.312).

And Fakhr al-Razi says:

The transferred sense (naql) is an exception to the rule [that the original primary meaning is presumed until proven otherwise], as is attested by various facts, one of which is that a transferred sense cannot be confirmed without there first having been an original primary meaning, then this meaning abrogated, then a different meaning established. As for the primary meaning, it is established by a single state—and something that depends on three separate things is outweighed by something that depends on only one (*al-Mahsul* (e75), 1.314).

In the case of interpreting the Qur'anic verse about facing the qibla, this means we must deal with "wherever" as it is, unless we can show that Allah intends something else by it than the word's original primary meaning. There is no objection to this in principle, but one must show that it has actually happened in the Arabic language. As we shall see below, the sphericality of the earth has been known to Islamic scholars for almost ten centuries, so if such a transfer of meaning had ever taken place, Arabic lexicographers would have noted it and attested to it in their works, while none has.

In other words, the above-mentioned interpretive principle of Sacred Law that "the transferred sense is an exception to the rule" (al-naql khilaf al-asl), together with the absence of any lexical evidence that such an exception has taken place, means that Allah's words about facing the qibla "Wherever you may be, turn your faces towards it" (Qur'an 2:144) must be interpreted in their original primary sense, as meaning "wherever on the actual earth you may be," for "wherever" has no other primary signification.

To say, as in the above difficulty, that the command to face the qibla should be interpreted "as if the world were flat, even though as we all know it is not flat" is thus unsupported by the interpretive methodology of fiqh. We have quoted the above principle from but three of the more well-known books on the bases of jurisprudence (usul al-fiqh); otherwise, there is scarcely a book in the field that does not mention it.

From their origin, the rulings of Sacred Law derive from Allah alone and apply to the world we find ourselves in, not an imaginary world, flat or otherwise. Scholars tell us that knowledge ('ilm) is an attribute that does not affect its object (al-ma'lum): whether we comprehend all of an object's particulars perfectly, or some of them imperfectly, or none of them at all, the object of our knowledge remains what it is. This is why human sense perception or common acknowledgment ('urf) as modes of knowledge have no effect, legal or otherwise, upon the geographical features of the real world in which Allah has commanded us to face the qibla.

Aside from this, common acknowledgement ('urf) is irrelevant to the discussion because first, it is not invoked when there is an unequivocal text (nass) like the word *haythu* or "wherever" in the above verse, which needs nothing additional from common acknowledgement in order for us to understand its precise referent, namely this world; and second, because common acknowledgement changes with time and place. When needed by ulema to spell out otherwise unspecified criteria of a legal ruling, such as whether something should be considered a fair stipulation in a contract, common acknowledgement refers to *contemporary* standards among people. And few people today regard the world as anything but round.

As for sense perception, it is merely the easiest way for human beings to learn how to go about obeying the commands of Allah in that world.

Sense Perception of the Earth

Moreover, the flatness of the earth is not a "given" of human sense perception, for the curvature of our planet's surface is visible to the naked eye in a number of situations. It is obvious, for example, when one is hiking in the mountains and there are several peaks of comparable height fairly close to one another. If one climbs to the top of one of them, all the other mountains appear to be lower than it. If one then climbs a neighboring peak of a similar altitude, the same thing happens, and the previous mountaintop appears lower than the present one. It is a palpable physical demonstration that the earth is round, which is further borne out when one lifts one's gaze to the horizons from such a mountaintop and sees the tops of all the mountains curving inexorably down lower and lower as they draw nearer to the horizons. Here, the curvature of the earth is mere sense perception.

It is equally perceptible when travelling at sea, out of sight of any land, and one comes into sight of a shoreline of high cliffs. The top of the cliffs always appears first, and then the rest, on down. The last thing one sees is whether there are any boats below them, because of the roundness of the earth. The same is true of meeting another boat at sea: the rigging is seen first, then the house, and then the whole boat. Here too, the roundness of the earth is a perceptible sensory fact.

For that matter, the shape of our planet is plain from the curved shadow of the earth that is cast upon the moon with monthly regularity by the light of the sun, observable to anyone who notes the stages of the moon. Finally, the shape of the earth is visible from the surface of the moon, which human beings have now travelled to and looked at the earth from and taken pictures to show the rest of us.

For all of these reasons it is far from clear how "direct sensory perception of reality" necessitates our dealing with the world as if it were flat.

The Ulema

Dealing with the earth as if flat was certainly not the perspective of previous centuries of Muslim scholarship. Fakhr al-Razi (d. 606/1210), for example, in his Qur'anic exegesis explaining the word of Allah in Sura al-Ghashiya "And [do they not look] at the earth, how it has been made level" (Qur'an 88:20), notes,

> There are people who have adduced this to prove that the earth is not round, which is weak, for if a sphere is absolutely tremendous in size, every portion of it will be just as if it were flat (*Mafatih al-ghayb* (e76), 31.158–59).

The six Shafi'i muftis of the Fatwa Council of Tarim, in Wadi Hadramawt, Yemen, write:

Because of what has been mentioned above about the qibla being something physical and tangible, whoever wants to know it must start from the fact that the earth is round, which is unanimously concurred upon by all geometers, astronomers, and even all Qur'anic exegetes—as the great scholar Muhammad al-Amin al-Shinqiti conveys in his Qur'anic commentary *Adwa' al-bayan* (9.202)—since that is how the earth is. As for flat maps, they are no more than a depiction of the earth's features, nothing else. They do not show how the earth actually is (*Fatwa* (e54), 12 September 2000, 2).

And Ibn Hazm (d. 456/1064) says:

Not a single one of the Imams of the Muslims who deserves the name Imam of Sacred Learning (Allah be well pleased with them) has ever denied the sphericality of the earth; nor from a single solitary one of them has any word rejecting it ever been learned. Rather, the proofs of the Qur'an and sunna show that it is round. Allah Mighty and Majestic says, "He winds the night around the day, and the day around the night" (Qur'an 39:5), which is the plainest explanation that they are wound around one another, the word being derived from the winding (kawwara) of the turban, meaning the wrapping of it around, this being an unequivocally clear scriptural proof (nass) that the earth is a sphere (*al-Fisal* (e41), 2.241).

Such was the state of Islamic knowledge nine hundred and fifty years ago. In the modern day, none of the twenty-two ulema from six Muslim countries who were asked for fatwas during the writing of the present work was found to believe that the earth was flat; nor has the author ever met a faqih who believes this, or that "direct sensory perception of reality" necessitates our dealing with it as if it were. As the Hanafi sheikh Hassan al-Hindi of Damascus says:

To stipulate [in fiqh] that the earth should be considered round is something taken for granted, because fuqaha investigate reality, not matters that contradict reality. So how should we require our minds to hypothesize a qibla on a flat earth merely because the fuqaha have not stipulated that the earth be considered round in determining the qibla? This too is one of the facts so obvious that they do not need an explicit fiqh text to state them. Rather, if the opposite were the case it would require an explicit text from them (*Fatwa* (e34), 20 July 2000, 4).

Fiqh, Perception, and Intellect

Those who have read fiqh realize that the true reason many of the rulings are based on direct sensory perception of reality is that fiqh is an *operationalization* of the Qur'an and sunna, and so must interpret the command of Allah in a way that the ordinary Muslim can easily grasp, easily accomplish, and easily see whether or not he has succeeded in doing so. Sense perception necessarily enters into the rulings because "Allah does not charge any soul except its capacity" (Qur'an 2:286), and one's capacity to understand the environment around one in order to apply the rulings of Allah normally entails using one's five senses.

Yet knowledge, cognition, memory, and other capacities of human reason also enter into the rulings of Sacred Law, which is why, for example, the mere knowledge that a drop of urine has fallen on one's clothes and now dried is sufficient according to scholars to necessitate washing away the filth that, although it is without discernible characteristic, the mind knows to be there.

Sense perception enters into fiqh rulings not because of any intrinsic significance it possesses, but rather for the certainty that it produces in the ordinary person about the ordinary situation. Other cognitive faculties can also produce this certainty. There is little difference, for example, in the certainty produced by testing how deep the water is at the muddy ford of a river by wading slowly and carefully across it, and the certainty produced by feeling ahead of oneself with a long stick. The end of the stick is like an extension of the body.

Similarly, the certainty afforded by mathematical calculation of the high risk of building a thermonuclear power plant at a particular location may well make it unlawful by the standards of Sacred Law to build there. Or the calculation of how many apples a schoolchild typically eats in a year make an orchardman's use of a particular pesticide unlawful. Rulings established by such kinds of certainty fall under the general rubric of *ta'abbud bi al-dhann* or "being morally responsible for what one believes to be the case," and are very common in Sacred Law. The point is that the outward rulings of Sacred Law are not applied in our world according to sense perception alone, but also through deduction, memory, inference from models, calculation, risk assessment, and other mental processes that produce subjective certainty in us about the particular worldly facts the rulings apply to.

Fiqh Texts and the Roundness of the Earth

As for the contention that "there is no text of fiqh that shows that knowing the earth is round is obligatory for someone finding the qibla," fiqh literature does indeed show that knowing the earth is round is obligatory, for "a judgement about something derives from the way it is conceptualized" (Taj al-Subki: *al-Ibhaj* (e85), 1.172), and only by using a globe as a conceptual model of the world is it possible to make geographically accurate ijtihad about the qibla in the Western Hemisphere. Without it, the would-be mujtahid falls into the kinds of mistakes inventoried in the present work. The proof that it is obligatory is the methodological precept of Sacred Law (asl) expressed by Taj al-Subki (with Jalal al-Din al-Mahalli) as,

> Anything possible which something obligatory cannot be accomplished without is itself obligatory (M: whether it be a necessary reason (sabab) for it or a precondition (shart)) (*Jam' al-jawami'* (e84), 1.192–93).

It is possible to know the world is round, the direction of Mecca from North America cannot be accurately ascertained without it, and so it is obligatory. Imam Ibn 'Abidin explicitly says in his *Radd al-muhtar,* the foremost fatwa resource for the late Hanafi school:

> The matter of the qibla is only to be ascertained by the principles of applied geometry (*handasa,* lit. "engineering") and mathematics, through knowing the distance of Mecca from the equator and from the west [i.e. its position latitudinally and longitudinally] as well as that of the city in question, it then being calculated according to these principles to ascertain the actual direction (samt) of the qibla [which forms the basis of the approximate direction (jiha)] (*Radd al-muhtar* (e37), 1.289).

That is, according to the Hanafi school, the direction of the qibla may only be determined by a geographer capable of using the principles of applied geometry (lit. "engineering") and mathematics to find the exact direction (samt). Our analysis on pages 56–66 above of the many geographic mistakes fostered by the Mercator projection map shows why it is impossible to geometrically ascertain the exact direction (samt) of the qibla in North America if one believes the world corresponds to such a map. And this Hanafi text entails that one must know the earth is round to do so, because the "principles of applied geometry and mathematics" exclude anyone who does not. The Shafi'i Imam Taqi al-Din al-Subki says:

> The Imam of the Two Sanctuaries [al-Juwayni (d. 478/1085)] says when mentioning the proofs of the qibla, "Experts have authored works on it, so let the evidences of the qibla be sought in their works." I say: this is the Imam of the Two Sanctuaries, with his renown in the Sacred Sciences, directing those who seek the evidences of the qibla to works by experts on it. Is there then no sense of embarrassment in the person who denies the necessity of referring to such works out of his ignorance, his inexperience in the field, his belief that he is a scholar of fiqh and that fiqh contradicts them? Is there no sense of compunction in the unlearned person who impugns scholars of Sacred Knowledge and the other sciences, presuming he is right and everyone else is wrong? Is there no sense of shame in both, for speaking about something they encompass not in knowledge? (*Fatawa al-Subki* (e87), 1.150).

If, as Imam al-Juwayni declares, one must refer to "experts" on the subject who have authored "works" on determining the qibla, someone who does not know the world is round hardly fits this description. The Hanafi scholar Dr. Muhammad Hisham al-Burhani of Damascus says:

> Total certainty that the world is round has become a commonplace of today's knowledge, and one must examine the subject of facing the qibla on this undeniable basis. Whoever deviates from it, departing from this premise and orientating mihrabs on the earth as though it were flat as it appears on drawn maps, has made a tremendous mistake, missed the truth, and failed to benefit from

the achievements of science and civilization (*Fatwa* (e19), 29 June 2000, 1).

Dr. Muhammad Sa'id al-Buti writes:

Without a doubt, Islamic jurists defer to the laws of geometry and astronomy and calculations based on them to explain what is meant by "facing the qibla"—as in any other ruling of Sacred Law that relates to a point of scientific knowledge, as with medicine, for example. This is something that is well known and perfectly sound.

Thus, ascertaining the direction of the qibla is accomplished on the basis that the earth is round, for this is what scientific evidence proves, and indeed Qur'anic evidence as well; as in the word of Allah Most High "And the earth He thereafter outspread" (Qur'an 79:30), and His word "And the earth We outspread, and cast upon it firm mountains" (Qur'an 15:19) [he adds in a footnote:] (the meaning of "outspread" in the verse is not limited to partial extension—for there is nothing possessing a surface that is not partially extended— in which case the words would have little special significance; rather their sense is to draw attention to the earth's being characterized by total extension: i.e. if one goes east, its extension never comes to an edge or limit, and likewise if one goes west, north, or south—the scientific explanation of which is that its unending extension is due to the continuous curvature that constitutes a spherical shape).

It is not the way of Islamic jurists, when they note that it is obligatory to face the qibla in prayer, to speak of the sphericality of the earth or its flatness. Their one concern is to clarify the necessity to face the Kaaba itself or its direction (according to their difference of opinion that I have previously noted)—whereupon mathematical and geometrical references are relied upon to determine just how it should be faced in light of how the earth actually is and its real nature (*Fatwa* (e20), 7 March 2000, 1).

Dr. Muhammad Ramadan, the Dean of the Faculty of Islamic Sciences at the University of Baghdad, writes:

Facing the actual Kaaba itself in prayer is not obligatory except for those close to the Kaaba. As for those remote from the Kaaba, they are only obliged to face its direction (jiha), and its direction is determined by experts who are scientists of applied geometry (lit. "engineering") and geography: they are "those who know well (ahl al-dhikr)" in this matter, and Allah Mighty and Majestic has said, "Ask those who know well, if you know not" (Qur'an 16:43). The qibla in respect to North America is to the northeast, not the southeast, in accordance with what experts on this matter have determined based on the sphericality of the earth, which no one denies but someone bereft of all acquaintance with geography (*Fatwa* (e72), 10 October 2000, 1).

At the level of the communal obligation (fard kifaya), some members of the community must be able to accomplish this geographical ijtihad, without which ascertaining the qibla would be impossible, or all would be guilty of serious sin. Dr. Wahbeh al-Zuhayli writes:

> Determining the qibla is accomplished through the cooperation of scholars of applied geometry (handasa), astronomy, and Sacred Law. The fuqaha in general utilize what these scholars decide.
>
> Determining the direction of the qibla is effected on the basis that the earth is round, not flat, in deference to what actually exists and the shortest distance, which is what is actually seen in practice, even if the fuqaha have not explicitly stated it (*Fatwa* (e102), 21 March 2000, 1).

And this is what has taken place in North America, where Muslim mathematicians have calculated the qibla in most cities using spherical trigonometry the same in its essential principles, as previously noted, as the methods used by the mathematician al-Biruni in Ghazna, Afghanistan, nearly a thousand years ago. The application of *spherical* trigonometry in finding the qibla, for those of us whose mathematical acumen may have slipped a little since school, presupposes a *sphere,* that is, the roundness of the earth.

In point of history, a sampling of seventy-two Muslim compendiums of geographical coordinates of latitude and longitude dating from al-Masha'allah (d. ca. 164/780) to al-Mawsili (d. ca. 1143/1730) yields some 2,500 names of locations for which they were calculated by Muslims of past centuries (Kennedy and Kennedy: *Islamic Sources* (e51), xiv)—which shows that determining the qibla by such means was not a rare scientific curiosity, but quite widespread. As we shall see below in chapter 13, the Maliki Imam Ahmad ibn Idris al-Qarafi (d. 684/1285) explicitly states that latitude and longitude are "the strongest evidences" for qibla determination (*al-Dhakira* (e66), 2.123–24).

If these are the methods of the geometers and mathematicians to whom the fuqaha have consigned the responsibility for establishing our mihrabs, it is hardly accurate to say that "there is no text of fiqh that says that knowing the earth is round is obligatory for someone finding the qibla." They have certainly not given the job to someone who thinks the earth is flat.

Conclusions

Urging that the North American qibla be determined on the basis of the earth being round in reality but flat for religious purposes cannot be regarded as good fiqh. Aside from the proofs that it is not an interpretive possibility for the Qur'anic verses at all, and the words of the fuqaha that necessitate knowing the world is round, it will only dismay thinking Muslims to learn that they have to practice their religion in a way that contravenes physical reality. The pitting of faith against reason has never been found in Islam, and there is no reason to put it there.

8

The Stars and the Qibla

—

DIFFICULTY

O NE of the visiting scholars looked at the sky at night, as ulema do in his native land, and on the basis of the stars established that the direction of the qibla is to the southeast, adducing the words of Allah Most High in Sura al-Nahl "And by the stars they are guided" (Qur'an 16:16).

RESPONSE

Those with some acquaintance with the stars of the night sky know that in the Northern Hemisphere, all of the stars appear to revolve around Polaris, the North Star, which is fixed in the northern sky and does not move. The reason for this is that the axis of the earth's rotation, the imaginary line passing straight through the earth and coming out at the north and south poles, points in the present epoch almost directly to Polaris. By any measure, the discovery of a fixed star at the north celestial pole by ancient man was a tremendous blessing because it showed him the direction of north, from which the other directions could be inferred. For this reason, the star was of the utmost practical importance to travellers and others before the discovery of the compass (which for its part could be used on cloudy nights, and in the Southern Hemisphere), which is why Allah mentions it in the Qur'an to remind man to be grateful for divine blessings. Fakhr al-Razi comments on the above verse, "The point of this verse is to mention some of the blessings that Allah Most High has created on earth" (*Mafatih al-ghayb* (e76), 20.7).

The North Star, however, gives no information about the direction of one physical thing on the earth's surface from another, except what a man may infer from the fact that the direction of Polaris is north, and thus the other compass directions—which must be combined with the geographical knowledge he *already has* of the whereabouts and specific direction of his object. That is, the North Star gives exactly the same information as the compass, neither more nor less. So knowing the direction of north from the stars lends no support, Qur'anic or otherwise, to one's subsequent judgement that the qibla is to the east.

The qibla from America certainly does appear to the east or southeast on a flat map of the world. If one draws a straight line with a pencil and ruler on the Mercator projection map from, for example, San Francisco to Mecca, it indicates a southeast, or more properly speaking, east-southeast direction, as shown in figure 23 below.

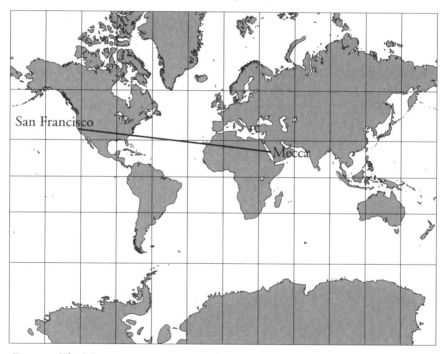

Figure 23. The Mercator projection map, showing the "rhumb line" or constant compass bearing from San Francisco to Mecca, giving the impression the qibla is to the east-southeast

But when examined with a straight-edge flexible ruler on a world globe, the east-southeasterly direction from San Francisco turns out

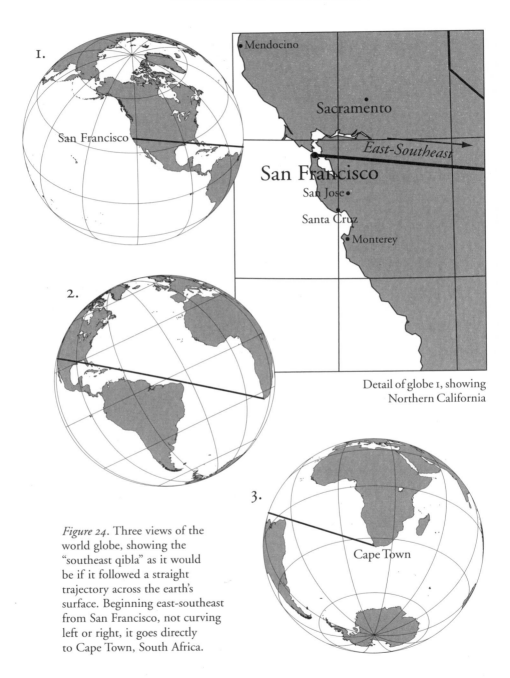

Detail of globe 1, showing
Northern California

Figure 24. Three views of the
world globe, showing the
"southeast qibla" as it would
be if it followed a straight
trajectory across the earth's
surface. Beginning east-southeast
from San Francisco, not curving
left or right, it goes directly
to Cape Town, South Africa.

94

to be facing Cape Town, not Mecca, as shown in figure 24 on the opposite page. Here, we have to turn to our visiting scholar again and ask, "Why do you feel that facing Mecca means facing southeast?" If he says, "Morocco is northwest of Mecca, and America is north-west of Morocco," this is but a verbal version of the flat map, and fails in the face of our physical reality on the earth's surface. Such an impression of course cannot be dispelled by knowledge of the stars, which are orientational; but only by knowledge of the earth, which is geographical.

A second traditional means of using the stars for direction finding involves the *matali'* (sing. *matla'*) or "places of ascent" of certain star constellations on the horizon. Man early noticed that star constellations appear to revolve around the North Star, which in most of the Northern Hemisphere lies obliquely to the north in the sky and not directly overhead, so while the constellations adjacent to it are always visible, other more distant constellations revolving around it appear to "rise" and "set" at specific points on the horizon at certain times of night, depending on the seasons of the year. The specific points on the horizon where they rise, termed in Arabic *matali'*, furnish another means of direction finding, which was also used by Muslims to orient themselves to the qibla. This is because when one knows where the qibla is, and then finds the constellation that rises at that point of the horizon, it furnishes an accurate, nightly recurring means for facing the qibla anywhere in the region.

We say "anywhere in the region" because it is plain that when the direction of Mecca corresponds to such a point on the eastern horizon, for example, as it would in Western Sahara and the lands between it and Mecca, then if one were to travel all the way east to Mecca, and then beyond it for a few miles, the point of the constellation's rising (matla') would still be in front of one on the eastern horizon, but the Kaaba would now be in back of one, in the opposite direction. This is because the *matali'*, like the North Star, do not indicate the direction of the Kaaba as such, but only a particular compass direction, which may or may not, according to the area one is in, correspond to the actual direction of Mecca. If the direction to Mecca is east in one's area, and a particular constellation also rises in the east, it will be an infallible guide to the qibla. But if one is in a different part of the world where that point of the horizon does not correspond to the actual physical direction of the qibla, it will be of no relevance whatsoever. A constellation's rising on the horizon merely indicates particular direction, as a compass does.

In other words, whether using Polaris or rising constellations, the stars are not the "Qur'anic method" for finding the qibla, but one method among others for finding directions.

The Qur'an

The original context of "And by the stars they are guided" in the Qur'an appears to have been to mention the blessing of stars for finding the correct direction of *travel* rather than the qibla. The verse was not considered to specifically refer to the qibla by any of the Companions (Sahaba) or their students (tabi'in) from whom al-Tabari (d. 310/922), the sheikh of transmission-based Qur'anic exegetes, relates its meaning. Out of nine separate reports he conveys from the earliest generations of Muslims, not one mentions the qibla. Rather, they mention finding one's way while travelling (*Jami' al-bayan* (e89), 14.91–92). Fakhr al-Razi says,

> If it be wondered why His word "[And He cast on the earth firm mountains] lest it shake with you" (Qur'an 16:15) speaks to those present, and His word "And by the stars *they* are guided" (Qur'an 16:16) speaks of those absent, we say the reason is that the Quraysh travelled a great deal seeking wealth, and whoever's journeys are many, his knowledge of the benefits of guidance through the stars is greater and more complete, so "by the stars they are guided" (Qur'an 16:16) is a reference to the Quraysh, for the reason we have just mentioned (*Mafatih al-ghayb* (e76), 20.10).

There is a purported hadith about the North Star (Ar. al-Jady) and the qibla in the exegesis of al-Qurtubi to the effect that Ibn 'Abbas (Allah be well pleased with him) asked the Prophet (Allah bless him and give him peace) what star was meant by the above Qur'anic verse, and he supposedly said,

> "It is Polaris (al-Jady) O Ibn 'Abbas: your qibla is based on it, and by it you are guided on land and sea" (*Ahkam al-Qur'an* (e71), 10.92),

which al-Qurtubi adopted from the exegesis of al-Mawardi, but it is spurious, being without a chain of transmission, or indeed, as revealed by an electronic search for the key word "Polaris" (al-Jady) in 1000 hadith works from Bukhari on down, any mention anywhere. The Imams whose business it is to know every hadith of the Prophet (Allah bless him and give him peace) do not know this hadith, which relieves Muslims of having to consider it. If it had any basis, which it does not, as the Maliki scholar Dr. Muhammad al-Tawil of the Qarawiyyin in Fez notes, after mentioning it as a possible evidence:

> The former position [that the verse "by the stars they are guided" (Qur'an 16:16) refers to travel, not to finding the qibla] fits the sura better, for it was revealed in Mecca, while the qibla and facing the Kaaba were only made obligatory after the Hijra [to Medina] (*Fatwa* (e90), 10 March 2000, 6).

In short, it was not because using the stars was a method legislated by Allah in the Qur'an or sunna for finding the qibla that it won the confidence of early Muslims, but rather because with the coming of Islam, Muslims welcomed an accurate direction-finding means that had proven itself to travellers since pre-Islamic times. And in the six centuries between the revelation of the Qur'an and the first use of the compass among the Arabs, the stars remained among the best ways of finding directions. As Imam Shafi'i said:

> Allah Mighty and Majestic says, "It is He who has made the stars for you to be guided by, in the darknesses of the land and sea" (Qur'an 6:97), and He says, "And [He has placed on earth] landmarks, and by the stars they are guided" (Qur'an 16:16), and says to His prophet (Allah bless him and give him peace), "Wherever you come forth, turn your face towards the Holy Mosque; and wherever you all may be, turn your faces towards it" (Qur'an 2:150).
>
> So Allah Mighty and Majestic raised the House (Kaaba) and the Mosque for them, such that when they saw it, they had to face the House, because the Messenger of Allah faced it and the people around it [faced it] with him from every direction. He [Allah] directed them, through the signs He created for them and the intellects He placed within them, to face straight (qasd) towards

the Sacred House and the Holy Mosque, [the latter specifically] meaning facing straight towards the Sacred House—so it is obligatory for every person praying a prescribed prayer, a supererogatory prayer, a funeral prayer, or making a prostration for thanks or Qur'an recital to make sure that he is facing the House" (*al-Umm* (e80), 2.101).

We have thus been given a command from Allah to face the Kaaba, and signs and intellects to help us do so; and neither the Qur'an nor the sunna indicates the preferability of stars over other signs. The stars were originally mentioned, as we have seen, not in the context of finding the qibla, but as a reminder to men to be grateful to Allah for guiding travellers. Unlike the specific prophetic command to sight the new moon that marks the beginning and end of Ramadan

Fast when you see it, and cease fasting when you see it, and if it is too overcast [to be seen], complete Sha'ban as thirty days (*Bukhari* (e18), 3.34–35: 1909. S),

there is nothing in the Qur'an or sunna that specifically recommends looking at the stars as a means for finding the qibla, other than their general suitability for direction finding. Early jurists like Shafi'i mention them in their books not because of the stars' inherent religious significance, but rather for their practical utility, which was that before the discovery of the compass they were the most accurate means available to find true north.

In any case, the above difficulty loses all force when one realizes that the stars do not point the direction to the Kaaba for someone who does not already know which compass direction it should be, and so mean nothing until this is agreed upon.

Ijtihad: Orientational and Geographical

What we have just said about stars applies equally to the other physical signs for finding the qibla that are traditionally mentioned in books of Islamic jurisprudence. They are explained in perhaps the greatest detail in a section of Imam Ghazali's *Ihya' 'ulum al-din* that tells how to use them. He says:

As for the evidences of the qibla, they are of three types: [1] terrestrial, such as inference from mountains, towns, and rivers; [2] atmospheric, such as inference from the north, south, east, and west winds; and [3] celestial, meaning the stars.

As for the terrestrial and atmospheric evidences, they differ with the various areas. There might be a route on which there is a high mountain that is known to lie to the right of one when one is facing Mecca, or to one's left, or behind one, or in front, so one should know and comprehend this. And likewise the winds, which might indicate [the direction] in some areas, so one should understand this. We are unable to exhaustively discuss this, as each area and each region is a separate case.

As for the celestial evidences, they are divided into those of the day and those of the night. Those of the day consist in the sun, so one should note before leaving town where the sun lies from oneself at noon (dhuhr): is it between one's eyebrows, or upon the right eye, or the left, or does it incline more towards the forehead?— for in northern lands, the sun does not go beyond these. If one memorizes this, then whenever one knows that noon has come through the signs we shall mention [below], one thereby knows the qibla. Likewise one should heed the position of the sun from oneself at midafternoon ('asr), for one will necessarily need to know the qibla at both of these times [as travel is usually continuous during the day, and the need to find the qibla will renew itself as one comes to a new place]. This also is impossible to treat exhaustively because different areas differ. As for the qibla at sunset, it can be seen by where the sun sets, namely by memorizing whether the sun sets to the right of the person facing the qibla, or whether this inclines toward his face, or the back of his head . . . . (*Ihya' 'ulum al-din* (e26), 2.232–33).

A moment's reflection on this passage will disclose what sort of ijtihad is expected of someone "finding the qibla" in this context. The traveller must note where the sun and other phenomena are in relation to himself at prayer times when standing at a place where the correct direction *is known* to him, such as beside the mosque of the last town passed through, so that he can correctly orient himself again to that direction when out in places where the correct direction *is not known* to him, such as when travelling. Every single "evidence" Imam Ghazali mentions is clearly but a means to do this. This may seem a simple point, but the discussion in North America about the scriptural authority of the stars to find the qibla shows how poorly it has been understood.

Once again, none of the "natural" evidences of the qibla named by the jurists, be it the dawn, sunset, stars, or sun, discloses the location of Mecca to a person who does not already know which direction it should lie from the region he is in, and no amount of "ijtihad" with such evidences will give such a person the slightest information about which way to face. For there are two kinds of ijtihad at work in facing the qibla to pray:

(1) the "geographical ijtihad" of establishing where one's region lies on the earth's surface in relation to Mecca, and what is the unique direction that Allah has created between the two places; and

(2) the "orientational ijtihad" of finding out how, at a given location in one's region, to point oneself towards this correct direction once one knows it.

The natural evidences given in fiqh books, and frequently the word *ijtihad* itself in this context, clearly pertain to the second of these two types. This is apparent from the fiqh rulings of jurists such as the Maliki Imam Ahmad al-Dardir, who says (with the commentary of al-Sawi (S:)):

> The person praying [outside of Mecca] should face that approximate direction (jiha) [of the Kaaba] through ijtihad, namely by means of ijtihad if he is able to do so with evidences indicating the direction such as the dawn, the last light of sunset, the sun, Polaris or other stars; and also the easterly, southerly, northerly, or westerly winds. It is not permissible for him to merely follow (taqlid) another (S: person who is himself making [such] ijtihad, or the mihrab of *other than a mosque in a city* [emphasis the translator's]) when he is able to do ijtihad (*al-Sharh al-saghir* (e21), 1.295).

The exception to such a person's needing to make ijtihad in "a mosque in a city" is plainly in deference to the normal presumption of the superiority of the "geographical ijtihad" of a collectivity of Muslims over that of an individual, even one capable of the "orientational ijtihad," to which alone the natural evidences mentioned in this passage pertain. We shall return to this in greater detail drawn from works of the Maliki and other schools in the coming chapters.

Imam Ghazali is even plainer, saying at the beginning of the section translated above, entitled "Tasks One Must Repeatedly Do Because of Travelling":

> They consist of knowing the qibla and prayer times, which is also obligatory when not travelling, although when not travelling, there are other means available to accomplish these for one, in [the form of] an agreed upon mihrab, freeing one from the need to find the qibla; and in a muezzin to keep track of the prayer times, freeing one from the need to know them—while a traveller could be uncertain of the qibla and unsure of the time, so he needs to know the evidences of the qibla and prayer times (*Ihya' 'ulum al-din* (e26), 2.232).

CONCLUSIONS

There is no evidence in the verse "And by the stars they are guided" (Qur'an 16:16) or the understanding of it by the earliest Muslims that Allah has legislated using the stars as the means to orient oneself towards the qibla in the way that, for example, He has legislated sighting the new moon to legally establish the coming of Ramadan. They are merely one means of direction finding among others.

Moreover, the stars, like the other natural evidences mentioned in books of fiqh such as the sun, winds, dawn, and sunset, do help one find a particular compass direction, but give no information at all about whether this is the correct direction of Mecca unless one already knows which direction Mecca lies from one's area, and is merely using them to face it. That is, such means provide the same knowledge a compass does. Someone who is mistaken about where Mecca lies in relation to his position will only be guided by them to the direction of his error, as our visiting scholar unwittingly was.

This led us to distinguish between two distinct operations of ijtihad at work in facing the qibla, the "geographical ijtihad" of establishing which direction Mecca actually lies from one's region, and the "orientational ijtihad" of finding out how, at a given location in one's region, to point oneself towards this direction once one knows it. The latter does not inspire much confidence without the former, since one cannot generally turn towards a direction one does not know.

9

Fuqaha and Engineers

===

THE qibla is determined by fuqaha, not engineers. Those who follow the visiting scholars by praying to the east or southeast are following methods taken from competent fuqaha, while the northeast is an entirely different qibla that engineers have determined by methods not one of the Sahaba or early Muslim jurists would have understood, since spherical trigonometry was not invented in their times. Moreover, Bukhari relates from Ibn 'Umar that

> the Messenger of Allah (Allah bless him and give him peace) said, "We are an unlettered nation, we neither write nor reckon; the month is such-and-such and such-and-such"—meaning at one time twenty-nine [days] and at another, thirty (*Bukhari* (e18), 3.35: 1913. S),

which al-Qastallani explains as meaning that

> we are not responsible, in defining the times of fasting and our worship, for that which we would need calculation or writing for. Our worship is but based on clear signs and plain, obvious matters equally familiar to mathematicians and non-mathematicians (*Irshad al-sari* (e67), 3.359).

Imam al-Shatibi says that this hadith reflects the essence of the Sacred Law, which is meant to be comprehended by literate and illiterate people, especially in things that everyone is obliged to know how to do, such as knowing prayer times, and fasting. He says,

> Among them [i.e. the principles inferable from the "unletteredness" (ummiyya) of the Sacred Law, which is interpreted according to the understanding of those to whom it was first revealed; namely, the Arabs] is that moral responsibilities, both of faith and practice,

must be within the power of the illiterate person to conceive of (taʿaqqul) (*al-Muwafaqat* (e81), 2.397),

which spherical trigonometry is not, but clearly beyond any illiterate person's capacity to conceive of or use. The northeast qibla in North America is thus too difficult for such a person to understand or to work out for his own prayer, and so is inadmissible because Allah "has not placed any hardship upon you in religion" (Qur'an 22:78).

And if al-Shatibi's above words are true of the illiterate person as regards responsibilities such as finding prayer times, they apply with still better right to those like the scholars visiting North America, who are internationally recognized Islamic jurists of the highest order, who know the earth is round, and whose ijtihad leads them to conclude that the qibla is to the east or southeast. How can it not be permissible to follow their ijtihad, even if it should contradict the direction of the mosques already built there on the basis of mathematical calculation?

RESPONSE

This difficulty has three main ideas, which we will deal with each in turn before summarizing together.

Fuqaha and Engineers

"The qibla is determined by fuqaha, not engineers. Those who follow the ijtihad of visiting scholars by praying to the east or southeast are following methods taken from competent fuqaha, while the northeast is an entirely different qibla that engineers have determined by methods not one of the Sahaba or early Muslim jurists would have understood, since spherical trigonometry was not invented in their times."

We saw at the end of the last chapter that there are two kinds of ijtihad involved in finding the qibla, (a) the "geographical ijtihad" of establishing the unique direction that Mecca lies on the earth's surface in relation to one's position, and (b) the "orientational ijtihad" of finding out how to orient oneself towards this unique direction once it is established.

We also found that many of the kinds of evidences given in fiqh books as means of ijtihad, and frequently the word *ijtihad* itself in the context, clearly pertain only to the second of these two types. As Sheikh Nuh 'Ali Salman al-Qudah says,

> What the scholars have mentioned as evidences indicating the qibla are actually evidences that indicate the directions. When the direction is known, and the location of the person praying in relation to the Kaaba is known, it is possible to determine the qibla (Fatwa (e70), 13 March 2000, 3).

That is, the "natural evidences" mentioned in the fiqh texts cited from Ghazali's *Ihya' 'ulum al-din* and the Maliki Imam Ahmad al-Dardir's *al-Sharh al-saghir*—such as wind, stars, or landmarks—while permitting one to orient oneself towards a particular direction, do not tell whether one is then facing the qibla unless one already knows which direction Mecca is supposed to be, and is merely using them as a means to face it. In other words, they concern orientational ijtihad rather than geographical ijtihad.

It might be wondered, "Why don't Imam Ghazali, al-Dardir, and other fiqh authors distinguish between these two types of ijtihad, or even mention that their evidences are merely orientational and do not geographically tell where Mecca lies on the surface of the earth in relation to one?" The answer is that in Islamic lands like those of the authors, the general direction of Mecca was so well-known that it was taken for granted. Their countries were connected to Mecca by frequently travelled trade and hajj routes that made the direction to Mecca common knowledge, verified by yearly throngs of travellers whose agreement constituted *tawatur* or "complete consensus of witnesses." In other words, in the Islamic heartlands, there was little to discuss about the general geographical direction of Mecca.

We have mentioned above that the relative closeness of these lands to Mecca, which made negligible the differences between a line on a flat map and a line on a globe, was a historical circumstance specific to the age when many of the fiqh books, in all four Sunni schools, were first written.

The rulings of Sacred Law, however, are not limited by specific historical circumstances, but apply everywhere until the end of time. The world changes, and part of fiqh is understanding the rule of

Allah concerning new things, among them the spread of Islam to far continents which, if known to Allah from preeternity, were undreamt of by the early fuqaha. To apply their words and judgements to something essentially different from anything they intended or envisioned is to risk many mistaken conclusions.

For example, to convey *ijma'* or "binding scholarly consensus," as one fatwa on the North American qibla recently did, from ancient commentaries on Imam Nawawi's *Minhaj al-talibin* to the effect that "the people of the west (ahl al-maghrib) must face east for their qibla," is clearly meaningless in North America. For one thing, it was a ruling by the scholars of the time about *ahl al-maghrib,* the people of north and west Africa. To present an ijma' about the direction of prayer in North Africa as a proof for the direction of prayer thousands of miles away in North America, a place that the scholars who effected the consensus did not have the slightest knowledge of—let alone intend—is to completely misrepresent their consensus. For another thing, the distances involved entail an essential qualitative physical difference in the qibla of the two regions that prevents any analogy other than purely verbal.

In words, it is all very well to reason, as one scholar did, that "Morocco is to the northwest of Mecca, and North America is to the northwest of Morocco." But in actions, of which facing the qibla is one, impressions born of flat maps are misleading. We have seen above in figure 24 on page 94 that praying "east-southeast" from Northern California means facing Cape Town.

That is to say, sound orientational ijtihad cannot take the place of sound geographical ijtihad. If a visiting scholar is familiar with the orientational evidences of the books of his school, but his geographical ijtihad, while adequate in his home country because of its closeness on a global scale to Mecca, is not applicable to North America, then those who follow him are not "following methods taken from qualified fuqaha." They are following a mujtahid on a question he is unqualified to make ijtihad about. For someone who does not know the facts of the question he is trying to apply his ijtihad to is not a mujtahid on that question. Ijtihad means expending one's utmost effort to determine the ruling of Allah about something in the real world. Someone unaware of the facts of the real world is not capable of ijtihad about it. Imams of *usul* or "methodological bases of Sacred Law" such as al-Razi in his *al-Mahsul* ((e75), 2.224), al-Amidi in his *al-Ihkam* ((e6), 1.136), al-Taj al-Subki in his *al-Ibhaj* ((e85), 1.172), and others all affirm the fundamental principle of ijtihad

> A judgement about something derives from the way it is conceptualized,

meaning that the validity of the mujtahid's ruling about a state of affairs cannot exceed the validity of his understanding of it. That is, to the precise extent that he does not know what he is talking about in the real world, he will be unable to understand the ruling of Allah concerning it.

As for orientational ijtihad, its means are numerous, and anyone who has learned one or more of those necessary for it can master it in a comparatively short time. But as for geographical ijtihad, it is plain that any one of a number of misconceptions about the nature of the real world and of directionality at intercontinental distances excludes one from being qualified to make ijtihad about the qibla on continents far from Mecca. These include:

(1) the belief that "straight lines" of intercontinental distances drawn on a Mercator projection map do not curve to the right or left on the actual surface of the earth;

(2) the belief that a line which curves right or left can be the "direction" of anything;

(3) the belief that "lines of latitude" other than at the equator do not curve right or left;

(4) the belief that such lines and their corresponding direction names ("east" or "west") can constitute the direction between two things at intercontinental distances in the real world;

or any of the other major geographical fallacies we have detailed above. As the Hanbali mufti and teacher of Duma, Syria, Sheikh Isma'il Badran says,

The matter of determining the direction of the qibla is to be left to the skilled Muslim scholar of geodesic geometry, it being obligatory to make the calculation on the basis that the earth is round (*Fatwa* (e10), 1 May 2000, 1),

which, if more imperative at global distances than for lands closer to Mecca, does point up the fact that an Islamic scholar qualified to make ijtihad in the question of the qibla in North Africa or South Asia may not necessarily be qualified to do so in North America, for basic qualitative geographical differences between the two continents may well necessitate additional geographical knowledge before true ijtihad is possible. Dr. Ahmad Muhammad al-Balisani, Hanafi scholar and professor of fiqh at the University of Baghdad writes:

The location of the Kaaba, which the Lawgiver has made a qibla for Muslims in their prayer, is an ordinary physical matter, while the obligation of knowing which direction it is in, in order to face it in prayer, is a religious matter. This religious matter, knowing its direction, relies upon conventional means: someone close to the Kaaba relies upon the naked eye; someone a little farther depends upon ordinary evidences; and so on, as one becomes farther and farther from it. The farther the distance is, the more scientific the means required to determine the direction of the qibla, while the overwhelming majority of scholars of the Muslims concur that it is permissible to rely upon scientific means to determine the qibla. So while the qibla is an Islamic legal matter, its determination is only accomplished by conventional means, by which I mean scientific means, which are the special province of specialists in astronomy and geography who know this matter. As for whether the qibla should be determined according to whether the earth is spherical or not, it should be determined according to the findings of science about the shape of the earth, as it is in reality, which is also subject to the scientists who are specialists in this field. The conditions for determining the qibla must be geometric scientific conditions, so that the determination can be correct (*Fatwa* (e11), 12 October 2000, 1).

Idris Muhammad al-'Alami, the Maliki professor of qibla and prayer-time determination (tawqit) at the Qarawiyyin in Fez, says:

Know, O questioner, Allah have mercy on you, that the matter of the qibla is a juristic-geometrical (fiqhi-handasi) subject, which is why the scholar of Sacred Law is best qualified to speak of it, provided he is knowledgeable in the means of applied geometry (handasa lit. "engineering") that enable him to ascertain the truth about the particular case at hand; followed [secondly] by the scholar who does not know the means of applied geometry—even though a scholar in his fatwa does actually refer to the established bases of fiqh and detailed commentaries that explain them, which are mainly based upon the rules of applied geometry. As for the geometer (muhandis), if he is not a jurist and does not know the subject he is dealing with from a religious standpoint, only his scientific expertise is utilized, provided he is reliable, meaning unbiased against the religion.

Know also that those who contributed to the science of geometry—plane, spherical, and spatial—and developed the science of trigonometry were the ulema of the Muslims. They only did so out of service to the Islamic religion and to comprehend the verses of the Noble Qur'an with the aim of worship, particularly in determining prayer times and the exact direction of the qibla anywhere on the face of the earth. They were truly jurist geometers. The day will come, Allah willing, when the direction of the qibla from such and such a planet or from absolute outer space will be asked about.

In reality, the earth is round. So whoever wants to find the direction of the qibla—so that the Muslims' prayer can fulfill the conditions of validity, Allah willing—must take the fact of the earth's sphericity into consideration, especially if the question concerns the regions of North America mentioned, for it is inadequate for a person to put a geographic map in front of himself to determine the direction of the qibla (*Fatwa* (e5), 8 March 2000, 1).

So it is not a matter of the fuqaha having one qibla in North America and the engineers another, but rather that the only true mujtahid on the issue is someone who knows the evidences essential to ascertain the direction that Allah has created between North America and Mecca. These evidences are both geographical and orientational. While detailed geographical evidences may have historically proved unneeded in the Islamic heartlands, the major errors we have described above made by those unaware of them in North America show that this is not the case there.

And if the books of Imam Ghazali and Ahmad al-Dardir do not mention the means of geographical ijtihad, other scholars ancient and modern do, as we shall see below.[1] But let us now consider the second idea of the difficulty.

Precision Direction Finding Is Foreign to Islam

"Precision means and calculations for finding the qibla are repudiated by the hadith in Bukhari, 'We are an unlettered nation, we neither write nor reckon,' meaning according to al-Shatibi that 'moral responsibilities must be within the power of the illiterate person to conceive of,' which spherical trigonometry is not, but clearly beyond any illiterate person's capacity to conceive or use. The northeast qibla in North America is thus too difficult for such a person to understand or to work out for his own prayer, which is inadmissible because Allah 'has not placed any hardship upon you in religion' (Qur'an 22:78)."

Islam is set in the real world, among whose undeniable realities is human society with its division of labor. We depend on each other for almost everything. We speak and think, for example, in a language we did not invent but received from others. Almost none of the things in our homes are made by us, and few of us, if asked, could even describe except in the vaguest terms how they are made. This poses little problem, because other people exist who know how to make them, and are willing to give us the benefit of their knowledge. In short, we live in a world of other people, who if occasionally difficult to live with, are impossible to live without.

In many ways our world is the sum of the shared expertise of the people in it, only a little of it known to the individual, most of it known to others, but nonetheless within the power of all of us to

---

[1] Not surprisingly, the schools that seem to have dealt most explicitly with geographical ijtihad predominated in lands far from Mecca, such as the Hanafi school in the Indian subcontinent, and Central Asia.

conceive of, as is borne out by the ease with which we utilize the world to accomplish our projects in it. The conceivability (ta'aqqul) of large areas of experience whose particular details are unknown to us but which we nonetheless exploit through the expertise of others is a fact of human life, implicitly acknowledged by the Qur'an with the words,

"Ask those who know well, if you know not" (Qur'an 16:43).

Similarly, the Sacred Law is a large body of knowledge "conceivable" in its practical details to virtually anyone, intelligent or simple, but fully known, properly speaking, only through a division of labor among scholars, whether in regard to the specific content of these details, or to proving that they are truly part of the religion. Few Muslims know the particulars of either of these, though every Muslim must be able to conceive of them in general before he can direct his will to carry them out.

As for specific content, only a minority of Muslims probably distinguish, for example, the obligatory elements of ablution (wudu) from those not strictly obligatory, though most are able to conceive of and carry out what they are supposed to do. The details are accessible through scholars.

And as for proving that particular details are actually part of the religion, if we want to know, for example, whether the hadith "When you hear the call [to prayer], repeat after the muezzin" (*Bukhari* (e18), 1.159: 611. S) is really from the Prophet or not (Allah bless him and give him peace), it is sufficient for most of us to know that it has been related in *Sahih al-Bukhari*. Though we have little idea of the particular steps of Bukhari's methodology in dealing with a hadith's chain of ascription (sanad), we do know enough to benefit from it. That is, we can adequately "conceive of" the meaning of the authenticity rating of the hadith by the mere fact that we can accurately use it, without knowing precisely why or how it came about.

For Imam al-Shatibi, the "conceivability" of the details of the religion, be it for the literate or illiterate, seems to refer merely to our ability to accomplish them successfully and be certain that we have done so. This is plain from his examples. He says:

Among them [the principles inferable from the "unletteredness" (ummiyya) of the Sacred Law] is that moral responsibilities, both of faith and practice, must be within the power of the illiterate person to conceive (ta'aqqul), so that their ruling may apply to him.

In matters of faith, this comes about by their being readily understood and easily intelligible, so that all people may hold them in common, be they sharp of intellect or dull. For if these could not be understood except by the elite, the Sacred Law would not be for all people, and would not be "unlettered," though it in fact is, so the meanings that are obligatory to know and to believe in must be easy to grasp . . . .

As for matters of practice, the observance of "unletteredness" therein entails that people's moral responsibility for them comes about through unmistakably plain criteria (jala'il) in works and in the approximations acceptable in matters, so that the majority of people can comprehend them; just as the times of the prayers are known through things actually perceptible to them, such as being defined by [the length of] shadows, the coming of dawn, sunrise, sunset, and the disappearance of twilight (al-Muwafaqat (e81), 2.397, 399).

As for the direction of Mecca from a particular geographical location, the real question for those who adopt al-Shatibi's view is whether the northeast direction of the qibla is within the power of the illiterate person to conceive of (ta'aqqul) or not. Now, the illiterate people whom the present writer knows are not unintelligent, but merely untaught in reading and writing. All of them can tell time from clocks, use telephones, and understand detailed explanations (and give them) as well as the literate can. Our question becomes: "Could an illiterate person in North America turn towards the northeast in his prayers with certainty that he is facing the right direction?"

If the northeast qibla could only be *conceived of* through the spherical trigonometry used in the articles published by Muslim astronomers in North America in recent years that mathematically prove the correctness of the northeast qibla, this would indeed be of the hardship (haraj) that in al-Shatibi's view is rejected by Sacred Law, for it would then be beyond the capacity of most people to understand.

But there is no hardship in understanding that Allah has created the world as a sphere, or that, as described at the end of chapter 1, the sun is directly above the Kaaba two times a year; or that the sun was actually seen this year (1421/2000) on the northeast horizon by Muslim witnesses at those times from Boston and Montreal in North America, proving that the Kaaba is in that direction and no other.

Nor is there anything challenging to illiterate people in the three other physical proofs the author has given in chapter 1, of which the first was the "flexible ruler on a globe" proof, the second the "concentric circles of worshippers around the Kaaba" proof, and the third the "vertical rod on Mecca" proof. Each is based on mere *sense-perception*, and hence accessible to everyone.

Even if we assume with al-Shatibi that the illiterate person must be able to conceive of the correctness of the northeast direction of the qibla, the distinction drawn in previous chapters between geographical ijtihad and orientational ijtihad has hopefully clarified that the usual way ordinary Muslims have historically known which direction Mecca lies from their lands is not through personally checking the geographical evidence, which many people might not know how to do, but rather by being *informed* of it by those who do know, which returns us to the verse "Ask those who know well, if you know not" (Qur'an 16:43). That is, geographical ijtihad in many lands is probably best conceived as a communal obligation (fard kifaya), and if this is the case in North America, then there is no problem in specialists fulfilling it for the rest of us. Imam al-Shatibi's words do not seem to entail that there are no communal obligations which scholars undertake for the rest of us.

Regarding the question of "hardship" for the ordinary Muslim who learns of the northeast direction of Mecca from those of geographical ijtihad, there is none, for one can easily find this direction and turn towards it by the various methods of orientational ijtihad mentioned in the books of fiqh. Moreover anyone, literate or illiterate, can buy a hiker's compass at a sporting goods store and learn how to use it to find the northeast in five minutes, which is less time than it takes most people to learn the Fatiha, so there is no hardship in it that religiously matters. We shall see in the following chapter that according to Imam Ibn Siraj, there is no offensiveness (karaha) for the Maliki school in using instruments to determine the approximate direction (jiha) of the qibla. If the exact direction is difficult—and one need not be very exact in either the Hanafi or Maliki schools, as we have seen—one can go to one's local mosque, align the compass with the mihrab, and pray that direction wherever one is in the region.

As for the hadith of Ibn ʿUmar

> The Messenger of Allah (Allah bless him and give him peace) said, "We are an unlettered nation, we neither write nor reckon; the month is such-and-such and such-and-such"—meaning at one time twenty-nine [days] and at another, thirty (*Bukhari* (e18), 3.35: 1913. S),

Imam Taqi al-Din al-Subki writes:

> His word (Allah bless him and give him peace) "We [are an unlettered nation]" refers to the Arabs, among whom this was prevalent, even if some of them did know how to write and reckon. And their neither writing nor reckoning was a distinction for them, because of their being destined in Allah's knowledge from beginningless eternity to be the nation of the Prophet (Allah bless him and give him peace) who was unlettered, an incontestable miracle in respect to him [as he was given the Qur'an, which far surpassed the works, knowledge, and learning of the literate] and an honor for them because they possessed one of his attributes.
>
> He made this [the counting to twenty-nine or thirty by the illiterate person referred to in the hadith] an indicator in Sacred Law to designate the month in order to furnish a criterion through something perceptible that was knowable to anyone and unsubject to mistakes, as opposed to mathematics, which only a few people know, and errors frequently occur in because it is inadequately known and because of the abstruseness of its premises, some of which are often purely theoretical. So the divine wisdom and the tolerant pure Sacred Law entailed that things should be made easy for His servants, and that legal rulings should be conjoined with something that could be readily accomplished by people, namely their sighting [the new moon] or completing the number to thirty [full days].

The meaning of the hadith is not to forbid writing or calculation, nor to censure or belittle them; indeed, they are an excellence and virtue among us (*al-'Alam al-manshur* (e86), 5–6).

The Maliki scholar Muhammad al-'Amrawi of Fez expresses it even more plainly:

Without a doubt, the hadith "We are an unlettered nation, we neither write nor reckon" merely informs about a state of affairs which actually existed. That state of affairs could change, the ruling in Sacred Law changing with the reason for it, in existing or not existing, as is corroborated in its proper place in methodological bases of jurisprudence (*Fatwa* (e7), 28 June 2000, 1).

So al-Shatibi's deriving the normative principle from the hadith's description of an "unlettered nation" that the rulings of Sacred Law must be simple enough to be conceivable by an illiterate person is not an opinion unanimously concurred upon by all scholars. Rather, some scholars see in the hadith a mere description of the state of the Arabs at the time of the revelation, a state which may well change with the coming in our times of nearly universal literacy, or, as in the case at hand, education about facts of geography.

Even if we concede al-Shatibi's point, the northeast qibla does not depend upon spherical trigonometry alone, but is also borne out by the other proofs of sense perception we have mentioned above that can be appreciated by anyone of ordinary intelligence, literate or illiterate. And even if only experts in geographical ijtihad could understand the proofs, which is not the case, this would not negate the ability of an illiterate person to *conceive of* that which he is obliged to do in facing northeast to the qibla, which he could learn about from another, something the Qur'an permits by telling us,

"Ask those who know well, if you know not" (Qur'an 16:43).

Finally, asking North American Muslims to understand something that the overwhelming majority of them have understood and practiced for the last thirty years imposes no discoverable hardship upon anyone. We now turn to the third main idea in the difficulty, which is as follows.

A Visiting Scholar Can Be Followed in His Ijtihad

"The 'unletteredness' of the Sacred Law entails with still better right that the ijtihad of an internationally recognized Islamic scholar visiting North America is legally valid both for himself and for other Muslims who wish to follow him, even if it should contradict the direction of mosques already built there on the basis of mathematical calculation."

As we saw in (1) above, sound orientational ijtihad, which a visiting scholar may well be proficient at, is insufficient if his premises obviate sound geographical ijtihad. Wrong premises lead to wrong conclusions. Someone who believes that the "straight lines" drawn to depict intercontinental distances upon a Mercator projection map do not curve to the right or left on the actual surface of the earth, or any number of other major geographical fallacies, is not a mujtahid qualified to make geographical ijtihad on the qibla in North America. Even if he is a recognized scholar in other areas of Islamic jurisprudence, he is not a scholar on the determination of the qibla who can be asked, because he does not "know well" what is necessary in order to issue a ruling about the qibla at intercontinental distances.

The clear need we have demonstrated above, for anyone who speaks about the qibla in North America to know the evidences of geographical ijtihad, necessarily enters into and qualifies the position of the Maliki school that Dr. Muhammad al-Tawil of the Qarawiyyin explains by saying:

> In respect to the first paragraph [of "The Fourth Question" on page 228] concerning the faqih whose ijtihad leads him to [pray to] a direction other than that of the mihrabs established in an area by reliable people knowledgeable in applied geometry (handasa) and calculation—one must realize that the matter of the qibla according to the Maliki school is dependent upon knowledge of the evidences of the qibla. So if the faqih is knowledgeable in the evidences of the qibla and able to know them through himself and his own means, he is not obliged to follow the mihrabs placed by others, according to the soundest position in the Maliki school, as has been conveyed without disagreement by al-Wansharisi in *al-Mi'yar,* 1.118, and

adopted by the commentaries on [*Mukhtasar*] *Khalil* by al-Ban-nani and al-Dusuqi (see *al-Dusuqi*, 1.226).

If he chooses to simply follow them (taqlid), he may do so. But if he exercises ijtihad, and his ijtihad leads to other than the direction of the mihrabs, he must follow his ijtihad, and may not simply follow another after having actually made his own ijtihad. Should he contravene his own ijtihad and pray to a different direction, his prayer is invalid, in view of the basic fiqh principle that a mujtahid may not simply follow another after having exercised his own ijtihad. Those who previously set the mihrabs did so through ijtihad, whereas he is a mujtahid like them who has contravened their ijtihad, so he may not leave his own ijtihad for another's; which is expressed in Khalil's words as, "A mujtahid may not simply follow another, nor [follow] mihrabs unless they are those of a major city" (*Fatwa* (e90), 10 March 2000, 7–8).

The key to the relevance of this Maliki position in North America is deciding whom the term "mujtahid" meaningfully applies to under the geographical circumstances there, for "a judgement about something derives from the way it is conceptualized" (*al-Ibhaj* (e85), 1.172), and whoever cannot conceptualize the geographical situation cannot be termed a "mujtahid like them" in any sense to which this Maliki position could meaningfully apply. Someone else is intended by these words. This is why the Hanafi Mufti of Aleppo Sheikh Muhammad Khalil al-Karmi conveys (*Fatwa* (e50), 10 September 2000, 1–2) from the Hanbali Imam Ibn Qudama al-Maqdisi:

> The mujtahid qualified to determine the qibla is he who knows the evidences for it, even if he is ignorant of the rulings of Sacred Law—for someone who knows the evidences for something is a mujtahid concerning it, even if ignorant of other things—and because he is the one who is capable of facing it because of his evidence. He is thus a mujtahid, like the faqih [who knows the evidences] is. And if a faqih is ignorant of its evidences, or is blind, then he is a non-mujtahid, even if he is knowledgeable in other things (*al-Mughni* (e43), 1.440–41).

This text has been cited by other contemporary scholars, such as the late Sheikh al-Azhar Jad al-Haqq in his *Buhuth wa fatawa* ((e48),

1.160) in a fatwa (unrelated to the Azhar Fatwa of chapter 2 of the present volume) on determining the qibla in lands far from Mecca, and it clearly ties ijtihad on the qibla with knowledge of its evidentiary bases, not mere competence in fiqh.

Moreover, those who have lived in an area for a long time have more familiarity with the relevant geographical evidences than a visitor would, even if a scholar, as Dr. Wahbeh al-Zuhayli of Damascus writes:

> The opinion of a scholar who is a stranger to an area is not adopted, because the people of the area know better what is around them, so the conclusions of their own specialists in applied geometry (handasa), geography, astronomy, and so forth are what is applied. It is incumbent upon someone arriving in a town to accept and follow the practice of the people there.
>
> It is obligatory upon ordinary Muslims to adopt what is decided by experts who have specialized knowledge in applied geometry and mathematics, while utilizing the observations of the fuqaha. Common Muslims are not entitled to adopt a merely personal view or the opinion of a single individual, but are obliged to do what the collectivity holds, for [the Prophet (Allah bless him and give him peace) has said,] "The hand of Allah is over the group: keep to the overwhelming majority; whoever diverges from them departs to the hellfire" [al-Mustadrak (e31), 1.115. H]—all of which is out of concern to preserve the unity of the Muslims (Fatwa (e102), 21 March 2000, 2).

Such unity is surely more consonant with the divine wisdom in gathering the Muslims together in the mosque five times a day to pray in a single group. Allah tells us, "Hold fast to Allah's bond together, and do not divide apart" (Qur'an 3:103). In the circumstances that obtain in North America, it is not only permissible but obligatory for Muslims of the Maliki school or any other to follow the vast majority of mihrabs that face to the northeast. The Maliki mufti Dr. Muhammad al-Rugi of Fez writes:

> When Muslims have mihrabs, they must be adopted and relied upon as evidence [in orientational ijtihad] to find the qibla, for the basis is that they have been placed there by people of knowledge

and expertise in the qibla. If a Muslim traveller comes to a place and finds mihrabs, he must conform to them in his prayer. If he contravenes them because of his own ijtihad he has made a mistake, for that which the collectivity is following and has persisted upon for a length of time is sounder and stronger than the ijtihad of a single individual, since Allah Most High says, "Whoever [. . .] follows other than the way of the believers, We shall consign him to hell, and how evil an outcome" (Qur'an 4:115), for this would be a kind of sowing of discord (shiqaq), since it opposes a collective ijtihad that Muslims follow with a solitary ijtihad against it.

Ordinary Muslims of the commonality who are not mujtahids must follow a faqih who is a mujtahid, and the mujtahid faqih must utilize those knowledgeable in applied geometry (handasa) and with expertise in calculation and the directions. A faqih may not merely make ijtihad according to his own preference and taste, but must rely on experts and specialists in order to conceptualize what is relevant to matters before he reaches a judgement about them.

If the mistake of the person whose opinion is being followed becomes apparent, it is not the fault of the ordinary Muslims, and they need not repeat the prayer, since Allah Most High says, "Wherever you turn, there is the countenance of Allah" (Qur'an 2:115).

In circumstances where there are two different directions being faced, one of which 90 percent or more [of the Muslims] pray towards, then that is the direction that Muslims must adhere to; the minority must follow the majority, as this instance is like the one described above; namely, that when there are mihrabs in an area, it is not permissible to make an individual ijtihad and contravene these mihrabs (*Fatwa* (e77), 10 March 2000, 3).

CONCLUSIONS

If the "unletteredness" (ummiyya) mentioned by al-Shatibi above is indeed an aspect of Sacred Law, it is of the excellences of the religion that an illiterate and unschooled Muslim can easily conceive what he is supposed to do in most acts of worship. But his capacity to *conceive of* his moral responsibilities, *ta'aqqul* in al-Shatibi's terms, does not mean that he is qualified to either legally prove or to provide the specific details of these responsibilities, which is the special province of the mujtahid, and is not termed *ta'aqqul* or "conceiving of" but rather *fiqh* or "understanding the details of."

As people vary in their ability to do ijtihad in fiqh, so too they vary in their ability to do ijtihad in the matter of the qibla, which requires both orientational ijtihad and geographical ijtihad. Ijtihad applies only to reality, and an adequate grasp of reality demands that both of these be taken into consideration. The existence of major geographical fallacies in a scholar's reasoning, be he internationally recognized or not, disqualifies his opinion from being genuine ijtihad, because "a judgement about something derives from the way it is conceptualized." For himself or followers, a mujtahid without the facts cannot be a mujtahid about the facts.

10

Instruments and Sacred Law

═══

DIFFICULTY

THE evidences of the northeastern qibla that require a globe—whether explicitly, as do the proofs of the flexible ruler on the globe, the concentric circles of worshippers around Mecca, or the rod rising from Mecca; or whether implicitly, as do the mathematics of spherical trigonometry—are unacceptable from a fiqh point of view, since the globe, like the compass and other devices, is an *instrument* for finding the qibla, and such instruments are offensive in the Maliki school.

The great compiler of fatwas from Muslim Spain and North Africa Ahmad ibn Yahya al-Wansharisi [d. 914/1508] conveys that the Maliki mufti of Granada Abul Qasim ibn Siraj [d. 848/1444] has said:

> As for seeking the direction with instruments, it has not been conveyed from the pious early Muslims (Allah be well pleased with them), so they [instruments] are unnecessary to refer to, and may not be made the criterion governing the evidences of Sacred Law (*al-Mi'yar al-mu'rib* (e96), 1.121–22).

RESPONSE

Ibn Siraj's argument is not against using instruments or precision direction-finding means as such, but rather against imposing more precision upon Muslims than Sacred Law requires, since the position of his school is that the approximate direction (jiha) is what is required, not the exact direction (samt). This is apparent from the fact that after noting that instruments

> are unnecessary to refer to, and may not be made the criterion governing the evidences of Sacred Law (ibid., 122),

he adds,

It is sufficient for someone who uses instruments as evidence to merely establish the approximate direction (jiha), since it is known through inference that one can correctly ascertain the approximate direction by them (ibid.).

This entails that they are acceptable for finding the general direction (jiha) that according to the Maliki school constitutes the obligation of the person praying. Dr. Muhammad al-Tawil of the Qarawiyyin in Fez, after quoting this passage in his fatwa, says:

> It is clear from this that the one responsible for determining the qibla is he who knows its evidences—whether he be of the fuqaha or others capable of knowing its direction (jiha) through the evidences of traditional jurisprudence or other evidences from the geometrical sciences, this [knowledge] not belonging exclusively to either group.
>
> It has long been the practice of the kings of Morocco to enlist both fuqaha and astronomers to establish or to correct mihrabs, as is fully authenticated of 'Ali ibn Tashifin [d. 537/1143], al-Mawla Isma'il [d. 1139/1727], al-Mawla al-Rashid [d. 1082/1672], and others: Hashiya Gannun, 1.355 (Fatwa (e90), 10 March 2000, 4).

In view of the possibility of misunderstanding Ibn Siraj's words above, the author asked the Mauritanian Maliki sheikh 'Abdullah al-'Alawi al-Shinqiti, who teaches at the Shari'a College in Tarim, Hadramawt, in Yemen, to clarify the place of Ibn Siraj's position within the larger framework of Maliki fiqh literature, and explain the "offensiveness" that some Malikis today ascribe to using precision instruments to determine prayer times or the direction of the qibla. He replied:

> As for what you have mentioned about the offensiveness (karaha) of the use of instruments in the school of Malik and the words quoted in the Mi'yar from Ibn Siraj, the probable source is what al-Hattab [d. 954/1547] mentions in his commentary on [Mukhtasar] Khalil, where he says, concerning determining prayer times with devices: "It was deemed offensive by [al-Qadi Abu Bakr] Ibn al-'Arabi [d. 543/1148] because the early Muslims did not do it." Al-Hattab, however, did not accept this "offensiveness," but rejected the opinion by saying, "I reply: the words of al-Mazari [d. 536/1142] have

been given above, and do not state that there is any offensiveness, but rather that this is a means of knowing it [a prayer's time]—the fuqaha not mentioning it either because it was too difficult or because it might lead to astrology. So reflect [on this]." (*Mawahib al-Jalil* (e32), 1.385).

Ibn Siraj mentions at the end of his words that you have quoted, which are adduced by those who would prove with them that instruments are offensive: "It is sufficient for someone who uses instruments as evidence to establish merely the approximate direction (jiha), since it is known through inference that one can correctly ascertain the approximate direction by them" [*al-Mi'yar al-mu'rib* (e96), 1.122]. So he did not see any harm in using them to determine the general direction (jiha), which is what is under discussion here. We will now mention the texts that explicitly state they are permissible.

Al-Hattab says, after mentioning that noon (zawal) is known by the increase in [an object's midday] shadow: "This is the familiar method which fuqaha mention in their books because of its ease and familiarity to everyone. Were one to determine the time by other instrumental means such as the quadrant [an early instrument for measuring the altitude of celestial bodies at a graduated 90° angle, shown in figure 25 below], the astrolabe [an instrument

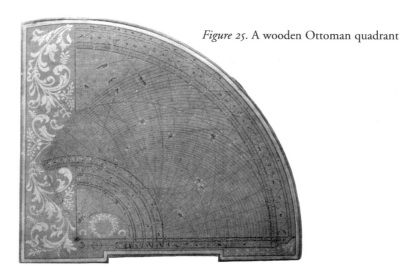

Figure 25. A wooden Ottoman quadrant

for measuring their position, shown in figure 26 below], or something else, it would be permissible, as al-Mazari and others have
mentioned" (*Mawahib al-Jalil* (e32), 1.385).

Figure 26. The astrolabe of al-Khujandi,
made in Baghdad in 374/984–85

And in the *Mi'yar al-jadid* by al-Wazzani [d. 1181/1767] it says,
citing Imam al-Tawudi ibn Sawda: "Instruments have a basis in
Sacred Law, and merely clarify what the Lawgiver has asked be done
and facilitate it without being an addition to it. Whenever someone
who knows [a prayer's time] from instruments disagrees with another about whether a prayer's time has come, his position is more
correct, and adopting it is fitter and more trustworthy" (*al-Mi'yar
al-jadid* (e97), 1.223–24).

The same work cites the great [Moroccan Maliki] scholar Sayyidi
Ahmad al-Ghurfi as saying: "Because these instruments, the quadrant, the astrolabe, and others have been introduced to Islam and
Muslims, and have been tested and found to provide complete
certainty [of prayer times] to the person who knows how to use
them when they are properly made in themselves, it is obligatory for
anyone without knowledge of them to follow without question

(taqlid) the person who has knowledge of them, and to act upon what he says—though one should take some precautions when the sky or horizon is overcast [preventing accurate enough observation of celestial bodies to furnish reliable results with such instruments]. This is what all people have adopted from east to west, as al-Hattab conveys from al-Qarafi [d. 684/1285], and others, so no one condemns relying upon instruments except an ignorant person whose view counts for nothing" (ibid., 223).

And Sheikh al-Sanusi himself, with the greatness of his rank, and his level of Islamic knowledge and practice, considered the astrolabe a blessing that Allah Most High had bestowed upon Muslims (ibid., 228) . . . .

It is well known that the astrolabe which the fuqaha have declared permissible and not mentioned any offensiveness regarding is an instrument whose functions include, together with determining prayer times, finding the exact direction (samt) of the qibla. Al-Qinnawji's *Abjad al-'ulum,* where it discusses the use of the astrolabe, says, "It is a noble science that affords knowledge of how to derive astronomical functions from the astrolabe through a specific operation, which is also a beneficial knowledge that many functions derive from, including the altitude of the sun, the location on the horizon of celestial ascents (matali'), the ascendants (tawali'), prayer times, and the exact direction of the qibla" (*Abjad al-'ulum* (e69), 2.385) . . . .

So if our ancient scholars received the instruments existing in their times with acceptance, as mentioned above, and considered them a blessing from Allah Most High—despite the humble scientific resources available in those times—what should one think of the age of the scientific boom and technological revolution? (*Fatwa* (e82), 21 September 2000, 1–3).

The texts al-Shinqiti cites here leave little doubt that even if we consider mathematically precise means of direction finding available today such as spherical trigonometry to be "instruments," their use does not conflict with the recorded positions of the Maliki school.

When asked this very question a few weeks later some 3,558 miles away in Fez, Morocco, Dr. Muhammad al-Tawil independently located and cited the same texts by al-Tawudi, al-Hattab, and al-Ghurfi from the *Mi'yar al-jadid* that al-Shinqiti had, and confirmed that there is no offensiveness in the Maliki school in using instruments for determining prayer times or the direction of the qibla. He said:

(1) Regarding knowledge of prayer times, the strongest position in the Maliki school is that it is only a communal obligation (fard kifaya), it not being obligatory for everyone to individually determine that a prayer's time has come, whether by instruments or anything else. It is sufficient to merely follow (taqlid) someone who knows, whatever may be his means of ascertaining the times, which is a condition for the validity of the prayer.

Scholars however disagree about the use of instruments, [Abu Bakr] Ibn al-'Arabi having said they are offensive because the early Muslims (salaf) did not use them, and al-Mazari averring that the astrolabe is offensive, though the reason for its offensiveness has been disagreed upon, as Sheikh Gannun conveys in his commentary (hashiya) on *al-Rahuni* (1.284).

Al-Barzali nevertheless states, "We hold that the soundest view in the Maliki school (dhahir al-madhhab) is that it is unconditionally valid to accept the information of a knowledgeable, morally upright muezzin who knows prayer times through instruments such as hourglasses, mechanical clocks, or other means," an opinion he reports from Ibn Yunus and others.

And this is the authoritative position in Maliki fiqh and what is adopted in practice, as has been explicitly stated by a number of later scholars who knew of these instruments, were fully acquainted with them, realized their precision and accuracy, and considered them superior to other evidences, of whom it suffices us to record the explicit statements of but a few:

Sheikh al-Tawudi [ibn Sawda, d. 1209/1794] says: "Instruments have a basis in Sacred Law, and merely clarify what the Lawgiver has asked be done and facilitate it without being an addition to it. Whenever someone who knows [a prayer's time] from instruments disagrees with another about whether a prayer's time has come, his position is more correct, and adopting it is fitter and more trustworthy" (*al-Mi'yar al-jadid* (e97), 1.223–24).

Al-Hattab says, after mentioning the way of the fuqaha in knowing the noontime (zawal) by shadow: "This is the familiar method which the fuqaha mention because of its ease and familiarity to everyone. Were one to determine the time by other instrumental means such as the quadrant, the astrolabe, or other, it would be permissible, as al-Mazari and others have mentioned" (ibid., 226).

The great scholar [Ahmad ibn 'Abdullah] al-Ghurfi says: "Because these instruments, the quadrant, the astrolabe, and others have been introduced to Islam and Muslims, and have been tested and found to provide complete certainty [of prayer times] to the person who knows how to use them when they are properly made in themselves, it is obligatory for anyone without knowledge of them to follow without question (taqlid) the person who has knowledge of them, and to act upon what he says—though one should take some precautions when the sky or horizon is overcast [preventing accurate enough observation of celestial bodies to furnish reliable results]. This is what all people have adopted from east to west, as al-Hattab conveys from al-Qarafi [d. 684/1285], and others, so no one condemns relying upon instruments except an ignorant person whose view counts for nothing" (ibid., 223).

(2) In relation to using instruments to find the qibla, I did not find an explicit text stating that it was offensive, even though the above-mentioned reason given by Ibn al-'Arabi that they were not used by the early Muslims is possible to apply here to the subject of prayer times.

The words of al-Qurtubi, however, may indicate that they are permissible, as he says of the means of knowing the qibla by someone who cannot see the Kaaba: "The other [case] is where the Kaaba is not visible, when one must turn towards its way and its direction by means of evidences, namely the sun, moon, stars, winds, and anything else through which one may discover its direction" (10.62) [(Ahkam al-Qur'an (e71), 10.92)].

His saying, "anything else through which one may discover its direction," generally, in this way, comprises every instrument that guides to the qibla.[1] So they are permissible to use and to take as

---

[1] Compare these words of al-Qurtubi to the previously translated citation from Imam Ibn 'Abd al-Barr conveying the *ijma'* of Islamic scholars that "whoever is out of sight of the Kaaba, be he far or near, must face towards it by every means in his power to discover its direction, whether through the stars, mountains, winds, or anything else" (*al-Istidhkar* (e35), 7.215), the last two words of which add scholarly consensus (ijma') to Dr. al-Tawil's case here that they are permissible to use and take as evidence.

evidence, since the signs of the qibla are only ways and means of finding it, there being no religious significance in which particular ones are used—as is also true of the means of warfare [in jihad]; it not being obligatory to use only those [weapons] which existed in the times of the Prophet (Allah bless him and give him peace). (*Fatwa* (e91), 3 November 2000, 1–2).

The Maliki scholar Muhammad al-'Amrawi of Fez says:

> The only [additional] point that might be brought to the attention of the person you are addressing is the immense gulf between applied geometry (handasa) in ancient times and this science in the present day. Matters are no longer as Imam Ibn Siraj (Allah have mercy on him) conceived them, or any one else who came in history before Imam al-Wansharisi [d. 914/1508, who quotes Ibn Siraj's above words]. This field of knowledge, like other rational, empirical, and natural sciences, has advanced so tremendously that we declare our full confidence in its results and rely upon them with complete conviction to decisively solve certain matters [that were hitherto the subject] of ijtihad (*Fatwa* (e7), 26 June 2000, 1).

Times change, and the world changes. Islam, as the true religion of that world, takes people and their ability to obey the commands of Allah Most High as they are, giving realistic consideration to their human social context and its collective achievements. The Iraqi Hanafi mufti Dr. 'Abd al-Malik al-Sa'di says:

> One's personal certitude suffices for "facing the direction of the qibla," and it is not necessary that one be absolutely sure or certain of it. If one finds an expert who determines its location and direction, one no longer has the right to make ijtihad, since an expert's determination comes under the general rubric of having to accept the factual report of someone religiously upright. If one finds a geometer (lit. "engineer"), geographer, or other person with expertise in determining directions, and they are religiously upright, ijtihad is not legally valid in the face of their determination, especially in this age, when the latest scientific methods have appeared which specify directions and locations precisely.
>
> The marks and signs that the fuqaha have mentioned for reaching personal certainty of the direction are but indicators; they are not specifically obligatory in themselves, but merely the means

available to them in those times. When something more accurate in determining the qibla exists, it should be relied upon, and they [the less accurate means] should be abandoned (*Fatwa* (e78), 20 October 2000, 2).

It is a truism of fiqh that the validity of a fatwa may well change with the *makan wa zaman wa ikhwan*—place, time, and brethren—it concerns. That times change points up the special relevance of Muhammad al-'Amrawi's above words about "the immense gulf" between ancient and modern applied geometry to all "instruments."

Compasses

Instruments disclose reality, not create it. A compass, for example, reveals the strong magnetic field generated by the earth at its northern end. This field is a natural phenomenon that is already present, though human beings cannot sense it without a compass. Other creatures, such as homing pigeons, which Allah has created so they return home no matter how many thousands of miles away they are released, sense the field directly, because they have submicroscopic crystals of a substance called magnetite on the surface of their brains which, "like a compass tells them the exact direction of the earth's magnetic field, enabling them to navigate with their astonishing precision" (Becker: *Cross Currents* (e13), 74–75).

That is, the compasses we use merely disclose a reality that, if normally unnoticed by human beings, is as much a part of the natural environment as the sun, wind, stars, landmarks, and other means of orientational ijtihad listed by the fuqaha are. This is why when compasses came to be used among Muslims, scholars of the Shafi'i school recognized that they could be relied upon to find the direction of Mecca. The six muftis of Tarim, Hadramawt, write:

> It is permissible to rely upon compasses in determining the direction of the qibla, as Imam Shams al-Din al-Ramli explicitly states in the *Nihaya al-muhtaj* (1.443) saying, "It is permissible to rely on compasses (bayt al-ibra) for determining prayer times[1] and the

---

[1] A prayer's time can be determined with a compass by seeing the sun in the same direction as seen at the correct prayer time on the previous day.

qibla, because it affords probabilistic knowledge of these, just as ijtihad does. This was the legal opinion (fatwa) given by my father (Allah have mercy on him), and it is plain,"—his father being Sheikh al-Islam Shihab al-Din Ahmad al-Ramli (d. 1004/1596) (*Fatwa* (e54), 12 September 2000, 3).

This is the explicit position of the Shafi'i school on compasses, and it agrees with what the Maliki scholars cited above have said on determining the qibla with instruments in general and determining prayer times with the quadrant and astrolabe in particular. In a word, they found nothing objectionable in using something that merely tells one what one needs to know in order to pray properly.

Clocks and Prayer-Time Calendars

Modern instruments for determining prayer times are another example. The Maliki scholars cited above in al-Shinqiti's and al-Tawil's fatwas mention the quadrant and astrolabe, which disclose prayer times by measurement of the position of the sun and celestial bodies from the horizon, and which fuqaha of previous times like Imam al-Sanusi saw as a blessing from Allah to mankind.

In the present age, Allah has brought forth devices that measure time. For a few hours' wages, one can buy a watch that tells the time of day with complete accuracy for all ordinary purposes. This is religiously significant because of the temporal regularity of the physical phenomena that govern prayer times.

Sunrise is observable and sunset is observable, and they happen every day. The time of *dhuhr* or "midday" occurs just after the sun has reached its zenith or high point in the sky, midway along its daily trek from horizon to horizon. As the earth's rotation does not appreciably speed up or slow down in a given day, the sun reaches the midpoint of its journey at its midpoint in *time* between sunrise and sunset. Since the latter two events are observable facts that respectively happen at the same time on any given calendar date, year after year, and since we can measure time with accurate timepieces, there is little mystery today as to when the sun reaches its zenith for anyone who knows when sunrise and sunset happen, and can add up the minutes between, divide by two, and look at his watch.

If one erects a ten-foot pole in one's yard and looks at it on a sunny day, as the present writer has, and marks its shadow at the sun's zenith on a tablet of paper under it, and thereafter every half minute or so, it is plain that the shadow moves from its place noticeably and perceptibly on the paper within the space of less than one minute. At any latitude in North America, one only has to try this on a sunny day at noon to see it for oneself. As the call to prayer (adhan) seldom takes less than two minutes, if one waits till after this midpoint in time between sunrise and sunset by the interval it takes to give the call to prayer, it is plain that the time for the midday prayer (dhuhr) has entered, because the increase in the shadow's length has become perceptible to the senses. It happens every day. Imam Ghazali says about erecting such a vertical *shakhs* or "upright marker" to observe the sun through the movement of its shadow:

> When the sun passes its utmost height, the length of the shadow starts to increase. As soon as the increase becomes perceptible to the senses, the time for midday prayer (dhuhr) has come. One knows with total certainty that the moment of the sun's passing its zenith [known only] in the knowledge of Allah Most Glorious took place before this, but moral responsibilities are only based on that which enters into sense perception (*Ihya' 'ulum al-din* (e26), 1.174).

The observation that no one can know the exact moment of the sun's zenith (zawal) except Allah, though true of His absolutely precise divine knowledge, no longer applies at the practical level because Allah has effectively lifted this limitation with the coming of the age of the wristwatch. Accurate time measurement has become, for all practical purposes, a fact of human sense perception.

Since the noon prayer is not valid before this *zawal* or "zenith," some ancient books of fiqh recommend looking at one's shadow on the ground and waiting until it has moved on from its position at high noon by at least a *shibr* or "span" (around nine inches), entailing about forty minutes or so at some latitudes. Such ijtihads accomplish one of the main tasks of fiqh, which is to provide simple criteria that give ordinary Muslims an adequate margin of safety in works of worship to prevent mistakes due to uncertainty; here, the mistake of praying the noon prayer before the sun has moved on from its zenith. But these ijtihads come from a different environment than most Muslims find themselves in today.

In the desert there are few cloudy days. Sunrise and sundown, the coming of dawn, the departure of the last redness of sunset, and of the last light of twilight are all manifest to one's eyes. In such circumstances, it would be strange to print up prayer-time calendars and distribute them to the bedouin.

But most Muslims today live in large cities, an environment that is equally valid to live in and equally indifferent in the eyes of a Sacred Law which applies to all places until the Last Day. Modern lighting in large cities eliminates the possibility of accurately observing the dawn, or the disappearance of the red of sunset that marks the beginning of the time for nightfall prayer ('isha) according to the Maliki, Shafi'i, and Hanbali schools, or the disappearance of the last light of twilight that marks nightfall prayer in the Hanafi school. The author can attest that in our times one must not only travel to the desert, but miles and miles into it to get far enough from the effects of the lights of cities and towns to accurately observe these daily events. This is not possible for most people today.

Providentially, Allah has created through human intelligence schedules of the motions of the sun and earth that render these times knowable to everyone who possesses a watch. They are useful for people living in the midst of cities like Cairo with high buildings, to whom sunrise and sunset are not visible, and for Muslims in most of the Northern Hemisphere, where noon or midafternoon are not visible daily because of clouds. Here, even if the sun were shining, merely earning a living would prevent most Muslims from being able to stand under it for forty minutes at noon to observe their shadows.

For them to do so for no other reason than its being "in the books" cannot be regarded as fiqh, since Allah Most High "has not placed any hardship upon you in religion" (Qur'an 22:78), and the fuqaha who originally made the ijtihad only specified such palpable, daily observable criteria in order to make it *easier* for ordinary Muslims of their times to perform their prayers.

To specifically mandate a means of knowing prayer times that can only exist far from the metropolitan areas where most Muslims now live is to impose the utmost hardship upon them. Rather, it is plain that instruments such as wristwatches and calculation-based prayer-time calendars—with the all-important proviso that their results be validated by empirical observation—are also means of knowledge, and do not produce the times that Allah has created for prayers and fasting, but only reveal them.

Spherical Trigonometry

Similarly, spherical trigonometry is a calculative means of disclosing the unique direction Allah has created between any place on earth and the Kaaba in Mecca. It is based on a mathematical model of the earth as a perfect sphere, which it is not, though its non-sphericality is negligible: the earth's north-south circumference is 42.73 miles shorter than its girth at the equator (*World Almanac* (e64), 731), so it is a few miles wider than it is tall.

With an estimable error factor of no more than 1 degree (out of 360), spherical trigonometry is very accurate. The Muslims who measured the direction of the sun earlier this year (1421/2000) from Boston, Montreal, and Amman when it was above Mecca found the observed compass bearing corresponded exactly and with no perceptible error to the qibla directions from those places calculable by spherical trigonometry. That is, like other instruments that are accurate, it discloses reality and does not create it.

The judgement of the handful of Maliki fuqaha we have quoted above who found fault with instruments must accordingly be understood for what it is: an ijtihad from previous times that considered the then-available instruments insufficiently simple and accurate to furnish information on which Muslims could base their worship. According to all the scholars we have asked, times have changed.

The reader may remember our conclusion (at the end of chapter 3 above) that the words of the Prophet (Allah bless him and give him peace) to the people of Medina "Everything between where the sun rises and sets is a qibla" (*Tirmidhi* (e93), 2.173: 344. S) referred to situations where certitude was not possible. Among the evidences for this was that when a Muslim is in sight of the Kaaba and ocular certainty exists as to its direction, the hadith by consensus of all fuqaha does not apply because certainty has taken its place. This is significant in our times, as the Hanafi sheikh Hassan al-Hindi says:

> In the matter of the qibla, the fuqaha referred people to astronomy and applied geometry (handasa), despite their considering these two sciences merely probabilistic; giving them precedence over mere personal judgement (taharri), so how should it be today, when we see the strength of these sciences and the greatness of their accuracy that reduces their error factor to a minimal fraction?
>
> Nor can it be said that Sacred Law has not obliged us to use this technology in determining the qibla. Rather, we say that the Sacred Law did not make it obligatory upon us when it did not exist: as for now that it is in front of us and available, who says we are not obliged to use it? [The Hanafi Imam] al-'Ayni mentions in *'Umda al-qari*, 4.126, that "there are three positions about having to learn the evidences of the qibla; the first being that it is a communal obligation (fard kifaya); the second that it is a personal obligation (fard 'ayn), though this is incorrect; and the third that it is communally obligatory unless one wishes to travel, in which case it is [personally] obligatory to learn the evidences of the qibla, among which are the laws of astronomy and applied geometry" (*Fatwa* (e34), 20 July 2000, 4).

And the Hanafi sheikh Dr. Muhammad Hisham al-Burhani further clarifies:

> It is not permissible for someone who can see the Kaaba or who is praying in a direction established by authoritative transmission [that the Prophet (Allah bless him and give him peace) prayed towards it] to make his own ijtihad. Nor may someone make ijtihad whose qibla has been determined by exact modern scientific means.
>
> Someone who is not any of the above may make his own ijtihad, and whatever he deems most probably correct suffices to be "facing the direction."
>
> Of an absolute certainty—in this age and the things actually daily seen in it, such as air traffic, the satellites that have filled space, and the fact that every single point on the earth and even the planets, stars, and asteroids travelling through space can be targeted and

made a determinate destination with limitless precision—is that the location of the Kaaba on earth, thus transformed by modern science into a small village, has become known and determinable by precise coordinates with infinitesimal accuracy.

Man has therefore become capable of knowing without the slightest doubt or hesitation his location in relation to the Noble Kaaba. It is therefore incumbent upon him to face the Kaaba itself, and it is insufficient for him to merely pray towards its approximate direction (jiha), as Allah is my witness, unless he is remote from actual civilization and its data, or this is inaccessible to him because of some excuse.

For it is obligatory to act upon the primary basis [of the divine injunction "Wherever you may be, turn your faces towards it" (Qur'an 2:144)] in order to apply the fundamental Shari'a rules and principles that state: "One may not have recourse to a substitute unless one is unable to use the first choice," just as dry ablution (tayammum) may not be used unless one is lacking water, whether actually [as when none exists] or virtually [as when it exists, but it may not be used for fear of thirst or illness]. Or just as ijtihad may not be resorted to on an issue already decided by an unequivocal scriptural text (nass). Or just as uncertainty must be disregarded when certainty exists.

Lastly, we should not omit to mention an important issue, namely that whoever prays towards a direction knowing with certainty that he is thereby plainly turned away from the correct direction, and has intentionally left it—his prayer is not legally valid, unless he has left it for some excuse. Indeed, the Hanafis say that whoever prays [towards a direction] by his ijtihad and believes that he has actually faced the exact direction (samt) of the qibla, this suffices him, and his prayer is valid. But the question here is: If he intentionally turns away from what he believes is the direction of the Kaaba, is his prayer valid? I am completely convinced it is not; and Allah Most High knows best.

In closing, I say that the qibla in the United States of America and other countries is the direction indicated by scientific experts who direct the movement of travel and transportation between the countries of the world; and that whoever contradicts this should be completely ignored. And Allah Most High knows best (*Fatwa* (e19), 29 June 2000, 3).

CONCLUSIONS

Our scholars say that first, there is nothing in the Maliki school (or any other) which entails that it is reprehensible to know that the world is round or to use a globe to understand the geographical direction of the qibla. Rather, this is *obligatory* for someone finding the qibla far from Mecca through ijtihad, since Allah has said, "Wherever you all may be, turn your faces towards it" (Qur'an 2:144), and our being on the face of the planet earth, as we have seen, physically affects our compliance with this command as much as the coming of a prayer's time physically affects our ability to perform the prayer.

Secondly, we saw that instruments, whether physical ones such as compasses, or calculative ones such as mathematical models for finding prayer times or the qibla direction from one's location, create nothing, but merely disclose a reality already created by Allah. As such, their ruling in Sacred Law is that of their empirical accuracy: if they work, there is no religious reason, according to any of the Islamic scholars we have asked, why Muslims should not use them.

Even if a handful of scholars once deemed instruments for finding the qibla or prayer times offensive, one cannot invoke their centuries-old texts without being guilty of a fatal ambiguity, for what we mean by "instruments" today is very different from anything within the technical possibilities they could conceive of or intend by their words.

Finally, the values exemplified in their fiqh ijtihads about instruments include not only certainty and accuracy, but simplicity, for they explicitly shunned the imposition of unnecessary complication on Muslims in their prayer and fasting times as well as in finding the qibla. In our times we have come full circle, and to advocate the religious superiority today of the means of this simplicity to the people of those times, such as direct observation of the sun's motion—easy in the desert but impossible for contemporary Muslims in cities for most daily prayers—imposes a complication and hardship upon them that has little to do with fiqh.

II

The Exact Direction

DIFFICULTY

THE exact direction (samt) determinable by spherical trigonometry and other precision means and instruments is not a condition for the qibla according to the majority of the fuqaha, including those of the Hanafi, Maliki, and Hanbali schools, and even some Shafi'is, such as Imam Ghazali. Rather, the scholarly majority say that the approximate direction (jiha) is the criterion. The Maliki Imam Ibn Siraj says:

> As for the exact direction (samt), the Sacred Law has not indicated that it should be observed, so it is of no consideration (*al-Mi'yar al-mu'rib* (e96), 1.122).

So the present work's arguments for the exact direction (samt) are of little significance to anyone but Shafi'is who follow that position.

RESPONSE

In ordinary language there are a number of meanings bound up in the word "direction."

The primitive use of the word "direction" is to locate something accurately enough to be able to point at it and say, "It is there," and for this to be considered true by conventional standards ('urf). In this primitive sense, a direct line from one's finger or one's eye to the object seems to be meant. It does not mean a geometrically precise trajectory—for which reason it is notoriously difficult for an unpracticed hand to hit something with a pistol that it is considered by any conventional standards to be "pointing" at it—but rather that which is conventionally acknowledged as "the direction" between the two. In Arabic this direct line is the *samt,* usually rendered in the present work as "exact direction," but only within these conventional limits of "exact."

From this meaning derives the concept of "facing" something, which in its primitive sense means orienting the face and the front of the body towards the object's unique direction. Here, convention seems to require less precision, although one does have to be within certain limits of conformity to the exact direction or one is not said to be facing it. The direction one is "facing" is termed in Arabic *jiha,* deriving, as in English, from the word "face" or *wajh,* and translated in the present work as "the approximate direction."

As mentioned above, this approximate direction logically derives from the exact direction, because the approximate direction either applies or does not apply to something on the basis of the criterion of *inhiraf* or "divergence" from the object one is trying to face. And if we think about this divergence, it is nothing besides an agreed upon permissible variance from the actual direction (samt). This is what we find in all four Sunni schools of jurisprudence.

All agree that when in sight of the Kaaba one must face it, or be part of a row of whom some face it. As for places far from Mecca, the Hanafi, Maliki, and Hanbali schools which use the approximate direction (jiha) as their qibla implicitly define it by reference to divergence from the exact direction, while the Shafi'i school does so explicitly. The acceptable amount of divergence varies with the school.

The Four Schools

In the Hanafi school, Imam Khayr al-Din al-Ramli explicitly states that the approximate direction (jiha) sought by his school means that one may not diverge more than 45 degrees to the left or right of the exact direction (samt), making a total of 90 degrees, since the 360 degrees around a person divided into the four bodily directions (right, left, forward, and backward) means there will be 90 degrees for each direction, including the front direction intended by "facing the qibla" (*al-Fatawa al-Khayriyya* (e73), 1.18). The Hanafi sheikh Dr. Muhammad Hisham al-Burhani, whose fatwa we have quoted above, believes that this ruling exclusively applies to situations in which one does not know the exact direction, and that if known one must face it.[1] Imam

---

[1] However, for mihrabs of already existing mosques the position of the Hanafi school according to Sheikh Muhammad Yusuf al-Bannuri is that "it is permissible

Ghazali argues for the same degree of divergence for the qibla as the Hanafi school does, and for the same reasons, and says that more precision than this imposes unnecessary hardship upon ordinary Muslims (*Ihya' 'ulum al-din* (e26), 3.233–35).

In the Maliki school we have seen in the quotation from Imam Malik translated above in chapter 3 that the degree of permissible divergence is about 90 degrees on either side of the exact line direction (*al-Mudawwana* (e55), 1.92). We also saw that Malik and other scholars of his school understand the dispensation of the hadith "Everything between where the sun rises and sets is a qibla" (*Tirmidhi* (e93), 2.173: 344. S) to apply to someone who believes he is facing the correct direction, not someone who is certain that he is turned away, even if only somewhat, from the correct direction. The Maliki Mufti Dr. Muhammad al-Rugi of Fez says:

> The *qibla* in its lexical sense means the "approximate direction" (jiha), and in its Islamic legal meaning a particular approximate direction; namely, that of the Kaaba, the physical meaning of "shortest path" entering into the legal sense. So if you are unable to place the shortest path between yourself and the Kaaba, there is no hardship, for the legal aim is to be sure that one is facing and directed towards the Kaaba and its approximate direction; and the more accurately we can do this, the closer it is to the aim of the Sacred Law (*Fatwa* (e77), 10 March 2000, 1).

The criterion for the Hanbali school is something between the approximate direction (jiha) and exact direction (samt), for although the term *jiha* is used, the exact direction is the basis, from which a "slight divergence" is allowable (al-Buhuti: *Kashshaf al-qina'* (e17), 1.305).

---

to turn [even if intentionally] somewhat aside (inharafa) from the exact direction (samt) of the qibla determined by the evidences of mathematical geography, if one does this by way of simply following (taqlid) the mihrabs of the commonality of Muslims, even though following the exact direction determined [by mathematical evidence] is fitter (awla)" (*Bughya al-arib* (e12), 100). This is a mercy to Hanafis whose local imam is unable (or undesirous) to correct the prayer direction—provided it is within 45 degrees of the exact direction to begin with, beyond which would be outside of the *jiha* or "approximate direction" that Hanafis hold obligatory to face.

In the Shafi'i school, one must be "in line with the exact direction, though by conventional rather than absolute standards ('urfan la haqiqatan)" (al-Haytami: *Tuhfa al-muhtaj* (e33), 1.484), and "with certitude (yaqinan) if one is close [enough to see the Kaaba], but to the best of one's belief (dhannan) if one is far" (al-Shirwani: *Hashiya* (e33), ibid.).

It is clear from these citations that the direction (samt) which is the physical basis for both the approximate direction (jiha) of the Hanafi, Maliki, and Hanbali school on the one hand, and the exact direction (samt) of the Shafi'i school on the other, is not the *scientifically* exact direction meant by mathematicians when they use the word *samt,* but rather the conventionally ('urfan) exact direction that is humanly possible under normal circumstances. Ibn Siraj acknowledges this by saying:

> As for the exact direction (samt), the Sacred Law has not indicated that it should be observed, so it is of no consideration, since "exact direction" means, for users of instruments, that if a straight line were imagined to be drawn from a person's place it would lie straight towards the Kaaba, whereas the jurists [such as Shafi'is] who hold that the exact direction (samt) is what is required do not construe it so narrowly, but deem it sufficient that one merely be "in line" (musamit) with the Kaaba as one is with something one sees, as stars line up with each other. While the two [conceptions of exact direction] are similar in meaning, there is a narrowness in the terminology of instrument users that is not found in the terminology of the fuqaha (*al-Mi'yar al-mu'rib* (e96), 1.122).

The passage clarifies that the meaning of the "exact direction" which the author repudiates as a criterion for the qibla is the *scientifically* exact direction (samt haqiqi), which, as we have seen, none of the schools of fiqh holds to be required of the person praying; nor is this advocated by the Azhar Fatwa translated above, which states that

> someone praying who can see the Kaaba must face the Kaaba itself, though if far from it, it is sufficient to face the direction of the Kaaba, and one need not face the Kaaba itself (*Fatwa* (e47), 25 February 1998, 1).

That is, one need not face the scientifically exact direction, which rather provides the physical basis for the less precise "approximate direction" (jiha) that Muslims must face. The fatwa also says:

> The approximate direction of the qibla in the regions of North America is the northeast, the angle varying from one location to another with the longitude and latitude, as experts have determined.
>
> Someone facing towards the southeast in these regions is so far off that he is in danger of not facing the direction of the Kaaba, and he does not fulfill the legal condition of facing the qibla (ibid., 2).

CONCLUSIONS

The above difficulty is immaterial, since there is no one who considers facing the scientifically exact direction (samt haqiqi) to be mandatory for someone performing the prayer: not the four Sunni schools, the Azhar Fatwa, or anyone else. The exact direction, however, *is* the implicit physical basis for the approximate direction (jiha) of all the schools, since the approximate direction is but a specified amount of divergence from it; and this is its critical importance for all Muslims.

12

The Traditional Direction of Mosques

DIFFICULTY

THE scholars of all four schools of Sunni jurisprudence have taken into consideration the authority of the traditional direction of the qiblas of mosques that have been built in the communities where they are found, and the traditional direction of mosques in the Western Hemisphere is to the east.

RESPONSE

Even if we grant this, a hemisphere is a big place, and will necessarily contain a great many directions to Mecca. It is no more possible for one point of the compass to be the direction towards Mecca from all places in the Western Hemisphere than it is possible from all places in the Eastern Hemisphere.

If we mean by "traditional direction" that of mosques in relatively long-established Caribbean Muslim communities such as those in Trinidad and Guyana, the eastern direction they face is close enough to the physical direction of Mecca to be valid according to the Hanafi school that most follow there.[1] But if by "traditional" we mean to include the mosques built in the United States and Canada in the twentieth century, this argument fails for a number of reasons. We must realize that Islamic jurists have taken into consideration the direction that most mosques face in a Muslim *city* (as opposed to a hemisphere or a continent) not because each mosque is to be taken as if it were one vote in a referendum, but for two very different reasons.

The Presumption of Accuracy

The first reason is that the fact that mosques in a Muslim city all face the same direction argues they have been built that way out of *ijtihad*

---

[1] According to the position just mentioned in the footnote on pages 138–39 above.

or "expert reasoning" using proofs that are significantly factually accurate, since large communities of Muslims in Islamic lands have seldom been without experts and scholars. Al-Wansharisi conveys that when the Maliki mufti of Granada Abul Qasim ibn Siraj, whom we have quoted above, was asked about an outcry that had resulted from a local imam's turning considerably from the angle that a mosque was facing in order to correct it, he said:

> The imam should not turn aside in the way asked about, because a mihrab set up in a large [Muslim] city has obviously been built with the consensus of many people and scholars, which is a proof that it is correct and has been constructed on the basis of expert reasoning. Scholars have explicitly stated (Allah be well pleased with them) that the mihrabs of major areas are valid to follow without checking evidences (yasihhu taqliduha) (al-Mi'yar al-mu'rib (e96), 1.117).

The Hanbali Imam Ibn Qudama al-Maqdisi says,

> And so too if one is in a large city or village: what is obligatory for one is to face their mihrabs and their established qibla, because these mihrabs are ascertained by people of expertise and knowledge, [to follow the results of] which is the same as being correctly informed of it, so it suffices in place of personal reasoning (ijtihad) (al-Mughni (e43), 1.439).

Ibn 'Abidin, the Imam of the late Hanafi school says,

> The people of a city possess knowledge of the direction of the qibla based on evidences that indicate it, such as stars, or other than the stars, and so that [knowledge] takes precedence over what may be ascertained by personal investigation (taharri), as is also the case when one finds mihrabs established in a city (Radd al-muhtar (e37), 1.291).

And Imam Nawawi says:

> As for mihrabs, one must rely upon them [for the main direction, though in the Shafi'i school, one may correct it by turning slightly to the right (tayamun) or left (tayasur)], and one may not use personal reasoning (ijtihad) where they exist. The author of al-Shamil ['Abd al-Sayyid ibn al-Sabbagh, d. 477/1084] has conveyed

scholarly consensus (ijma') of Muslims on this point, and our colleagues adduce for it that mihrabs are not built except in the presence of a number of people who possess knowledge of the position of the planets and of other evidences, and so are as [obligatory to accept as] being informed by someone who knows.

Know that a mihrab is obligatory to rely upon if it is in a large city or in a small village that many travellers pass through, such that they would not merely confirm an error, though if it is in a small village that not many travellers pass through it is not permissible to rely upon (al-Majmu' (e63), 3.201).

The reason for the latter distinction—between a village that many travellers pass through and one that they do not—is the same reason that one may rely on the consensus of many mihrabs in a large city; namely, the expectation of factual accuracy based on the expertise and knowledge of the builders, and rechecked (in the case of a village) by others, that the direction they have been built to is the direction of Mecca.

The Shafi'i ulema of the Fatwa Council of Tarim convey in their fatwa, quoting the Mufti of Hadramawt 'Abd al-Rahman Ba-'Alawi (d. 1251/1835):

"Mihrabs may be divided into [two kinds:] those fully authenticated as having been prayed towards by the Prophet (Allah bless him and give him peace) . . . , and those not authenticated as having been prayed towards by him (Allah bless him and give him peace).

"If the latter are [1] in a place where whole generations (qurun) of Muslims have been born and bred, or many have travelled through, such that they could not have confirmed a mistake, and [2] the direction has not been objected to, then it is not permissible to make ijtihad about the general direction (jiha), although one may do so in respect to turning slightly right or left (though this is not obligatory, according to the soundest view). If either stipulation is unmet, it is unconditionally obligatory to make ijtihad. 'Turning slightly right or left,' as previously mentioned, means not diverging from the general direction (jiha) in which the Kaaba lies" [Ba-'Alawi: Bughya al-mustarshidin (e9), 40].

As for his words "generations of Muslims," the hadith master (hafiz) Suyuti says in his Fatawi: "The meaning of 'generations'

[Ar. *qurun,* also meaning "centuries"] of Muslims is certainly not "three hundred years" or a hundred years, or half of that, but merely that whole groups of Muslims have prayed towards that mihrab, and no one is recorded to have criticized it . . . .

"The criterion is the number of people, not the length of time, and the disagreement of a single person is adequate if he mentions evidence for it or is a scholar in determining the qibla and prayer times; for such a disagreement excludes it from being of the certitude that makes ijtihad impermissible" (*Fatwa* (e54), 12 September 2000, 3–4).

So the above difficulty's using the "traditional direction" of mosques in the Western Hemisphere is only valid as a proof for the correctness of the eastern qibla if we can show that their mihrabs, like the mihrabs of the large Muslim cities referred to by the above quotations, have been built by people of knowledge and expertise.

This is certainly not the case in North America, where in the early part of the twentieth century there were very few mosques, undoubtedly less than 1 percent of the number today, and those who built them were not intellectuals or professionals, but the ordinary laborers and businessmen who first brought Islam to this land and who had little special expertise in the evidences of finding the qibla far from Mecca.

This knowledge vacuum explains not only why they first thought to pray to the east, but also why, within two decades of the building of the Islamic Center in Washington, D.C., towards the northeast in 1953 on the basis of the sphericality of the earth and the calculations of professional engineers at the Egyptian Ministry of Works, Muslims of the United States and Canada welcomed the new information and built their mihrabs to correspond to it. As previously noted, fewer than one-half of 1 percent of the some 3000 mosques in North America today face any other direction.

As for the previous "traditional direction" in North America, even if the mere passage of time were significant—which, according to the above fiqh works cited, it is not, because of the fewness of Muslims who were there—the first mosque actually built in North America was completed in Cedar Rapids, Iowa, in 1934 (*Islam in Iowa* (e92), 8–9), only nineteen years before the Islamic Center in Washington, D.C., was built towards the correct direction, an interval not typically regarded as long enough to establish a "traditional direction."

Fitna

The second reason that the consensus of mihrabs in a city is taken into consideration by jurists is because of the *fitna* or "strife" resulting among ordinary people from disagreement about the direction. Islam is a religion of peace and psychic equilibrium, and strongly prohibits anything that sows discord among hearts. The Prophet (Allah bless him and give him peace) foretold the strife that would break out after him and condemned it by saying:

> There shall be troubles (fitan) in which he who sits shall be better than he who stands, he who stands better than he who walks, and he who walks better than he who runs. Whoever even raises his head [to see what is happening] in them shall be felled by them. So let whoever finds shelter from them take refuge in it" (*Muslim* (e62), 4.2211–12: 2886. S).

Abul Hasan 'Ali al-Quryani mentions that when the Andalusian ruler al-Hakam ibn 'Abd al-Rahman wanted to correct the direction of the Friday Mosque of Córdoba, "he was prevented from doing so by the enormity in the eyes of the common people of contravening that which their forefathers had always done" (*al-Mi'yar al-mu'rib* (e96), 1.118). In present day North America, where over 99 percent of the mosques face the northeastern direction, the *'illa* or "reason" for this decision by a Muslim ruler, namely to prevent strife and disunity among Muslims, is an argument *against* changing to any other direction. Anas ibn Malik (Allah be well pleased with him) heard the Messenger of Allah (Allah bless him and give him peace) say,

> Make things easy [for people], not difficult; quieten them and do not repel them (*Muslim* (e62), 3.1359: 1734. S),

while it is hard to think of something more disquieting to a group of Muslims than being unable to agree about which direction to pray together.

CONCLUSIONS

The two reasons why the fuqaha take into consideration the "traditional direction" of the qibla in a major city are that first, it argues that
it has been placed that way in agreement with evidence known to be
accurate by people of knowledge and expertise, and second, because
turning the qibla around would cause strife among ordinary people.
For neither of these reasons is an easterly "traditional direction" applicable or relevant to mosques in North America.

The first reason is inapplicable because, as we have seen, it was
only after professionals and men of expertise arrived in North America
that they agreed, under the aegis of the Islamic organizations that
sprang from Muslim student groups in the sixties and seventies, that
all the mosques should face the physical direction of Mecca, to the
northeast. Aside from the Caribbean countries, which we have treated
above, the prayer niches that existed in the handful of North American
cities with mosques before the mid–twentieth century were not put
there by people with credentials to do so or expertise, but by amateurs
with little familiarity with the issues and proofs.

The second reason, to obviate strife and disunity among Muslims,
is not an argument against the northeast qibla but an argument for it.
The physical direction of Mecca is now plain to the overwhelming
majority of those who pray in North America, their mihrabs face that
direction, and to require them to now change, flouting both physical
fact and their consensus, would cause unparalleled strife.

This is not because of the level of intolerance today among North
American Muslims due to their ignorance of fiqh or ijtihad, but simply
because everyone, scholar and nonscholar, realizes that the qibla in any
given place should be one. In the course of gathering material for the
present work, when the author told scholars across the Arab world
from all four Sunni schools of jurisprudence that in America last year
(1420/1999) three groups of Muslims prayed at a convention center
facing three different directions in the wake of opinions by visiting
scholars, not a single one found this even remotely acceptable or
regarded it as an outcome of valid scholarly differences. They regarded
it only as *fitna.*

The Mauritanian Maliki sheikh 'Abdullah al-'Alawi al-Shinqiti writes:

> A tempest of headstrong opinions besets most Muslims today; schools and sects divide them until nothing remains to unite them but the qibla. If it splits into a number of directions in a single city, it is a religious disaster. By means of collective ijtihad, returning to experts, and the use of accurate instruments, this problem can be overcome. Muslim unity is a key aim of Sacred Law (*Fatwa* (e82), 21 September 2000, 4).

Unity is of prime importance, and the east being termed the "traditional direction" in North America for the qibla cannot be an obstacle to it, because a handful of mosques constructed without expertise before the vast majority of Muslims arrived in America and built their mosques to the correct direction is of no discoverable significance in Sacred Law.

13

The Four Directions of the World

—

DIFFICULTY

A MUSLIM of the Maliki school finding the qibla for himself far from Mecca may only face one of the four "cardinal directions," either north, south, east, or west, depending on which is closest to the actual physical direction of the Kaaba. The northeast qibla is none of these.

Moreover, physical arguments for the northeast qibla such as those of the present work do bear out the northeast qibla, but all contain the same basic flaw, which is the idea that the Kaaba itself ('ayn al-Ka'ba) is what is meant by facing the qibla, and that directions are relative and not absolute. Imam Ghazali clearly states that the directions are absolute and they are four by scholarly consensus. He claims *ijma'* for this or "complete scholarly consensus," and if this is the case, we cannot claim that the directions are relative. It is still the *'urf* or "common acknowledgement" of the people of the earth to view the four directions as absolute.

Finally, if they are absolute, the northeast qibla is unacceptable because it is a "compound direction"—a line that changes its direction from northeast, to east, to southeast—rather than a true direction.

RESPONSE

With this final difficulty, we have returned to the original question of the present volume; namely, whether a Maliki must pray to one of the four cardinal directions. This question in turn raises two related issues about the nature of directions. We will deal with each in turn before summing them up.

Maliki Fiqh and the Cardinal Directions

"A Muslim of the Maliki school finding the qibla for himself far from Mecca may only face one of the four 'cardinal directions,' either north, south, east, or west, depending on which is closest to the actual physical direction of the Kaaba. The northeast qibla is none of these."

In the past few years, this position seems to have been taught in both England and America, for the author has heard it from a number of Western Malikis, teacher and student alike, including the young man mentioned in the preface. Upon checking, the author has found that it has no basis. Neither the Maliki school nor any other advocates praying to one of the four cardinal directions when one knows with certainty that the actual physical direction of the Kaaba lies elsewhere. This is shown by four separate proofs from Maliki fiqh literature.

(1) The most exhaustive treatment of qibla issues the author knows of in a major Maliki work is in the fourteen-volume *al-Dhakhira,* in which Imam Ahmad ibn Idris al-Qarafi (d. 684/1285) states that the directions possible to take as one's qibla consist in every single point in 360 degrees around one, depending on where the Kaaba physically lies. He says:

> The direction of the Kaaba may be east in one region and west in another. Every single point imaginable, north or south, between where the sun rises and where it sets is the direction of the Kaaba for some people or another, in 360 degrees—the exact determination of which is drawn from the above-mentioned ways of determining the qibla (*al-Dhakhira* (e66), 2.131).

"Every single point imaginable" in 360 degrees flatly contradicts the idea of a "cardinal direction qibla" restricting the qibla exclusively to the four cardinal points of the compass. Moreover, al-Qarafi explicitly says that the "strongest" (aqwaha) of the "above-mentioned ways" he refers to in this passage are "latitude and longitude, combined with the 'geometer's circle' or other geometrical forms, as is expounded in the science of prayer-time and qibla determination ('ilm al-mawaqit)" (ibid., 123–24). Plainly, in Imam al-Qarafi's view, praying towards a "cardinal qibla" when the Kaaba is known to lie in another more precise direction is simply praying in the wrong direction.

(2) Praying to a cardinal direction when a more precise direction is known is also rebutted in Maliki legal literature by the *ijma'* or "consensus" of the eighty Companions of the Messenger of Allah (Allah bless him and give him peace) who were with 'Amr ibn al-'As (Allah be well pleased with him) when he built his mosque in Cairo to the southeast.

Maliki books term such a direction of prayer *qibla al-ijma'* or "qibla of unanimous consensus [of the Sahaba]," which the southeast-facing mosque of 'Amr ibn al-'As is cited as an example of by Imam al-Kharashi in his *Sharh 'ala Khalil* (e52), 1.255–56; Imam al-Sawi in his *Bulgha al-salik* (e21), 1.292; and by Sheikh Muhammad al-'Ulaysh in his *Minah al-Jalil* (e95), 1.140–41.[1] Al-Wansharisi also notes that the southeast was the direction of the mosques of Andalusia, the predominantly Maliki lands of Muslim Spain (*al-Mi'yar al-mu'rib* (e96), 1.121).

The southeast direction of these qiblas, which no Maliki regards as a mistake, is not one of the four cardinal directions.

(3) One looks in vain for any mention of a "cardinal qibla" in Maliki reference works. The position is not in: Imam Malik's four-volume *al-Mudawwana* (e55); Ibn Abi Zayd al-Qayrawani's fifteen-volume *al-Nawadir wa al-ziyadat* (e68); 'Abd al-Wahhab al-Maliki's *al-Ma'una* (e56); Ibn 'Abd al-Barr's thirty-volume *al-Istidhkar* (e35) or his *al-Kafi* (e36); Ibn Rushd's twenty-volume *al-Bayan wa al-tahsil* (e44) or his *Muqaddimat Ibn Rushd* (e55); Muhammad al-Mazari's two-volume *Sharh al-Talqin* (e60); Ibn al-Hajib's *Jami' al-ummahat* (e39); Ahmad ibn Idris al-Qarafi's fourteen-volume *al-Dhakhira* (e66); Qasim al-Tanukhi's *Sharh 'ala matn al-Risala* (e101); the two-volume *Sharh Hudud Ibn 'Arafa* (e74) by Muhammad al-Rassa'; Muhammad al-Mawwaq's *al-Taj wa al-iklil* (e32); Ahmad Zarruq's two-volume *Sharh*

---

[1] Some Maliki texts such as Ibn Hamdun's *Hashiya* upon Muhammad Mayyara's *Sharh* of Ibn 'Ashir's *al-Murshid al-mu'in* challenge the claim that the eighty Sahaba present were legally sufficient to effect a *unanimous* consensus upon the direction of the mosque of 'Amr ibn al-'As—as not *all* the Sahaba were present—(*Hashiya Ibn Hamdun* (e40) 1.149), but no Maliki has ever denied the legal *validity* of the southeastern direction that those present agreed upon, which is what is under discussion here.

'ala matn al-Risala (e101); 'Ali ibn Nasir al-Din al-Manufi's three-volume *Kifaya al-talib al-rabbani* (e57); Muhammad al-Hattab's six-volume *Mawahib al-Jalil* (e32); Muhammad al-Kharashi's eight-volume *al-Kharashi 'ala Khalil* (e52); Ahmad al-Dardir's four-volume *al-Sharh al-saghir* (e21); Muhammad al-Dusuqi's six-volume *Hashiya al-Dusuqi* (e22); or Ahmad al-Sawi's *Bulgha al-salik* (e21).

If the "cardinal direction qibla" had ever existed, its very uniqueness among the four schools of Sunni jurisprudence would have made it the most famous of Maliki fiqh positions, and it would have required the spirited (and lengthy) defense typical of legal positions that a single school adopts apart from others, yet none of these Maliki Imams mentions a word about it.

The only question that it remotely resembles is that of the *mutahayyir* or "person with no idea where the qibla is," who some Maliki fuqaha say may pray successively in each of four directions to ensure that at least one of them is the right direction. And this is a weak position in the school, as noted by Imam al-Dardir in *Aqrab al-masalik* (e21), 1.296, and others. More tellingly, the question of the *mutahayyir* has nothing to do with the point here, which is *ijtihad* about the correct direction of the qibla, but rather concerns the opposite: what to do when ijtihad is impossible.

(4) The "cardinal qibla" is also refuted by the Maliki texts we have translated at the end of chapter 3 above from the works of Imam Ibn 'Abd al-Barr, Imam Malik, and Imam Khalil (Allah be well pleased with them). In the first passage we cited, Ibn 'Abd al-Barr said that by the unanimous consensus (ijma') of all scholars

> whoever is out of sight of it [the Kaaba], be he far or near, must face towards it by every means in his power to discover its direction, whether through the stars, mountains, winds, or anything else (*al-Istidhkar* (e35), 7.215).

And in the passage translated from the *Mudawwana* on page 49 above, Imam Malik said that three possible cases exist when trying to face the qibla for prayer through one's ijtihad: (a) having one's back to it (istadbara); (b) having one's right or left side to it (sharraqa aw gharraba)—in contemporary terms, being turned from the actual direction 90 degrees or more—or (c) being merely turned somewhat aside (inharafa) from it, meaning less than 90 degrees. As previously noted, Malik says of this third case,

> If a man prays turned somewhat away from the qibla (inharafa) without his right or left side being towards it [i.e. at less than a right angle], and he learns of this before finishing his prayer, he should turn back towards the qibla, then finish his prayer without stopping (al-Mudawwana (e55), 1.92),

which we said entails *a fortiori* that one should not intentionally *begin* one's prayer turned somewhat aside from it. Unsurprisingly, a Maliki who knows where the Kaaba is must face it, just as in other schools.

We also saw, from the *Mukhtasar* of Imam Khalil ibn Ishaq al-Jundi, that Maliki scholars term a person in circumstance (a) or (b) above to be *munharif kathiran* or "greatly turned" from the actual direction (samt), meaning 90 degrees or more—and in circumstance (c) above to be *munharif yasiran* or "merely turned somewhat aside" from it, meaning less than 90 degrees, and that each has his own ruling. Imam Khalil (with the commentary of al-Abi (A:)) says:

> If the mistakenness (A: of the qibla one is facing) becomes plain during a prayer, one stops praying [in order to begin again facing the right direction], unless one is blind or merely turned somewhat aside from the qibla (*munharif yasiran,* i.e. less than 90 degrees), in either of which cases one turns to face it (A: that is, face the qibla, and merely goes on to complete the rest of the prayer that one had begun facing away from it. If in either case one does not turn to face towards it, but merely completes the prayer facing the direction whose mistakenness has become plain, then the prayer is legally invalid for the blind person if he is turned greatly aside from the qibla (*munharif kathiran,* i.e. 90 degrees or more)—while such a prayer is legally valid for someone merely turned somewhat aside from the qibla (*munharif yasiran,* i.e. less than 90 degrees), whether sighted or blind, though for either [sighted or blind] to do so is unlawful)[1] (*Jawahir al-iklil* (e3), 1.45).

---

[1] To understand the distinction in this Maliki text between such a prayer being *valid* while nevertheless *unlawful,* one must realize the fiqh difference between the

From these texts it is plain that the Maliki school's wide tolerance on the qibla does not extend to someone making ijtihad who *deliberately* turns away from the actual position of the Kaaba according to his belief and ijtihad, even if only somewhat (munharif yasiran)—and even if towards one of the cardinal directions. Such a person is not doing something obligatory according to the Maliki school, but something unlawful.

It may be that Maliki sheikhs in Saharan lands such as northern Chad, Niger, Mali, and Mauritania teach local students that ijtihad on the qibla need not exceed trying to face east. If so, they are certainly correct, for Mecca lies due east of their countries, though for Western students to infer from this that facing the qibla anywhere and everywhere means nothing more than orienting oneself to a cardinal direction is unsupported by Maliki fiqh literature.

We have seen such a "cardinal direction qibla" rebutted first by Imam al-Qarafi's explicit statement that the qibla may be in any direction in 360 degrees; second, by the "qibla of ijma'" of 'Amr ibn al-'As, which was established, according to several main Maliki scholars, by the consensus of eighty Sahaba and which faces southeast in Cairo to this day; third, by the fact that none of the main authors of Maliki fiqh works knows anything about a mandatory "cardinal direction qibla"—including the twenty more famous ones listed above; and fourth, by Imam Ibn 'Abd al-Barr's, Malik's, and Khalil's words about facing the direction as best one knows, and al-Abi's explanation that anything else is unlawful (haram). In other words, the qibla of the Malikis is the same as the qibla of everyone else.

---

legally valid (sahih) and invalid (fasid) on the one hand, and the lawful (halal) and unlawful (haram) on the other. To clarify with an example, if one were to wrongfully seize another's home, it is of course unlawful for one to live there, and likewise to perform one's five daily prayers there. But if one performed the noontime prayer (dhuhr) in such a house, and the Islamic ruler's troops arrived at midafternoon time ('asr) to eject one and restore the house to its owner, then after exacting the damages from one, they could not additionally penalize one for the intentional nonperformance of the prayer, since it did actually happen in a technically valid (sahih) way, though it was unlawful (haram) for one to have prayed it there. Needless to add, the fuqaha are well aware that a prayer "valid" in this way while being unlawful (haram) is most unlikely to be accepted by Allah.

Thus, what has been has been taught to Malikis in England and the United States on this matter is a mistake, though perhaps the rationale for it is discoverable from the second part of the above difficulty, to which we now turn.

The Four Directions Are Absolute by Ijma'

"The physical arguments for the northeast qibla such as those in the present work do bear out the northeastern qibla, but all contain the same basic flaw, which is the idea that the Kaaba itself ('ayn al-Ka'ba) is what is meant by facing the qibla, and that directions are relative and not absolute. Imam Ghazali clearly states that directions are absolute and they are four by scholarly consensus. He claims *ijma'* for this or 'complete scholarly unanimity,' and if this is the case, we cannot claim that the directions are relative. It is still the *'urf* or 'common acknowledgement' of the people of the earth to view the four directions as absolute."

The claim that the basic flaw in the present work's argument is "the idea that the Kaaba itself ('ayn al-Ka'ba) is what is intended by facing the qibla," harkens back to an older fiqh controversy that the above difficulty has apparently confused with the present discussion, but which it has little in fact to do with. The controversy was whether, as Shafi'i believed, one must face the "Kaaba itself" ('ayn al-Ka'ba) when praying, or whether, as Abu Hanifa and Malik held, it is sufficient to face the "approximate direction of the Kaaba" (jiha al-Ka'ba). As pointed out in chapter 11, the implicit criterion for both of these is the exact direction (samt) of the Kaaba, which the Kaaba itself ('ayn) is in direct line with, and which the approximate direction (jiha) is but a specified amount of divergence from.

Raising this "basic flaw" demonstrates the above difficulty's confusion between the fiqh sense of *jiha,* the "approximate direction," and the quite different cartographic sense of *jiha* as "compass direction" or "direction name." We have detailed the differences between these two senses in chapter 4 above, "Mecca and the Mercator Projection," which shows that to identify the two is an *equivocation* between two distinct senses of a key term in the argument, which is a logical fallacy by any standards.

Reasons to confuse them certainly exist. The two separate senses of the word *jiha,* though distinct in themselves, are for all practical purposes almost identical at relatively short local distances in the real world, which is why flat maps are successful at depicting the lay of the land at a regional and national level. The difference only becomes obvious at global, intercontinental distances like that of the North American qibla. At such distances, the two above senses of *jiha* converge in one context alone: the Mercator projection map, which this difficulty seems based upon.

That the cardinal directions are physically relative and not absolute has been proven above by examples (A) and (B) on pages 9–14, as well as the discussion of the Mercator projection map on pages 56–66 and elsewhere in this work. We have also seen that east-west "lines of latitude" anywhere but at the equator are not straight, but rather lines curved to the left or right, and a curved line cannot be considered the direction of anything.

So in order to discover what Imam Ghazali may have meant by saying that the four directions are "absolute" and "four by scholarly consensus," let us turn to the text itself in the *Ihya',* where he writes:

As for the proof of the correctness of the diagram we have drawn [indicating the Kaaba in front of the person praying, within a permissible margin of divergence of 45 degrees on either side of its actual physical direction]—which [proof] is that the directions of the world are only four—it is the words of the Prophet (upon whom be blessings and peace) about the proper way to go to the toilet "Do not face the qibla when doing so or turn your backs to it, but face east or west," which he said in Medina, where the place of sunrise (east) is to the left of the person facing it [the Kaaba], and the place of sunset (west) is to his right.

So he forbade two directions and permitted two others, the sum total of which (majmu' dhalika) is four directions. Nor has it come into anyone's mind that the directions of the world are possible to construe as six, or seven, or ten: however many they might be, what would the rest be [except subsumed by the four, adding nothing meaningful to them]?

Rather, the directions are established in conceptions by the physical makeup of the human being, who has only four directions:

forward (quddam), *backward* (khalf), *right* (yamin), and *left* (shimal) [italics the translator's]. So the directions in relation to the human being are manifestly four, and Sacred Law is only based upon such considerations. It is thus plain that what is intended [for the person finding the qibla on his own] is the approximate direction (jiha) (*Ihya' 'ulum al-din* (e26), 2.234–35).

A careful reading of this passage shows that the directions Ghazali is talking about here have nothing at all to do with the cardinal directions of north, south, east, or west. Rather, he explicitly states that the directions everyone agrees to be four and nobody disagrees about are "forward, backward, right, and left."

The point of the passage as a whole is that the approximate direction (jiha) should be the criterion for the qibla instead of the exact direction (samt) that other Shafiʿi scholars advocate. As previously mentioned, he considers the approximate direction to be a 90-degree sweep in front of one, 45 degrees on either side of the exact line direction to the Kaaba.

The significance of the four bodily directions for his argument is that each of the four directions takes up a quarter of the circle around one, that is, a 90-degree corner-segment around a central line extending straight out from each of the four sides of the body, as shown here in figure 27.

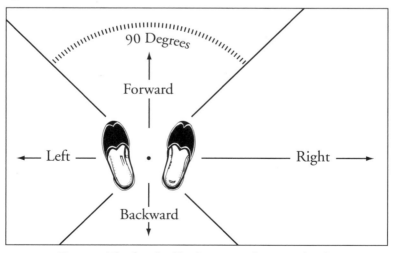

Figure 27. The four bodily directions of Imam Ghazali

When applied to *quddam* or "forward," the direction by which we face anything, this means a 90-degree angle approximately defined by two imaginary lines emanating, as he remarks in another passage, "[from the center of the brain] out the two eyes" (ibid., 233) and taking in everything in between. Whenever one orients oneself as best one can to the qibla, and the Kaaba is anywhere within this sweep, one is facing the "approximate direction" (jiha) that in Imam Ghazali's opinion suffices for the validity of prayer. Such a field obviously moves with one, and so is completely independent of the four compass directions.

That Ghazali's four bodily directions have nothing to do with the four cardinal points of the compass is also borne out by the above hadith he cites about going to the toilet. In such a case, if one is to the northwest of Mecca, for example, the four *bodily,* not cardinal, directions are obviously meant by the command not to turn one's front or rear towards it, but rather one of one's two sides towards it. The rest of the text merely underscores that the cardinal points of the compass have nothing to do with the example.

So the four bodily directions are what is meant, and if we call them "absolute" in the sense that they never go away as long as one is within one's body, they are nonetheless completely relative to which way one turns that body. When one faces another person, for example, one's left is to the other's right. Whose is more objective? The absoluteness of bodily directions is thus clearly a "relative absolute."

As for Ghazali conveying that their fourfold number is the subject of ijma', the text does not mention this anywhere. Perhaps the raiser of the difficulty read the passage long ago and mistakenly remembered the above words *majmu' dhalika* or "the sum total of which" as *mujma' 'alayhi* or "the object of scholarly consensus." This is a simple misreading, and easily corrected by a return to the text.

Regarding the contention that "it is still the *'urf* or 'common acknowledgement' of the people of the earth to view the four directions as absolute," if by "directions" we mean the bodily directions referred to by Ghazali, they are absolute only in respect to one's person, and change with one's bodily orientation. So they mean nothing in a discussion of ijtihad about the geographical position of Mecca in the real world.

And if by "directions" we mean the four cardinal directions, we have shown in chapter 4 that the constant compass bearings such as "east" (termed "rhumb lines"), anywhere but at the equator, or north-south lines of longitude, are lines curved toward the left or right, not straight. A curved line cannot be the direction of anything, which brings us to the third and last part of the difficulty.

The Northeast Is Not a True Direction

"The northeast qibla is unacceptable because it is a 'compound direction'—a line that changes its direction from northeast, to east, to southeast—rather than a true direction."

As we have clarified in chapters 1 and 4 above, this difficulty confuses direction names ("north," "south," "east," or "west") with directions. In terms of direction *names*, "compound directions" are the *rule* on this earth, while "true directions" in the sense of "a straight line of travel that does not change its direction name no matter how far one travels along it" are the rare exception, existing in the real world only at the equator, if one is travelling east or west.

We have seen above that Muslim geographers early discovered that the earth is round, and in consequence, any straight line between two points on the surface of the earth is in fact a segment of a "great circle," meaning that if such a line were extended indefinitely beyond the two points, it would ultimately go all the way around the globe and come back to itself (incidentally bisecting the earth). Every straight line towards anything on the face of the earth is part of such a "great circle."

It is worth reflecting on this fact for a moment, because if one does not understand it, one will not understand anything about the physical issues that relate to the qibla far from Mecca. People with a strong spatial imaginative faculty can work it out by picturing such a line in their minds as it proceeds around a globe. People with mathematical training can prove it by spherical trigonometry. The rest of us can establish its truth by conducting it repeatedly as a physical experiment on the surface of a world globe. It is a physical consequence of the fact that the world is round. A straight line between two points on the surface of the earth will always be found to be a segment of such a "great circle."

Knowing it enables us to see why the only examples in the real world of a "true direction" in the sense intended by the above difficulty as "a line of constant direction-name" are at the equator, which one can follow around to the east (or west) for the entire circumference of the globe, the entire "great circle" of that direction. Every other straight line of travel on the face of the globe will prove upon examination to be a "compound direction" which if followed far enough will change its direction name, for it must ultimately form part of a "great circle," upon which whatever goes north must eventually come south, and vice versa.

Lines directly north or directly south change their direction names at the poles, as in example (A) on page 10 of chapter 1 above; while travelling along a "line" to the east, for example, at other than the equator in the Northern Hemisphere, is not proceeding in a straight line (in the sense of going neither left nor right), but rather, as noted in example (B) above on page 11, actually moving along a segment of the circumference of a circle whose plane parallels that of the equator, a circle which if one wants to stay on it, in the case of going east, one must continually correct one's course by curving towards the left. In the Northern Hemisphere "going east" means nothing besides moving counterclockwise around the North Pole along such a circle, curving gradually but inevitably to the left, just as "going west" means continually correcting one's course by curving towards the right, clockwise around the Pole.

The only other conceivable example of a "true direction," in the sense intended by the above difficulty as "a straight line with a constant direction-name," is on a Mercator projection map. Here also, the direction name of a particular line of travel is absolute, meaning it retains its name (e.g. "east" or "northeast") until it reaches the edge of the map. This suffices to show us where the difficulty comes from—a flat conception of the earth—but in physical reality, it does not enter into our discussion at all, because we live on a planet, not a plane.

To summarize, the difficulty fails because being a "compound direction" in terms of *direction names* is no difficulty at all, but entirely usual for virtually all direction lines on the surface of the earth that extend for global distances.

CONCLUSIONS

We have seen that the difficulties pitting the absoluteness of the four cardinal directions against the northeast qibla are largely imaginary.

The first difficulty, the idea that Malikis must face one of the cardinal directions for prayer despite knowing that Mecca lies elsewhere, does not exist in Maliki fiqh literature. Rather, Maliki fiqh works confirm that their qibla is the same as everyone else's: the actual direction to Mecca as best one knows it.

The second, that the four directions are absolute by unanimous consensus of scholars (ijma') according to Imam Ghazali, was found upon scrutiny of the text to relate to the four *bodily* directions (forward, backward, right, and left), not the four *cardinal* directions (north, south, east, and west). Though the text does not mention scholarly consensus, it is plain that if the former are "absolute" in the sense that everyone with a body has them, they are also *relative* to the direction one turns the body, so they have no relevance to deciding which way Mecca is from North America.

The third, that the northeast qibla is a "compound direction," far from being an objection, is true of almost every direction on the face of the earth. And since according to Imam al-Qarafi the qibla is in all 360 points of the compass, most qiblas at global distances will be compound directions. So there is nothing in the difficulty to keep Malikis or anyone else from praying to the northeast from North America.

PART THREE

Muslim Unity

14

Port in a Storm

———

THE real fiqh question of this book is whether it is desirable or undesirable for all North American Muslims to pray towards the physical direction of Mecca.

In the first pages, we established by four separate proofs that the physical direction of Mecca from North America is to the northeast. The fourth of these proofs, the visible sighting by Muslim witnesses of the sun on the northeast horizon from Montreal on 16 July 2000 at the very same moment the sun was observed in Mecca straight above the Kaaba is probably the most significant physical detail in our discussion.

What does it mean? Think as one may, there is no other explanation than that Mecca lies in that direction, and that the way most mosques in North America face today is the direction of the Holy Kaaba itself. That the qibla of these mosques is correct is little cause for wonder, for the Prophet has said (Allah bless him and give him peace) in a rigorously authenticated (sahih) hadith:

> Adhere to the group (al-jama'a) and beware lest you separate, for the Devil is with one person, while he is farther from two. Whoever aspires to the midst of paradise, let him adhere to the group (*Tirmidhi* (e93), 4.465–66: 2165. S).

The present writer takes adhering to the group (al-jama'a) on the qibla in North America to mean agreement with them on at least three points: (1) that we have been commanded to face the direction of the Kaaba when we pray, (2) that the "direction" of anything on earth means the direct way to that thing, and (3) that the direct way to Mecca from North America is to the northeast.

The Fatwa of al-Azhar confirms the northeast qibla, and says, "All Muslims must cease discord and disagreement among themselves, and accept what scholars have finally agreed upon in this matter as mandatory and not permissible to contravene under any circumstance whatsoever" (*Fatwa* (e47), 5 March 1998, 3).

Here, a question poses itself that no serious exposition of the Azhar Fatwa can avoid: "What about the personal ijtihad on the qibla that some schools of fiqh say is obligatory?"

Personal Ijtihad and the Qibla

The ijtihad that books of fiqh say is obligatory for the person praying has a definite aim: to reach the strongest possible conviction that the direction one is facing is the direction of the Kaaba. As this is also the whole point of the present work, it serves as a convenient context to summarize our most important conclusions.

The text that perhaps best illustrates a number of aspects of the question is from Ibn Hamdun's *Hashiya* (Commentary) upon Muhammad Mayyara's *Sharh* (Exegesis) of *al-Murshid al-mu'in* by Ibn 'Ashir. Although a Maliki work, it is identical in many of its rulings about personal ijtihad with the Shafi'i and other schools, for the reason that all deal with our response as individuals to the fairly straightforward divine command "Wherever you all may be, turn your faces towards it" (Qur'an 2:144).

A careful reading of Ibn Hamdun's text below shows that personal ijtihad about the qibla is not viewed by Maliki scholars as an act of worship obligatory in itself, but rather obligatory because it is the only means to accomplish something else that is obligatory, namely knowing that one is fulfilling the command to face the direction of Mecca in prayer. This is evident from Ibn Hamdun's division of people into three categories: (1) those who *may not* use ijtihad because they are already certain that they are facing it; (2) those who *must* use ijtihad in order to be certain that they are facing it; and (3) those who *must follow* another's ijtihad because they are incapable by themselves of being certain they are facing it. The aim of each is identical: the strongest possible subjective certainty that they are complying with the divine command to face the direction of the qibla. In the section "The [Prayer] Condition of Facing the Qibla," Ibn Hamdun says:

People fall into three categories in relation to facing the direction of the qibla. The first is he whose obligation in facing it is complete certitude (yaqin), whether by actually seeing it, as the person does who is praying in the presence of the Kaaba; or by other than seeing it, as do those who live in Mecca and pray in their homes—because of the certitude that exists that they are facing straight towards the Kaaba, since it has long proven itself true.

There is complete scholarly agreement that ijtihad is not permissible for either of these two, because it is retreating from certitude (yaqin) to what one deems merely probable (dhann) . . . .

This ruling also holds for the mihrab of the Prophet (Allah bless him and give him peace) in Medina, for it faces the Kaaba of a certitude made absolute by Gabriel leading him in prayer, as *al-Sharh al-kabir* [Mayyara's larger commentary on the same text] reports; and so it is with every single mosque that the Messenger of Allah prayed in (Allah bless him and give him peace) (*Hashiya Ibn Hamdun* (e40), 1.149).

In these instances, personal ijtihad is not permissible according to this Maliki text because "retreating from certitude (yaqin) to what one deems merely probable (dhann)" is not valid or permissible.

The certitude of seeing the Kaaba when standing in front of it is clear. We have noted at the end of chapter 2 that the Hanafi, Hanbali, and Shafi'i schools explicitly state that the space directly above the Kaaba is legally the Kaaba, as high as it may go; and have documented that the sun has been sighted this year (1421/2000) occupying this space by a number of upright Muslim witnesses who saw it to the northeast from North America. According to these three schools, the Kaaba has been *seen* from there, and accordingly, for them, personal ijtihad has been superseded by observed fact.

Ibn Hamdun above adds to this category of visual certainty "those who live in Mecca and pray in their homes—because of the certitude that exists that they are facing straight towards the Kaaba, since it has long proven itself true." If we reflect for a moment on the houses of Mecca in olden times, it is well known that many lay in its various neighborhoods along the roads at the bottoms of its valleys (shi'ab) between hills. So for many, the legal "certitude" of the direction of the Kaaba referred to here merely meant that one knew which way one's house faced, and that if one went outside to go to the Sacred Mosque, after turning into a few streets, one would come within sight of it, and so could thereby infer the direction of the Kaaba back at one's home. For other houses, the exterior of the Sacred Mosque could doubtless be seen from a window or by stepping just outside the door; and from the direction of the Kaaba (which would still be out of view behind the mosque's exterior) one could infer the exact qibla within one's home. With continuous repetition over the centuries, such an inference would have "long proven itself true."

Maliki scholars deemed such "certitude"—which is in fact but an inference vindicated by long empirical trial and verification—sufficient to obligate Muslims to act upon it, and sufficient to make personal ijtihad about the qibla unlawful. The present author holds that the visual sighting of the sun directly above the Kaaba to the northeast from North America affords a certainty of its direction equal to or greater than that of those living inside their houses in Mecca beyond sight of the Kaaba, since someone who sees the sun and knows the Kaaba is directly beneath it knows the direction of the Kaaba. One cannot acknowledge the one certainty without acknowledging the other.[1]

As a separate but related issue, every scholar whom we asked during the course of the present work adds to the category of such physical certainty all modern scientific means of observation and calculation that have been empirically proven to disclose reality with accuracy equal to actually seeing something. This is why in previous times, as quoted above, the Moroccan Maliki scholar of Rabat, Ahmad ibn 'Abdullah al-Ghurfi, a contemporary of al-Wazzani, said:

> Because these instruments, the quadrant, the astrolabe, and others have been introduced to Islam and Muslims, and have been tested and found to provide complete certainty [of prayer times] to the person who knows how to use them when they are properly made

---

[1] As shown by our earlier quotation from Nasir al-Din al-Tusi on page 23, the sun has been observed by Muslims exactly above the Kaaba on two particular days of the solar year for more than seven and a half centuries, ample time to have "long proven itself true."

in themselves, it is obligatory for anyone without knowledge of them to follow without question (taqlid) the person who has knowledge of them, and to act upon what he says (*al-Mi'yar al-jadid* (e97), 1.223).

In our own times, as we have also conveyed earlier, the Hanafi scholar Dr. Muhammad Hisham al-Burhani of Damascus has written:

It is not permissible for someone who can see the Kaaba or who is praying in a direction established by authoritative transmission [that the Prophet (Allah bless him and give him peace) prayed towards it] to make his own ijtihad. Nor may someone make ijtihad whose qibla has been determined by exact modern scientific means.

Someone who is not any of the above may make his own ijtihad, and whatever he deems most probably correct suffices to be "facing the direction."

Of an absolute certainty—in this age and the things actually daily seen in it, such as air traffic, the satellites that have filled space, and the fact that every single point on the earth and even the planets, stars, and asteroids travelling through space can be targeted and made a determinate destination with limitless precision—is that the location of the Kaaba on earth, thus transformed by modern science into a small village, has become known and determinable by precise coordinates with infinitesimal accuracy.

Man has therefore become capable of knowing without the slightest doubt or hesitation his location in relation to the Noble Kaaba. It is therefore incumbent upon him to face the Kaaba itself, and it is insufficient for him to merely pray towards its approximate direction (jiha), as Allah is my witness, unless he is remote from actual civilization and its data, or this is inaccessible to him because of some excuse.

For it is obligatory to act upon the primary basis [of the divine injunction "Wherever you may be, turn your faces towards it" (Qur'an 2:144)] in order to apply the fundamental Shari'a rules and principles that state: "One may not have recourse to a substitute unless one is unable to use the first choice," just as dry ablution (tayammum) may not be used unless one is lacking water, whether actually [as when none exists] or virtually [as when it exists, but it may not be used for fear of thirst or illness]. Or just as ijtihad may not be resorted to on an issue already decided by an unequivocal scriptural text (nass). Or just as uncertainty must be disregarded when certainty exists (*Fatwa* (e19), 29 June 2000, 3).

We therefore conclude that the Azhar Fatwa's contention that accepting the northeast qibla as "mandatory and not permissible to contravene under any circumstance whatsoever" is, upon scrutiny, consistent with all four Sunni schools of jurisprudence, as is shown by three points which summarize the legal evidence just given:

(1) Geographical ijtihad about the compass direction of Mecca from North America is not permissible for a Muslim of the Hanafi, Shafi'i, or Hanbali school because of the legal certitude of *seeing* the Kaaba from North America by seeing the sun in the space above it to the northeast.

(2) Geographical ijtihad about the compass direction of Mecca is not permissible for a Muslim of the Maliki school because the sighting of the sun above the Kaaba from Montreal this year produces a legal certitude of the latter's direction equal to or greater than the certitude of those praying inside their houses in Mecca, which according to Malikis makes personal ijtihad impermissible.

(3) The Maliki scholar al-Ghurfi's statement that it is obligatory for the non-specialist to accept the results of someone knowledgeable in the use of the quadrant and the astrolabe, and Sheikh Hisham al-Burhani's statement "Nor may someone make ijtihad whose qibla has been determined by exact modern scientific means" entail that the certitude of determining the northeast qibla through modern scientific means, calculational or instrumental, also obviates personal geographical ijtihad, making it invalid and impermissible.

We say "*geographical* ijtihad" in each of these points because as the reader will remember there are actually two kinds of ijtihad involved in facing the qibla to pray: geographical and orientational.

"Geographical ijtihad" consists in establishing where one's region lies on the earth's surface in relation to Mecca, and what is the unique direction that Allah has created between the two places. This, for

North America, is the northeast qibla that the present work has established beyond a reasonable doubt with visible proofs, and which the Azhar Fatwa says is not permissible to contravene.

"Orientational ijtihad," on the other hand, consists in finding out how to point oneself from a given location in one's region towards this correct direction once one knows it. This remains obligatory for every Muslim who needs it to face the qibla.

The distinction between the two can be clarified by an example. Imagine being taken on an air flight for ten hours in an unknown direction to an unknown location on an unknown continent, and upon landing there, being shown the four directions with a compass, or from natural signs, and then told to ascertain the direction to Mecca. Without the knowledge of one's *location,* which is the basis of geographical ijtihad, the direction-finding means of orientational ijtihad are little better than useless. The reason for this is the intrinsic difference between these two types of ijtihad.

We saw in chapter 8 that very few of the traditional works of fiqh authored in the Muslim heartlands mention geographical ijtihad at all, probably because the geographic direction of Mecca from their lands was a commonplace of general knowledge that was taken for granted. In consequence, their lists of qibla evidences and even the word *ijtihad* itself in the context refer almost invariably to orientational ijtihad, because any other kind was unneeded. None of the evidences typically mentioned in their books—whether the dawn, sunset, sun, moon, North Star, other stars, landmarks, trade routes, or the east, west, north, or south winds—discloses the location of Mecca to anyone who does not already know which direction it should lie from the region he is in, and who is merely trying to use them to orient himself to it.

The ijtihad obligatory for such a person is simply to know how the sun or other natural phenomena are normally positioned in relation to someone facing the qibla in his region, so that by positioning them that way he can correctly reorient himself to that direction whenever needed. Such a person may not simply follow the results of another mujtahid's orientational ijtihad, because this would not produce the personal subjective certitude of facing Mecca which is the aim of such ijtihad. To produce this certitude, one's *own* orientational ijtihad is necessary with one's own knowledge of natural phenomena or other signs. This is the "ijtihad" obligatory for someone "who knows the physical evidences of the qibla," which is discussed in the next part of our Maliki fiqh text by Ibn Hamdun, who continues:

> The second category is he who *must* make ijtihad, namely someone not residing at the Meccan or Medinan sanctuaries, and who knows the physical evidences of the qibla or is capable of knowing them: it is obligatory for him to make ijtihad that will direct him to its approximate direction (jiha), as Ibn Rushd explains in the chapter on judicial decisions in *al-Muqaddimat,* and Khalil indicates by saying, "Otherwise (i.e. when not in Mecca), the sounder position is [that one must face] the approximate direction (jiha) determined through ijtihad" even if the Kaaba were razed—which is to say, the prayer is nullified if one contravenes this direction, even if one [inadvertently] prays facing the correct direction. One may not simply follow another mujtahid, or follow a mihrab, unless it is that of a city, "even," Ibn Qassar adds, "if one is blind but able to ask about the [physical] evidences [and thereby become capable of one's own ijtihad]."
>
> In inhabited cities in which prayers repeatedly take place, and the Imam of the Muslims is known to have determined its mihrab, or the people of the city have joined together to determine it, both the learned and unlearned may simply follow it (taqlid) [though ijtihad is still permissible for those capable] . . . .
>
> Ibn Shas and Ibn al-Hajib say, "The mujtahid makes his ijtihad anew for each prayer, since his ijtihad may change," though al-Tiraz says, "When two [successive] prayer times differ as to the qibla evidences available, he must make ijtihad again, though if not, then he need not," which is sounder than the view of Ibn Shas and Ibn al-Hajib . . . . (*Hashiya Ibn Hamdun* (e40), 1.149–50).

Whether such orientational ijtihad is and remains obligatory in one's particular circumstances is quite a separate issue from the obligatory character of accepting the *geographical* ijtihad of North America's northeast qibla. In light of the proofs presented in the present work, the latter may without exaggeration be termed not "geographical ijtihad," but simply "fact." Whoever does not know this fact does not know the most important of the evidences of the qibla in North

America. The scope of personal ijtihad is merely in trying to face it. This is no revolutionary new suggestion, but merely what Muslims actually do the world over: in North America, in the western Sahara, and in all the countries of the world. In every land where there are Muslims, the direction of Mecca is known, and people determine *whether they are facing it* through personal orientational ijtihad.

The final category of people mentioned by Ibn Hamdun consists of those incapable of ijtihad, who are permitted to simply follow another person presumed to be correct:

> The third category is the person whose obligation is to simply to follow (taqlid) another; namely, someone unable to make ijtihad because of not knowing the [geographical direction of the] qibla and being unable to learn the means of ijtihad. Such a person must simply follow someone who is legally responsible [to perform the obligation, i.e. not insane, juvenile, etc.], knowledgeable [in the means of determining the qibla], and morally upright. Or he may simply follow the direction of a mihrab, even if not in a city . . . . (*Hashiya Ibn Hamdun* (e40) 1.150).

In all three categories above, ijtihad exists for one purpose alone: to produce the strongest possible subjective certainty that one is facing the direction of the Kaaba.

For the first category of people mentioned by Ibn Hamdun who are at Mecca or Medina, ijtihad is not permissible because *objective* certainty already exists. Our physical evidence and a number of the fatwas cited by the present work add to this category the objective geographical certainty of Mecca's northeast direction from North America.

For the second category of people, ijtihad is obligatory because they are not objectively certain of facing the direction of the Kaaba, so are obliged to attain the strongest *subjective* certainty of this possible, through orientational ijtihad, provided that they know the geographical and other evidences necessary for it. In North America these evidences include first knowing which way Mecca lies; namely to the northeast, and second how to orient oneself to this direction according to the position of natural or other phenomena—whether observable directly, or whether through instrumental means that disclose such phenomena, as the compass does with the earth's natural magnetic field—which permit one to utilize one's knowledge of the geographical direction of Mecca by turning towards it. Without the latter knowledge, the former is not valid at all, for as mentioned earlier, "a mujtahid without the facts cannot be a mujtahid about the facts."

Finally, people of the third category, who are neither able to know the correct direction with objective certainty, nor to attain subjective certainty through personal ijtihad, must rely on another's ijtihad.

So when properly understood, there is no conflict between accepting the Azhar Fatwa and the obligation of personal ijtihad. The ijtihad that Maliki, Shafi'i, and other scholars hold to be personally obligatory in lands where the geographical direction of Mecca is common knowledge is in fact orientational ijtihad. And the ijtihad that is now finished for North America, obligatory to accept, and no longer a matter of ijtihad, is the geographical fact of Mecca's northeastern direction, since "retreating from certitude (yaqin) to what one deems merely probable (dhann)" is not valid or permissible, according to the Maliki school and others. Empirical reality may not be ignored.

CONCLUSIONS

The "port in a storm" of the present work's title is a place that is familiar to everyone: the real world. In it alone do the rulings of Islam apply, and on the basis of it alone is it possible to unite Muslims, on this question or others. If we believe that it can be whisked away by fiqh, authority, or primitivism, it will prove very difficult to avoid a morass of subjectivism and real and sharp differences, as Allah says of those who destroyed their religion through disunity, "each faction exulting in what was theirs" (Qur'an 23:53).

A non-Muslim watched two Muslims at prayer not long ago on a college campus in the United States, and when they finished, walked up and asked, "Why are you praying in two different directions?" And a Muslim lady who recently moved to the United States called the author to ask about the two qiblas in her home. She was praying towards one, and her husband towards another. This unsettled her, and she was unconvinced by the assurance that it was not an issue but rather the outcome of normal scholarly differences.

Most people realize that Islamic knowledge is not supposed to work like this.

Islam is spreading to the far corners of the earth, and if the only way we can establish the qibla of the new mosque in Tierra del Fuego, for example, is by the visit of an impressive scholar from Algeria and hearing his opinion, the qibla will only last until an even more impressive scholar from Iraq arrives and gives a contrary opinion. People in our times are unable to accept such a process. The real world and not subjective personal preference must be our home port, and we can only put into it with religion and intelligence.

Everything lawful that facilitates the worship of Allah is a blessing from Him that necessitates gratitude for it. And gratitude for Allah's giving us not only a heart and emotions but also a mind and objective knowledge of our world means using these things to best express our love and submission to Him. This must certainly be part of the divine wisdom in Muslims daily turning towards Mecca with body, heart, and soul.

Enlightenment, on this issue or others, can only come from Allah. May Allah make our qibla one, and may He give everyone who reads these words the sincerity to turn to it.

APPENDICES

Cited Arabic Texts

▬

PREFACE

p. xvi. Shafi'i: "Learning, among the virtuous . . . ."

العلم بين أهل الفضل والعقل رحمٌ متصل (الإمام الشافعي؛ نقله عنه الإمام الغزالي: إحياء علوم الدين ١: ٤١).

I. A QUESTION OF FACT

p. 5. Allah Most High: "We certainly see your . . . ."

﴿قد نرىٰ تقلب وجهك في السماء فلنولينك قبلة ترضٰها فول وجهك شطر المسجد الحرام وحيث ما كنتم فولوا وجوهكم شطره﴾ (البقرة: ١٤٤).

p. 6. Ibn Hajar al-Haytami: one must be "straight in line . . . ."

والمعتبر مسامتتها عرفاً لا حقيقة (الإمام ابن حجر الهيتمي: تحفة المحتاج ١: ٤٨٤).

p. 16. Allah Most High: "Turn your face . . . ."

﴿فول وجهك شطر المسجد الحرام وحيث ما كنتم فولوا وجوهكم شطره﴾ (البقرة: ١٤٤).

p. 23. Nasir al-Din al-Tusi: "There are many ways . . . ."

ولمعرفة سمت القبلة طرق كثيرة لا يليق إيرادها ها هنا، فلنقتصر علىٰ وجهٍ سهل وهو أن الشمس تكون مارة بسمت رأس مكة عند كونها في الدرجة الثامنة من الجوزاء، والثالثة والعشرين من السرطان وقت انتصاف النهار هناك. والفضل بين نصف نهارها ونصف نهار سائر البلدان يكون بقدر

179

التفاوت بين الطولين . فليؤخذ التفاوت ، ويؤخذ لكل خمسة عشر جزءاً ساعة ، ولكل جزء أربع دقائق ، فيكون ما اجتمع ساعات البعد عن نصف النهار . وليرصد في ذلك اليوم ذلك الوقت قبل نصف النهار إن كانت مكة شرقيةً ، أو بعده إن كانت غربية ؛ فسمت الظل ساعتئذٍ يكون سمت القبلة ، (نصير الدين الطوسي : التذكرة في علم الهيئة ٢٧٢) .

p. 24. Habib ‘Alawi: “On May 28 . . . .”

ففي يوم ٢٨ مايو و ١٦ يوليو (في أي سنة) نجد ميل الشمس من ناحية الشمال وخط العرض بمكة المكرمة متساويين ، وتكون الشمس رأسية بوقت الزوال علىٰ الأفق بمكة المكرمة . وعلىٰ أي التاريخين المذكورين إذا أقمنا عصا عمودية علىٰ سطح الأرض في وقت الزوال لمكة المكرمة ثم يمد خط علىٰ ظل العصا فالجهة المخالفة للظل تبين اتجاه الكعبة المشرفة . (الفلكي الحبيب علوي بن الشيخ أبو بكر بن سالم : رسالة تعيين اتجاهات الكعبة ١-٢) .

p. 25. Ibn ‘Abidin: “The criterion for the qibla . . . .”

والمعتبر في القبلة العَرَصة لا البناء فهي من الأرض السابعة إلىٰ العرش (الإمام ابن عابدين : رد المحتار ١ : ٢٩٠) .

p. 25. Mansur al-Buhuti: “The prayer is valid . . . .”

(صحت) الصلاة (إلىٰ هوائها) وكذا لو حفر حفيرة في الأرض ، بحيث ينزل عن مسامتة بنيانها صحت إلىٰ هوائها : لما تقدم أن المقصود البقعة لا الجدار (الإمام منصور البهوتي : كشاف القناع ١ : ٣٠١) .

p. 25. Ibn Hajar al-Haytami: “The meaning of the ‘Kaaba itself’ . . . .”

ليس المراد بالعين الجدار بل أمر اصطلاحي أي وهو سمت البيت وهواؤه إلىٰ السماء والأرض السابعة (الإمام ابن حجر الهيتمي : تحفة المحتاج ١ : ٤٨٤) .

p. 25. Mahmoud Jastaniah: [This letter was in English.]

CITED ARABIC TEXTS

2. THE AZHAR FATWA

p. 32. al-Azhar: [The complete fatwa appears in Appendix B on p. 215.]

3. THE QIBLAS OF THE SAHABA

p. 43. Hadith of Ibn 'Umar: "While people were praying . . . . "

[حدثنا شيبان بن فروخ حدثنا عبد العزيز بن مسلم حدثنا عبد الله بن دينار عن
ابن عمر ح وحدثنا قتيبة بن سعيد (واللفظ له) عن مالك بن أنس عن عبد الله
بن دينار] عن ابن عمر قال: بينما الناس في صلاة الصبح بقباء إذ جاءهم آتٍ
فقال: إن رسول الله صلى الله عليه وسلم قد أنزل عليه الليلة وقد أمر أن
يستقبل الكعبة فاستقبلوها. وكانت وجوههم إلى الشام فاستداروا إلى الكعبة
(مسلم: صحيح مسلم ١: ٣٧٥ (٥٢٦)).

p. 43. Ghazali: "they turned around . . . . "

[وأما فعل الصحابة رضي الله عنهم فما رُوِيَ أن أهل مسجد قباء كانوا في
صلاة الصبح بالمدينة مستقبلين لبيت المقدس مستدبرين الكعبة لأن المدينة
بينهما فقيل لهم الآن قد حُوِّلت القبلة إلى الكعبة] فاستداروا في أثناء الصلاة
من غير طلب دلالة ولم ينكر عليهم وسُمّي مسجدهم ذا القبلتين، ومقابلة
العين من المدينة إلى مكة لا تعرف إلا بأدلة هندسية يطول فيها النظر فكيف
أدركوا ذلك على البديهة في أثناء الصلاة وفي ظلمة الليل، ويدل أيضاً من
فعلهم أنهم بنوا المساجد حوالي مكة وفي سائر بلاد الإسلام ولم يُحضروا قط
مهندساً عند تسوية المحاريب، ومقابلة العين لا تدرك إلا بدقيق النظر
الهندسي (الإمام الغزالي: إحياء علوم الدين ٢: ٢٣٤).

p. 44. Hadith: "Everything between where the sun rises . . . . "

[حدثنا الحسن بن أبي بكر المروزي حدثنا المعلّى بن منصور حدثنا عبد الله
ابن جعفر المخرمي عن عثمانَ بن محمد الأخنسي عن سعيد المقبري عن أبي
هريرة] عن النبي صلى الله عليه وسلم قال: «ما بين المشرق والمغرب قبلة».
[قال أبو عيسى: هذا حديث حسن صحيح] (الترمذي: الجامع الصحيح
٢: ١٧٣ (٣٤٤)).

p. 44. Allah Most High: "Be as godfearing...."

﴿فاتقوا الله ما استطعتم﴾ (التغابن: ١٦) .

p. 48. Allah Most High: "Their way is consultation...."

﴿وأمرهم شوريٰ بينهم﴾ (الشوريٰ: ٣٨) .

p. 49. Ibn 'Abd al-Barr: "The ulema are in unanimous...."

وأجمع العلماء عليٰ أن القبلة التي أمر الله النبي صلى الله عليه وسلم وعباده بالتوجه نحوها في صلاتهم هي الكعبة البيت الحرام بمكة . قال الله عز وجل : ﴿فول وجهك شطر المسجد الحرام وحيث ما كنتم فولوا وجوهكم شطره﴾ (البقرة: ١٥٠) . وأجمعوا عليٰ أنه فرض واجب عليٰ من عاينها وشاهدها استقبالها بعينها وأنه إن ترك استقبالها وهو معاين لها فلا صلاة له . أجمعوا أن عليٰ من غاب عنها بعد أو قرب أن يتوجه في صلاته نحوها بما قدر عليه من الاستدلال عليٰ جهتها من النجوم والجبال والرياح وغيرها (الإمام ابن عبد البر: الاستذكار ٢١٥:٧) .

p. 49. Sahnun from Ibn Qasim: "Malik said, regarding someone...."

[قال مالك] فيمن استدبر القبلة أو شرق أو غرب فصليٰ وهو يظن أن تلك القبلة ثم تبين له أنه عليٰ غير القبلة فقال يقطع ما هو فيه ويبتدىء الصلاة. قال فإن فرغ من صلاته ثم علم في الوقت فعليه الإعادة (قال) وإن مضيٰ الوقت فلا إعادة عليه (قال) وقال مالك لو أن رجلاً صليٰ فانحرف عن القبلة ولم يشرق ولم يغرب فعلم بذلك قبل أن يقضي صلاته قال ينحرف إليٰ القبلة ويبني عليٰ صلاته ولا يقطع صلاته (الإمام سحنون عن الإمام ابن قاسم: المدونة الكبريٰ ٩٢:١) .

p. 50. Salih al-Abi: "If the mistakenness...."

وإن تبين خطأ (في القبلة التي هو مستقبلها) بصلاة قطع صلاة أعمى غير منحرف ومنحرف يسيراً فيستقبلانها (أي القبلة ويبنيان عليٰ ما صلياه إليٰ غيرها. وإن لم يستقبلا وأتماها إليٰ الجهة التي تبين خطؤها بطلت صلاة الأعمى المنحرف كثيراً، وصحّت صلاة المنحرف يسيراً، بصيراً كان أو أعميٰ مع الحرمة عليهما) (الإمام خليل بن إسحاق الجندي؛ وبين الأقواس شرح الشيخ صالح بن عبد

182

السميع الآبي : جواهر الإكليل شرح مختصر العلامة الشيخ خليل في مذهب الإمام مالك إمام دار التنزيل (٤٥ : ١) .

p. 50. 'Abd al-Rahman Ba-'Alawi: "The context of the approximate . . . ."

محل الاكتفاء بالجهة على القول به عند عدم العلم بأدلة العين إذ القادر على العين إن فرض حصوله بالاجتهاد لا يجزيه استقبال الجهة قطعاً وما حمل القائلين بالجهة على ذلك إلا كونهم رأوا أن استقبال العين بالاجتهاد متعذر فالخلاف حينئذ لفظي إن شاء الله تعالى لمن تأمل دلائلهم (الإمام عبد الرحمٰن باعلوي: بغية المسترشدين ٣٩-٤٠) .

p. 51. Allah Most High: "Be as godfearing . . . ."

﴿فاتقوا الله ما استطعتم﴾ (التغابن : ١٦) .

<h2>4. MECCA AND THE MERCATOR PROJECTION</h2>

[No Arabic citations.]

<h2>5. THE SHORTEST DISTANCE</h2>

p. 70. 'Abd al-Fattah al-Bizm: "The meaning of the 'direction' . . . ."

[قرر السادة الحنفية في كتبهم أن] المراد بجهة الكعبة الجانب الذي إذا توجه إليه الإنسان يكون مسامتاً للكعبة أو هوائها تحقيقاً أو تقريباً. ومعنى التحقيق: أنه لو فرض خط من تلقاء وجهه على زاوية قائمة إلى الأفق يكون ماراً على الكعبة أو هوائها. ومعنى التقريب: أن يكون منحرفاً عنها أو عن هوائها بما لا تزول به المقابلة بالكلية، بأن يبقى شيءٌ من سطح الوجه مسامتاً لها أو لهوائها (من فتوى الدكتور عبد الفتاح البزم مفتي دمشق بتاريخ ٢١ جمادى الأولى ١٤٢١/ ٢١ آب ٢٠٠٠؛ دمشق، نقلاً عن ابن عابدين [١ : ٢٨٧] عن صاحب معراج الدراية) .

p. 71. Hassan al-Hindi: "It has not been explicitly mentioned . . . ."

لم يذكر في كتب الفقه تصريح بأن الجهة هي أقصر طريق أو لا ، فهذه مسألة لم يذكرها الفقهاء بإثبات أو نفي ، وذلك لسببين :

الأول منهما: أن كل المناطق التي وضعوا لها قواعد القبلة لم يتصور فيها افتراق إلى جهتين إحداهما أطول والثانية أقصر بل كل ما ذكروه من الأمثلة كانت الجهة فيها هي الأقصر دائماً فالفقهاء كانوا في جزء صغير من العالم وهو المحيط بمكة.

والسبب الثاني: أن هذه المسألة لا تحتاج إلى نص فهي بدهية ولو كان الأمر على خلاف ذلك لوجب أن ينص الفقهاء عليه لأنه يخالف المتبادر للذهن.

وهذا التعريف بدهي يفهم من ظاهر كلام العرب فإن السائل عندما يسأل عن جهة بلد يريد أقصر مسافة موصلة إليها ولو لم يكن الأمر على هذا لصح من كان بحذاء الكعبة أن يوليها ظهره ويقول هذه الكعبة استناداً إلى أن الأرض سطح ممتد يصل إلى الكعبة من الطرف الثاني ولما كان لنا أن ننكر عليه (من فتوى الشيخ حسان الهندي: ص٦-٧؛ ١٨ ربيع الثاني ١٤٢١/ ٢٠ تموز ٢٠٠٠؛ دمشق).

p. 71. Muhammad al-Tawil: "The meaning of the 'approximate . . . ."

[والجواب أن] معنى الجهة عند القائلين باستقبالها هي الناحية التي توجد فيها الكعبة المشرفة بالنسبة للمصلي، بحيث يواجه بوجهه تلك الجهة والناحية وهو في صلاته، وقد تكون المشرق أو المغرب أو غيرهما من الجهات الأصلية أو الفرعية: الجنوب الشرقي أو الشمال الشرقي مثلاً، كما يدل على ذلك حديث (ما بين المشرق والمغرب قبلة). رواه الترمذي وصححه.

كما أن المعتبر في اعتبارها هو أقرب طريق بين الكعبة ووجه المصلي، لأنها جهته التي تواجهه، وإذا كانت نصوص الفقهاء ليس فيها ما يدل صراحة على اعتبار أقرب طريق أو أبعده فإن في كلامهم ما يستنتج منه ذلك بوضوح، وهو:

١ ـ إجماعهم على أن من استدبر القبلة في صلاته بطلت عليه، فإن هذا يدل على أن المراد أقرب جهة، لأن من استدبر القبلة في الجهة القريبة يكون مستقبلاً لها في الجهة البعيدة، نتيجة كروية الأرض، وبهذا نستطيع القول إن المعتبر هو أقصر طريق، لأنه لو كان المقصود أي طريق لما أجمعوا

علىٰ بطلان صلاة من استدبرها في الجهة القريبة .

٢ ـ حديث تحويل القبلة، فإنه لو كان المقصود استقبال الكعبة في الجهة القريبة أو البعيدة لما أمرهم الله تعالىٰ بتحويل القبلة، لأنهم حين صلاتهم لبيت المقدس كانوا مستدبرين لها من أقرب طريق ومستقبلين لها من أبعد طريق، لأن من استقبل بيت المقدس استدبر الكعبة، والعكس كما أشار لذلك ابن حجر في الفتح ١: ٥٠٧ .

وبالتالي فمستقبل بيت المقدس في الجهة القريبة مستقبل للكعبة في الطريق البعيدة ضرورة كروية الأرض . فالأمر بتحويل القبلة دليل علىٰ أن المعتبر أقرب طريق لا أبعده، وإلا ظهر أن دلالة لفظ الجهة علىٰ هذا المراد دلالة لغوية، لأن لفظ الجهة مشتق من المواجهة . يقال : واجهت فلاناً جعلت وجهي تلقاء وجهه، وهذا إنما يتحقق في مواجهته من الجهة القريبة فيما يبدو، وإلا كان مواجهاً لغيره إذا واجهه من الجهة البعيدة . (من فتوىٰ الدكتور محمد التاويل : ص١-٢؛ ٣ ذو الحجة ١٤٢٠/ ١٠ آذار ٢٠٠٠؛ فاس) .

p. 73. Fatwa Council of Tarim: "In respect to the question . . . ."

أما بالنسبة لقول السائل هل العبرة في تحديد جهة القبلة بأقصر طريق أم لا؟ فالجواب : أنّ أمر القبلة أمرٌ حسيٌ كما في تحفة المحتاج لابن حجر (١: ٤٩٦) وهو أي الحس المشاهدة كما في نهاية المحتاج للعلامة محمد الرملي (١: ٤٣٩) وعليه فيكون العبرة في تحديد جهة القبلة بأقصر طريق إلىٰ الكعبة إذ هو المسمىٰ جهة عُرفاً بخلاف أبعد طريق وهذا ما يُفهم من كلام العلامة أحمد بك الحسيني في كتابه دليل المسافر (ص٦٨) [. . . .] وقد صرّح مفتي تريم شيخنا الفقيه العلامة الشيخ فضل بن عبد الرحمٰن بأفضل رحمه الله تعالىٰ باعتماد أقصر طريق وأقربها في تحديد جهة القبلة حين سئل من بعض طلابه عن هذه المسألة بخصوصها فأجاب بذلك وأحال علىٰ كلام العلامة أحمد بك الحسيني في كتابه دليل المسافر (من فتوىٰ مجلس الإفتاء بتريم : ص١-٢؛ ١٣ جمادىٰ الآخرة ١٤٢١/ ١٢ أيلول ٢٠٠٠؛ تريم وادي حضرموت اليمن) .

p. 75. Allah Most High: "We certainly see your . . . ."

﴿قد نرىٰ تقلب وجهك في السماء فلنولينك قبلة ترضاها فول وجهك شطر المسجد الحرام وحيث ما كنتم فولوا وجوهكم شطره﴾ (البقرة: ١٤٤).

6. A TUNNEL THROUGH THE EARTH

[No Arabic citations]

7. CONSIDERING THE EARTH LEGALLY FLAT

p. 81. Allah Most High: "Wherever you all may be . . . ."

﴿وحيث ما كنتم فولوا وجوهكم شطره﴾ (البقرة: ١٤٤).

p. 81. Ghazali: "If a word . . . ."

إذا دار اللفظ بين الحقيقة والمجاز فاللفظ للحقيقة إلىٰ أن يدل الدليل علىٰ أنه أراد المجاز (الإمام الغزالي: المستصفىٰ من علم الأصول ١: ٣٥٩).

p. 81. Taj al-Subki: "It (M: i.e. the figurative) . . . ."

(وهو) أي المجاز (والنقل خلاف الأصل) فإذا احتمل اللفظ معناه الحقيقي والمجازي أو المنقول عنه وإليه فالأصل أي الراجح حمله علىٰ الحقيقي لعدم الحاجة فيه إلىٰ قرينة أو علىٰ المنقول عنه استصحاباً للموضوع له أولاً (التاج السبكي (بين الأقواس) وجلال الدين المحلي: جمع الجوامع ١: ٣١٢).

p. 82. Fakhr al-Razi: "The transferred sense (naql) . . . ."

النقل خلاف الأصل ويدل عليه أمور: أحدها: أن النقل لا يتم إلا بثبوت الوضع اللغوي، ثم نسخه، ثم ثبوت الوضع الآخر. وأما الوضع اللغوي فإنه يتم بوضع واحد. وما يتوقف علىٰ ثلاثة أشياء، مرجوح بالنسبة إلىٰ ما لا يتوقف إلا علىٰ شيء واحد (الفخر الرازي: المحصول في علم أصول الفقه ١: ٣١٤).

p. 84. Fakhr al-Razi: "There are people . . . ."

ومن الناس من استدل بهذا علىٰ أن الأرض ليست بكرة وهو ضعيف، لأن

الكرة إذا كانت في غاية العظمة يكون كل قطعة منها كالسطح (الفخر الرازي : مفاتيح الغيب ٣١: ١٥٨–١٥٩) .

p. 85. Fatwa Council of Tarim: "Because of what has been . . . ."

[. . .] علىٰ ما تقدم من أن أمر القبلة أمر حسي مشاهد فلا بد لمن أراد معرفتها من بناء الأمر علىٰ أن الأرض كروية كما وقع عليه إجماع علماء الهندسة والفلك بل والمفسرين كما قاله العلامة محمد الأمين الشنقيطي في تفسيره أضواء البيان (٩:٢٠٢) إذ هذا هو واقع الأرض . أما الخرائط المسطحة فلا تعدو كونها رسماً لمعالم الأرض لا غير ، فليست هي صورة لما عليه الأرض حقيقة (من فتوىٰ مجلس الإفتاء بتريم: ص٢؛ ١٣ جمادىٰ الآخرة ١٤٢١/ ١٢ أيلول ٢٠٠٠؛ تريم وادي حضرموت اليمن) .

p. 85. Ibn Hazm: "Not a single one of the Imams . . . ."

[قال أبو محمد: وهذا حين نأخذ إن شاء الله تعالىٰ في ذكر بعض ما اعترضوا به ، وذلك أنهم قالوا: إنّ البراهين قد صحّت بأن الأرض كروية والسماء كذلك ، والعامة تقول غير ذلك ، وجوابنا وبالله تعالىٰ التوفيق] أن أحداً من أئمة المسلمين المستحقين لاسم الإمامة بالعلم رضي الله عنهم لم ينكروا تكوير الأرض ، ولا يحفظ لأحدٍ منهم في دفعه كلمة ، بل البراهين من القرآن والسنة قد جاءت بتكويرها . قال الله عزّ وجلّ : ﴿يكور الليل علىٰ النهار ويكور النهار علىٰ الليل﴾ . وهذا أوضح بيان في تكوير بعضها علىٰ بعض ، مأخوذ من كور العمامة ، وهو إدارتها ، وهذا نص علىٰ تكوير الأرض (ابن حزم: الفصل في الملل والأهواء والنحل ٢:٢٤١) .

p. 85. Hassan al-Hindi: "To stipulate [in fiqh] that . . . ."

[وكذلك] اشتراط اعتبار كروية الأرض أمر بديهي وذلك لأن الفقهاء يبحثون في الواقع وليس في الأمور المخالفة للواقع فكيف نريد من عقولنا أن تفرض القبلة علىٰ أرض مسطحة لأن الفقهاء لم يشترطوا كروية الأرض في تعيين القبلة ، فهذا أيضاً من الأمور البديهية التي لا تحتاج إلىٰ النص عليها ولكن لو كان الأمر علىٰ ذلك لوجب أن ينصوا عليه (من فتوىٰ الشيخ حسان الهندي: ص٤؛ ١٨ ربيع الثاني ١٤٢١/ ٢٠ تموز ٢٠٠٠؛ دمشق) .

p. 86. Allah Most High: "Allah does not charge any...."

﴿لا يكلف الله نفساً إلا وسعها﴾ (البقرة: ٢٨٦).

p. 87. Taj al-Subki: "a judgement about something...."

الحكم علىٰ الشيء فرع تصوره (التاج السبكي: الإبهاج في شرح المنهاج ١: ١٧٢).

p. 87. Taj al-Subki: "Anything possible which something...."

[الفعل] (المقدور) [للمكلف] (الذي لا يتم) [أي يوجد] (الواجب المطلق إلا به واجب) [بوجوب الواجب] سبباً كان أو شرطاً (التاج السبكي (بين الأقواس) وجلال الدين المحلّي: جمع الجوامع ١: ١٩٢–١٩٣).

p. 87. Ibn 'Abidin: "The matter of the qibla is only...."

وأمر القبلة إنما يتحقق بقواعد الهندسة والحساب بأن يعرف بعد مكة عن خط الاستواء وعن طرف المغرب ثم بعد البلد المفروض كذلك ثم يقاس بتلك القواعد ليتحقق سمت القبلة (ابن عابدين: حاشية رد المحتار ١: ٢٨٩).

p. 88. Taqi al-Din al-Subki: "The Imam of the Two...."

قال إمام الحرمين في ذكر أدلة القبلة وقد ألف ذوو البصائر فيه كتباً فلتطلب أدلة القبلة من كتبها. قلت فهذا أمام الحرمين ومحله من علوم الشريعة قد علم يحيل في أدلة القبلة علىٰ كتب أهلها أفلا يستحيي من ينكر الرجوع إليها بجهله وعدم اشتغاله وظنه أنه من أهل الفقه وأن الفقه يخالفها وما يستحيي عامي من الإنكار علىٰ العالمين بعلوم الشريعة وغيرها ومن ظنه أنه علىٰ الصواب دونهم وأما يستحي الفريقان من الكلام فيما لم يحيطوا بعلمه (الإمام تقي الدين السبكي: فتاوىٰ السبكي ١: ١٥٠).

p. 88. Muhammad Hisham al-Burhani: "Total certainty...."

لقد أصبح من بدهيات العلم اليوم القطع بكروية الأرض، ويجب أن ينظر في موضوع التوجه إلىٰ الكعبة علىٰ هذا الأساس اليقيني، فمن شذ عن ذلك وخرج عن هذا الأصل فوجّه المحاريب في الأرض علىٰ أساس أنها مسطحة

كما تبدو في الخرائط المرسومة فقد أخطأ خطأً جسيماً جانب فيه الحق ولم ينتفع بمنجزات العلم والحضارة (من فتوىٰ الدكتور محمد هشام البرهاني: ص١؛ ٢٦ ربيع الأول ١٤٢١/ ٢٩ حزيران ٢٠٠٠؛ دمشق).

p. 89. Muhammad Saʿid al-Buti: "Without a doubt ...."

ما لا شك فيه أن الفقهاء يحيلون تفسير التوجه إلىٰ القبلة إلىٰ قواعد الهندسة والفلك وحسابهما كأي حكم شرعي آخر يتعلق بمناط علمي كالطب مثلاً ... وهذا أمر معروف وسليم.

وعلىٰ هذا فإن البحث عن جهة القبلة يتم علىٰ أساس أن الأرض كروية، لأن هذا ما أثبته الدليل العلمي بل الدليل القرآني أيضاً، وذلك في مثل قوله تعالىٰ: ﴿والأرض بعد ذلك دحاها﴾ وفي قوله: ﴿والأرض مددناها وألقينا فيها رواسي﴾ [ثم قال في تعليق له:] ليس المراد من الامتداد في الآية الامتداد الجزئي، إذ ما من شيء ذي سطح إلا ويوصف بالامتداد الجزئي، والكلام عندئذ غير ذي جدوىٰ، وإنما المراد لفت النظر إلىٰ أن الأرض تتصف بالامتداد الكلي، أي فإن اتجهت شرقاً فلن ينتهي امتدادها إلىٰ أي حافة أو طرف، كذلك إن اتجهت غرباً أو شمالاً أو جنوباً، والتفسير العلمي لذلك أنها مستمرة في امتدادها مع الانحناء المتواصل الذي يشكل منها حجماً كروياً.

وليس من شأن الفقهاء أن يتحدثوا ـ عند التنبيه إلىٰ وجوب الاتجاه إلىٰ القبلة في الصلاة ـ عن كروية الأرض أو تسطيحها، وإنما مهمتهم أن يوضحوا ضرورة التوجه إلىٰ عين الكعبة أو سمتها حسب خلافهم الذي ذكرته، ثم إن المراجع الحسابية والهندسية هي المعتمد في كيفية التوجه وذلك علىٰ ضوء واقع الأرض وطبيعتها (من فتوىٰ الدكتور محمد سعيد رمضان البوطي: ص١؛ ١ ذو الحجة ١٤٢٠/ ٧ آذار ٢٠٠٠؛ دمشق).

p. 89. Muhammad Ramadan: "Facing the actual Kaaba ...."

إصابة عين الكعبة في الصلاة لا تجب إلا علىٰ القريبين من الكعبة، وأما بالنسبة للبعيدين فلا تجب عليهم إلا إصابة جهتها، وجهتها يحددها الخبراء من العلماء بالهندسة والجغرافيا، وهم أهل الذكر في هذا الشأن، والله عز وجل يقول: ﴿فسئلوا أهل الذكر إن كنتم لا تعلمون﴾، فالقبلة بالنسبة لسكان

أمريكا الشمالية هي الشرق الشمالي لا الشرق الجنوبي، وذلك بناءً علىٰ ما حققه الخبراء في هذا الشأن استناداً إلىٰ كروية الأرض، وكروية الأرض لا ينكرها إلا من حرم من الاطلاع علىٰ العلوم الجغرافية (من فتوىٰ الدكتور محمد رمضان عبد الله: ص١؛ ١٢ رجب ١٤٢١/ ١٠ تشرين الأول ٢٠٠٠؛ بغداد).

p. 90. Wahbeh al-Zuhayli: "Determining the qibla...."

أمر تحديد القبلة يتم بتعاون علماء الهندسة والفلك والشريعة، والفقهاء يستعينون عادة بما يقرره هؤلاء العلماء.

يتم تحديد اتجاه القبلة علىٰ أساس أن الأرض كروية، وليست مسطحة، مراعاة لواقع الأمر وقصر المسافة، وهذا ملحوظ فعلاً وإن لم يصرح به الفقهاء (من فتوىٰ الدكتور وهبة الزحيلي: ص١؛ ١٥ ذو الحجة ١٤٢٠/ ٢١ آذار ٢٠٠٠؛ دمشق).

8. THE STARS AND THE QIBLA

p. 92. Allah Most High: "And by the stars...."

﴿وبالنجم هم يهتدون﴾ (النحل: ١٦).

p. 92. Fakhr al-Razi: "The point of this verse...."

[اعلم أن] المقصود من هذه الآية ذكر بعض النّعم التي خلقها الله تعالىٰ في الأرض (الفخر الرازي: مفاتيح الغيب ٢٠: ٧).

p. 96. Fakhr al-Razi: "If it be wondered...."

فإن قيل: قوله ﴿أن تميد بكم﴾ خطاب الحاضرين وقوله ﴿وبالنجم هم يهتدون﴾ خطاب للغائبين فما السبب فيه؟ قلنا: إن قريشاً كانت تكثر أسفارها لطلب المال، ومن كثرت أسفاره كان علمه بالمنافع الحاصلة من الاهتداء بالنجوم أكثر وأتم فقوله ﴿وبالنجم هم يهتدون﴾ إشارة إلىٰ قريش للسبب الذي ذكرناه (الفخر الرازي: مفاتيح الغيب ٢٠: ١٠).

p. 96. Hadith: "It is Polaris (al-Jady)...."

[قال ابن عباس: سألت رسول الله صلى الله عليه وسلم عن قوله تعالىٰ:

﴿وبالنجم هم يهتدون﴾ قال:] «هو الجَدْيُ يا ابن عباس، عليه قبلتكم وبه تهتدون في بركم وبحركم» [ذكره الماورديّ] (حديث موضوع أورده الإمام القرطبي: الجامع لأحكام القرآن ١٠: ٩٢).

p. 97. Muhammad al-Tawil: "The former position . . . ."

والأول أنسب بالسورة، فإنها مكية، والقبلة واستقبال الكعبة إنما فرضت بعد الهجرة (من فتوىٰ الدكتور محمد التاويل: ص٦؛ ٣ ذو الحجة ١٤٢٠/ ١٠ آذار ٢٠٠٠؛ فاس).

p. 97. Shafiʻi: "Allah Mighty and Majestic says . . . ."

[أخبرنا الربيع، قال: أخبرنا الشافعي، قال:] قال الله عز وجل: ﴿وهو الذي جعل لكم النجوم لتهتدوا بها في ظلمات البر والبحر﴾ (الأنعام: ٩٧). وقال: ﴿وعلاماتٍ وبالنجم هم يهتدون﴾ (النحل: ١٦) وقال لنبيه صلى الله عليه وسلم: ﴿ومن حيث خرجت فول وجهك شطر المسجد الحرام وحيث ما كنتم فولوا وجوهكم شطره﴾ (البقرة: ١٥٠).

[قال الشافعي رحمه الله تعالىٰ:] فنصب الله عز وجل لهم البيت والمسجد، فكانوا إذا رأوه، فعليهم استقبال البيت؛ لأن رسول الله صلى الله عليه وسلم مستقبله، والناس معه / حوله من كل جهة، ودلهم بالعلامات التي خلق لهم، والعقول التي ركب فيهم، علىٰ قصد البيت الحرام، وقصد المسجد الحرام؛ وهو قصد البيت الحرام، فالفرض علىٰ كل مصل فريضة أو نافلة أو علىٰ جنازة، أو ساجد لشكر، أو سجود قرآن؛ أن يتحرىٰ استقبال البيت، إلا في حالين أرخص الله تعالىٰ فيهما، سأذكرهما إن شاء الله تعالىٰ (الإمام الشافعي في الأم ٢: ١٠١).

p. 98. Hadith: "Fast when you see it . . . ."

[حدثنا آدم حدثنا شعبة حدثنا محمد بن زياد قال سمعت أبا هريرة رضي الله عنه يقول قال النبي صلى الله عليه وسلم أو قال قال أبو القاسم صلى الله عليه وسلم] صوموا لرؤيته وأفطروا لرؤيته فإن غُبّي عليكم فأكملوا عدة شعبانَ ثلاثين (رواه البخاري بهذا اللفظ في صحيحه: ٣: ٣٤-٣٥ (١٩٠٩)).

p. 99. Ghazali: "As for the evidences...."

أما أدلة القبلة فهي ثلاثة أقسام أرضية كالاستدلال بالجبال والقرىٰ والأنهار، وهوائية كالاستدلال بالرياح شمالها وجنوبها وصباها ودبورها، وسماوية وهي النجوم.

فأما الأرضية والهوائية فتختلف باختلاف البلاد فرب طريق فيه جبل مرتفع يعلم أنه علىٰ يمين المستقبل أو شماله أو ورائه أو قدامه فليعلم ذلك وليفهمه وكذلك الرياح قد تدل في بعض البلاد فليفهم ذلك ولسنا نقدر علىٰ استقصاء ذلك إذ لكل بلد وإقليم حكم آخر.

وأما السماوية فأدلتها تنقسم إلىٰ نهارية وإلىٰ ليلية أما النهارية فالشمس فلا بد أن يراعي قبل الخروج من البلد أن الشمس عند الزوال أين تقع منه أهي بين الحاجبين أو علىٰ العين اليمنىٰ أو اليسرىٰ أو تميل إلىٰ الجبين ميلاً أكثر من ذلك فإن الشمس لا تعدو في البلاد الشمالية هذه المواقع فإذا حفظ ذلك فمهما عرف الزوال بدليله الذي سنذكره عرف القبلة به، وكذلك يراعي مواقع الشمس منه وقت العصر فإنه في هذين الوقتين يحتاج إلىٰ القبلة بالضرورة وهذا أيضاً لما كان يختلف بالبلاد فليس يمكن استقصاؤه، وأما القبلة وقت المغرب فإنها تدرك بموضع الغروب وذلك بأن يحفظ أن الشمس تغرب عن يمين المستقبل أو هي مائلة إلىٰ وجهه أو قفاه (الإمام الغزالي: إحياء علوم الدين ٢ : ٢٣٢ – ٢٣٣).

p. 100. Ahmad al-Dardir: "The person praying...."

[وِجْهَتُها: أي الكعبة لغيره: أي غير من بمكة سواء كان قريباً من مكة كأهل منىٰ أو بعيداً كأهل الآفاق] فيستقبل المصلي تلك الجهة اجتهاداً أي بالاجتهاد إن أمكن الاجتهاد بمعرفة الأدلة الدالة علىٰ الجهة كالفجر والشفق والشمس والقطب وغيره من الكواكب، وكذا الريح الشرقي أو الجنوبي أو الشمالي والغربي. ولا يجوز التقليد (أي لمجتهد أو لمحراب غير مصر) مع إمكان الاجتهاد (أحمد الدردير مع تعليق (بين القوسين) لأحمد الصاوي: الشرح الصغير علىٰ أقرب المسالك ١ : ٢٩٥).

p. 101. Ghazali: "They consist of knowing...."

وهو علم القبلة والأوقات وذلك أيضاً واجب في الحضر ولكن في الحضر من

يكفيه من محراب متفق عليه يغنيه عن طلب القبلة ومؤذن يراعي الوقت فيغنيه عن طلب علم الوقت والمسافر قد تشتبه عليه القبلة وقد يلتبس عليه الوقت فلا بد له من العلم بأدلة القبلة والمواقيت (الإمام الغزالي: إحياء علوم الدين ٢: ٢٣٢).

9. FUQAHA AND ENGINEERS

p. 103. Hadith: "We are an unlettered nation . . . ."

[حدثنا آدم حدثنا شعبة حدثنا الأسود بن قيس حدثنا سعيد بن عمرو أنه سمع ابن عمر رضي الله عنهما عن النبي صلى الله عليه وسلم أنّه قال] إنا أمة أمية لا نكتب ولا نحسب الشهر هكذا وهكذا يعني مرة تسعة وعشرين ومرة ثلاثين (رواه البخاري بهذا اللفظ في صحيحه: ٣: ٣٥ (١٩١٣)).

p. 103. al-Qastallani: "we are not responsible . . . ."

فلم نكلف في تعريف مواقيت صومنا ولا عبادتنا ما نحتاج فيه إلىٰ معرفة حساب ولا كتابة إنما ربطت عبادتنا بأعلام واضحة وأمور ظاهرة لائحة يستوي في معرفتها الحُسّاب وغيرهم (القسطلاني: إرشاد الساري ٣: ٣٥٩).

p. 103. al-Shatibi: "Among them . . . ."

ومنها: أن تكون التكاليف الاعتقادية والعملية مما يسع الأمي تعقّلها، [ليسعه الدخول تحت حكمها] (الإمام الشاطبي: الموافقات ٢: ٣٩٧).

p. 104. Allah Most High: "has not placed any hardship . . . ."

﴿وما جعل عليكم في الدين من حرج﴾ (الحج: ٧٨).

p. 105. Nuh Ali Salman al-Qudah: "What the scholars . . . ."

ما ذكره الفقهاء من أدلة علىٰ معرفة القبلة هي في الحقيقة أدلة تعرف بها الجهات فإذا عرفت الجهة وعرف موقع المصلي من الكعبة أمكن أن تعرف القبلة (من فتوىٰ الدكتور الشيخ نوح علي سلمان القضاة: ص٣؛ ٧ ذو الحجة ١٤٢٠/ ١٣ آذار ٢٠٠٠؛ طهران).

p. 107. Taj al-Subki: "A judgement about something...."

الحكم على الشيء فرع تصوره (التاج السبكي: الإبهاج في شرح المنهاج
١: ١٧٢).

p. 108. Isma'il Badran: "The matter of determining...."

إن أمر اتجاه القبلة يترك إلى العالم بالهندسة الجيوديزية المسلم الحاذق
ويجب أن يتم الحساب على أساس أن الأرض كروية (من فتوى الشيخ
إسماعيل بن محمد بدران: ص١؛ ٢٨ صفر ١٤٢١/ ١ حزيران ٢٠٠٠؛ دوما
ـ سوريا).

p. 108. Ahmad al-Balisani: "The location of the Kaaba...."

إن موقع (الكعبة) الذي جعله الشارع قبلة للمسلمين في صلاتهم أمر عادي
(كوني) ووجوب معرفة اتجاههم لأجل استقباله في الصلاة أمر تعبدي، وهذا
الأمر التعبدي (وهو معرفة اتجاههم) يعتمد على الوسائل العادية، فالقريب
من الكعبة يعتمد على العين المجردة والأبعد قليلاً يعتمد على الدلالات
العادية وكذلك الأبعد فالأبعد. فكلما بعدت المسافة احتيج إلى وسائل أكثر
علمية لتعيين اتجاه القبلة... وجماهير علماء المسلمين على جواز الاعتماد
على الوسائل العلمية في تعيين اتجاه القبلة. لذلك فإن أمر تعيين القبلة أمر
شرعي لكن تعيينها يتم بالوسائل العادية أقصد العلمية وهو من اختصاص
المختصين بعلوم الفلك والجغرافية الذين يعرفون هذا الأمر. وأما كون أمر
القبلة يتم على أساس أن الأرض كروية أو لا فهذا يتم حسبما وصل إليه العلم
في تعيين شكل الأرض كما هي عليه في الواقع... وهو أمر منوط أيضاً
بعلماء الاختصاص بهذا المجال، وشروط تعيينها يجب أن تكون شروطاً
علمية هندسية لضبط التعيين (من فتوى الدكتور أحمد بن محمد الباليساني:
ص١؛ ١٤ رجب ١٤٢١/ ١٢ تشرين الأول ٢٠٠٠؛ بغداد).

p. 109. Idris al-'Alami: "Know, O questioner...."

اعلم أيها السائل يرحمك الله، إن أمر القبلة هو موضوع هندسي فقهي،
ولذلك يتكلم فيه بالدرجة الأولى الفقيه، إذا كان ملماً بالطرق الهندسية التي
توصله إلى تبين وجه الحق في النازلة، ثم الفقيه الذي لا يعرف الطرق

الهندسية، إن كان الفقيه في فتواه يعتمد على الرجوع إلى القواعد الفقهية المقررة، والشروحات المفسرة لها، وهي غالباً مبنية على قواعد هندسية. أما المهندس إذا لم يكن فقيهاً، ولا مدركاً للموضوع الذي يعالجه من الناحية التعبدية، فإنما يستفاد من خبرته العلمية، إذا كان أميناً، أي غير متحيز ضد الدين.

واعلم أيضاً، أن الذي خدم علم الهندسة ـ مستوية وكروية وفضائية ـ واستنبط علم المثلثات، هم علماء المسلمين، وما فعلوا ذلك إلا خدمة للدين الإسلامي، ولتفهم آيات القرآن الكريم، بقصد التعبد، وخصوصاً لتحديد أوقات الصلوات، وتعيين سمت القبلة في أي مكان على سطح الكرة الأرضية، فكانوا فقهاء مهندسين حقاً. وسيأتي إن شاء الله يوم يقع فيه السؤال عن القبلة من كوكب كذا أو كذا، أو من مطلق الفضاء.

الواقع أن الأرض كروية، ولذلك فعلى الذي يريد أن يتعرف على جهة القبلة ـ لتكون صلاة المسلمين مستوفية لشروط الصحة إن شاء الله ـ أن يضع في اعتباره موضوع كروية الأرض، وخصوصاً إذا كان الأمر يتعلق بالأقطار المذكورة من شمال أمريكا، لأنه لا يكفي أن يضع الإنسان بين يديه الخريطة الجغرافية ليحدد جهة القبلة (من فتوى الأستاذ إدريس محمد العلمي: ص١؛ ١ ذو الحجة ١٤٢٠/ ٨ آذار ٢٠٠٠؛ فاس).

p. III. Allah Most High: "Ask those who know well . . . ."

﴿فاسألوا أهل الذكر إن كنتم لا تعلمون﴾ (النحل: ٤٣).

p. III. Hadith: "When you hear the call . . . ."

[حدثنا عبد الله بن يوسف قال أخبرنا مالك عن ابن شهاب عن عطاء بن يزيد الليثي عن أبي سعيد الخدري أن رسول الله صلى الله عليه وسلم قال] إذا سمعتم النّداء فقولوا مثل ما يقول المؤذن (رواه البخاري بهذا اللفظ في صحيحه: ١: ١٥٩ (٦١١)).

p. II2. al-Shatibi: "Among them [the principles . . . ."

ومنها: أن تكون التكاليف الاعتقادية والعملية مما يسع الأميَّ تعقّلها، ليسعه الدخول تحت حكمها.

أما الاعتقادية: بأن تكون من القرب للفهم، والسهولة على العقل، بحيث

يشترك فيها الجمهور، مَن كان منهم ثاقب الفهم أو بليداً، فإنها لو كانت مما لا يدركه إلا الخواص لم تكن الشريعة عامة، ولم تكن أمية، وقد ثبت كونها كذلك؛ فلا بد أن تكون المعاني المطلوب علمها واعتقادها سهلة المأخذ [....].

وأما العمليات: فمن مراعاة الأمية فيها أن وقع تكليفهم بالجلائل في الأعمال والتقريبات في الأمور، بحيث يدركها الجمهور؛ كما عرف أوقات الصلوات بالأمور المشاهدة لهم، كتعريفها بالظلال، وطلوع الفجر والشمس، وغروبها وغروب الشفق (الإمام الشاطبي: الموافقات ٢ : ٣٩٧، ٣٩٩).

p. 114. Hadith: "We are an unlettered nation . . . . "

[حدثنا آدم حدثنا شعبة حدثنا الأسود بن قيس حدثنا سعيد بن عمرو أنه سمع ابن عمر رضي الله عنهما عن النبي صلى الله عليه وسلم أنّه قال] إنا أمة أمية لا نكتب ولا نحسب الشهر هكذا وهكذا يعني مرة تسعة وعشرين ومرة ثلاثين (رواه البخاري بهذا اللفظ في صحيحه : ٣ : ٣٥ (١٩١٣)).

p. 114. Taqi al-Din al-Subki: "His word . . . . "

وقوله صلى الله عليه وسلم (إنا): يعني العرب لأن الغالب عليها ذلك وإن كان قد يعلم بعضهم الكتابة والحساب. وكونهم لا يكتبون ولا يحسبون شرف لهم لما سبق في علم الله من أنهم أمة النبي الأمي فذلك معجزة له صلى الله عليه وسلم وشرف لهم لاتصافهم بصفة من صفاته.

وجعل ذلك عَلَماً في الشريعة علىٰ الشهر ليكون ضبطاً بأمر ظاهر يعرفه كل أحد ولا يغلط فيه بخلاف الحساب فإنه لا يعرفه إلا القليل من الناس ويقع الغلط فيه كثيراً للتقصير في علمه ولبعد مقدماته وربما كان بعضها ظنياً فاقتضت الحكمة الإلهية والشريعة الحنيفية السمحة التخفيف عن العباد وربط الأحكام بما هو متيسر علىٰ الناس من الرؤية أو كمال العدد ثلاثين.

وليس معنىٰ الحديث النهي عن الكتابة والحساب ولا ذمهما وتنقيصهما بل هما فضيلة فينا (الإمام تقي الدين السبكي: العَلَم المنشور في إثبات الشهور ٥-٦).

p. 115. Muhammad al-ʿAmrawi: "Without a doubt . . . ."

ولا شك أن حديث «نحن أمة أمية لا تكتب ولا تحسب» إخبار عن واقع،
وقد تغير ذلك الواقع، والحكم يدور مع العلة وجوداً وعدماً كما تقرر في
محله من علم الأصول (من فتوىٰ الشيخ محمد بن محمد العمراوي: ص١؛
٢٥ ربيع الأول ١٤٢١/ ٢٨ حزيران ٢٠٠٠؛ فاس).

p. 115. Allah Most High: "Ask those who know well . . . ."

﴿فاسألوا أهل الذكر إن كنتم لا تعلمون﴾ (النحل: ٤٣).

p. 116. Muhammad al-Tawil: "In respect to the first . . . ."

بالنسبة للفقرة الأولىٰ الخاصة بالفقيه الذي أداه اجتهاده إلىٰ جهة غير جهة
المحاريب المنصوبة في البلد علىٰ يد الموثوق بهم من ذوي العلم بالهندسة
والحساب يجب أن يعلم أن أمر القبلة عند المالكية منوط بمعرفة أدلة القبلة،
فإذا كان هذا الفقيه عالماً بأدلة القبلة، قادراً علىٰ معرفتها بنفسه، وبوسائله،
فإنه لا يلزمه تقليد المحاريب المنصوبة من طرف غيره علىٰ الصحيح في
المذهب المالكي. (حسبما نقله وسلمه الونشريسي في المعيار ١١٨:١
واعتمدته حواشي خليل: بناني والدسوقي. انظر الدسوقي ٢٢٦:١).

فإن اختار تقليدها فذاك، وإن اجتهد فأداه اجتهاده إلىٰ خلاف ما عليه
المحاريب وجب عليه العمل باجتهاده، وامتنع عليه تقليد غيره بعد اجتهاده
بالفعل، وإن خالف اجتهاده وصلىٰ لغيره بطلت صلاته، عملاً بالقاعدة
الأصولية والفقهية، أنه لا يقلد مجتهدٌ غيرَه بعد اجتهاده، فالذين سبقوه
لـوضع المحـراب وضعـوه بـاجتهاد، وهـو مجتهـد مثلهـم، خـالفهـم في
اجتهادهم، فلا يترك اجتهاده لاجتهاد غيره، ولهذا يشير خليل بقوله: ولا
يقلد مجتهد غيره ولا محراباً إلا لمصر (من فتوىٰ الدكتور محمد التاويل:
ص٧-٨؛ ٣ ذو الحجة ١٤٢٠/ ١٠ آذار ٢٠٠٠؛ فاس).

p. 117. [Taj al-Subki]: "a judgement about something . . . ."

الحكم علىٰ الشيء فرع تصوره (التاج السبكي: الإبهاج في شرح المنهاج
١٧٢:١).

p. 117. Ibn Qudama al-Maqdisi: "The mujtahid qualified . . . ."

والمجتهد في القبلة هو العالم بأدلتها وإن كان جاهلاً بأحكام الشرع، فإن كل من علم أدلة شيء كان من المجتهدين فيه، وإن جهل غيره، ولأنه يتمكن من استقبالها بدليله. فكان مجتهداً فيها كالفقيه. ولو جهل الفقيه أدلتها أو كان أعمىٰ فهو مقلد وإن علم غيرها (الإمام موفق الدين ابن قدامة المقدسي: المغني ١: ٤٤٠–٤٤١).

p. 118. Wahbeh al-Zuhayli: "The opinion of a scholar . . . ."

لا يعمل برأي فقيه غريب عن البلد، فأهل البلد أعرف بما لديهم، فيعمل بما توصل إليه علماؤهم المتخصصون في الهندسة والجغرافيا والفلك وغير ذلك. وعلىٰ القادم لبلد تقليد ما عليه عمل أهل البلد.

علىٰ العوام العمل بما يقرره أهل الخبرة من ذوي العلوم المتخصصة في الهندسة والحساب، مع الاستعانة بملاحظات الفقهاء، وليس للعوام الخيار في الأخذ برأي شخصي أو برأي واحد، وإنما عليهم العمل بما رآه الجماعة، فيد الله علىٰ الجماعة، وعليكم بالسواد الأعظم، ومن شذ شذ في النار، وكل ذلك للحفاظ علىٰ وحدة المسلمين (من فتوىٰ الدكتور وهبة الزحيلي: ص٢؛ ١٥ ذو الحجة ١٤٢٠ / ٢١ آذار ٢٠٠٠؛ دمشق).

p. 118. Allah Most High: "Hold fast to . . . ."

﴿واعتصموا بحبل الله جميعاً ولا تفرقوا﴾ (آل عمران: ١٠٣).

p. 119. Muhammad al-Rugi: "When Muslims have mihrabs . . . ."

إذا كان للمسلمين محاريب فيجب اعتمادها والاستدلال بها علىٰ القبلة، لأن الأصل أنها إنما توضع من أهل المعرفة والخبرة بالقبلة. فإذا دخل المسلم (المسافر) إلىٰ بلد وجد فيه محاريب، فعليه أن يعتمدها في الصلاة. فإن خالفها لاجتهاده فقد أخطأ، لأن ما عليه الجماعة وداموا عليه زماناً هو أصح وأقوىٰ من اجتهاد الواحد، ولقوله تعالىٰ: ﴿ومن يشاقق الرسول من بعد ما تبين له الهدىٰ ويتبع غير سبيل المؤمنين نوله ما تولىٰ ونصله جهنم﴾ (النساء: ١١٥) لأن هذا نوع من الشقاق ما دام يقابل اجتهاداً جماعياً عليه المسلمون باجتهاد فردي يخالفهم.

عامة المسلمين (أي العامة المقلدون) عليهم أن يتبعوا الفقيه المجتهد،
والفقيه المجتهد عليه أن يستعين بأهل الهندسة والخبرة بالحساب والجهات،
فالفقيه لا يجتهد لمجرد هواه وذوقه، بل لا بد أن يعتمد علىٰ ذوي الخبرة
والتخصص، فيما يتعلق بتصور الأمور قبل الحكم عليها .

وإذا تبين الخطأ في المتبوع فلا جناح علىٰ العوام وليس عليهم إعادة
الصلاة. لقوله تعالىٰ: ﴿فأينما تولوا فثم وجه الله﴾ (البقرة: ١١٥) .

في حالة وجود اتجاهين مختلفين، أحدهما يصلي إليه تسعون بالمائة أو
أكثر، فهذا هو الذي يجب أن يكون عليه المسلمون، ويجب علىٰ الأقلية أن
تتبع الأكثرية، لأن هذه الصورة كالصورة السابقة: أي عند وجود محاريب في
بلد، لا يجوز الاجتهاد الفردي ومخالفة تلك المحاريب (من فتوىٰ الدكتور
محمد الروكي: ص٣؛ ٣ ذو الحجة ١٤٢٠/ ١٠ آذار ٢٠٠٠؛ فاس) .

IO. INSTRUMENTS AND SACRED LAW

p. 121. Ibn Siraj: "As for seeking...."

وأما الاستدلال بالآلات فلم يرد عن السلف الصالح رضي الله عنهم، فلا يلزم
الرجوع إليها، ولا يجوز أن تجعل حاكمة علىٰ الأدلة الشرعية . (من فتوىٰ ابن
سراج التي نقلها الونشريسي: المعيار المعرب: ١ :١٢١-١٢٢) .

p. 121. Ibn Siraj: "[instruments] are unnecessary to refer to...."

[فـ] ـلا يلزم الرجوع إليها، ولا يجوز أن تجعل حاكمة علىٰ الأدلة الشرعية
(من نفس المصدر: ١ :١٢٢) .

p. 122. Ibn Siraj: "It is sufficient for someone...."

وحسب من يستدل بها أن يستخرج بها الجهة خاصة، لأنه قد علم بالاستقراء
صحة استخراج الجهة بها (من نفس المصدر: ١ :١٢٢) .

p. 122. Muhammad al-Tawil: "It is clear from this...."

وانطلاقاً من هذا يتبين أن المسؤول عن تحديد أمر القبلة هو العارف بأدلتها
من فقهاء وغيرهم ممن يمكنهم معرفة جهتها بالأدلة الشرعية أو غيرها من

العلوم الهندسية، ولا يختص ذلك بفريق دون فريق، وقد جرت عادة ملوك المغرب بإشراك الفقهاء والفلكيين في نصب المحاريب أو تصحيحها، كما ثبت عن علي ابن تاشفين، والمولیٰ إسماعيل، والمولیٰ الرشيد وآخرين، حاشية گـنون علیٰ الرهوني ١: ٣٥٥ (من فتویٰ الدكتور محمد التاويل: ص٤؛ ٣ ذو الحجة ١٤٢٠/ ١٠ آذار ٢٠٠٠؛ فاس).

p. 122. ʿAbdullah al-Shinqiti: "As for what you have mentioned . . . ."

أما ما ذكرتم من الكراهة في استخدام الآلات في مذهب مالك والكلام الوارد في المعيار عن ابن سراج فلعل منشأه ما ذكره الحطاب في شرحه لخليل، حيث قال عند ذكر معرفة الأوقات بالآلات: «وكرهه ابن العربي لأنه ليس من فعل السلف». ولم يسلم الحطاب هذه الكراهة بل رد هذا الكلام بقوله: «قلت: تقدم كلام المازري وليس فيه تصريح بالكراهة، بل ذكر أن ذلك طريق لمعرفته، ولكن لم يذكره الفقهاء إما لصعوبته أو لأنه يؤدي إلیٰ النظر في النجوم فتأمله» (مواهب الجليل: ١: ٣٨٥).

وقد ذكر ابن سراج في آخر مقولته التي نقلتم والتي استدل بها المستدلون علیٰ كراهة استعمال الآلات قال: «وحسب من يستدل بها أن يستخرج بها الجهة خاصة لأنه علم بالاستقراء صحة استخراج الجهة بها» فلم ير بأساً باستعمالها لاستخراج الجهة بها، وهو المبحوث فيه هنا.

وها نحن نذكر نصوص الأئمة المصرحة بالجواز:

قال الحطاب بعد ذكر أن الزوال يعرف بزيادة الظل: وهذا هو الطريق المعروف الذي يذكره الفقهاء في كتبهم لسهولته واشتراك الناس في معرفته ولو عرف الوقت بغير ذلك من الآلات كالربع والاسطرلاب وغيرهما لجاز ذكره المازري وغيره (مواهب الجليل: ١: ٣٨٥).

وفي المعيار الجديد للوزاني عازياً للإمام التاودي بن سودة: أن الآلات لها أصل في الشريعة وهي مبينة لما جاء عن الشارع وموصلة إليه لا شيء زائد عليه، وإذا اختلف العارف المستند في معرفته للآلات مع غيره في دخول الوقت كان قوله أحق والاستناد إليه أولیٰ وأوثق. (المعيار الجديد: ١:٢٢٤).

وفيه أيضاً عازياً للعلامة سيدي أحمد الغُرْفي: وحيث دخلت هذه الآلات من ربع واسطرلاب وغيرهما في الإسلام وعند أهله فوجدت تفيد اليقين

للعارف بها إذا أتقنت في نفسها وجب تقليد العارف بها لمن لا علم له بها والعمل على قوله مع أنه ينبغي له بعض الاحتياط عند غيم السماء والأفق وعليه عمل الناس في المشارق والمغارب كما نقله الحطاب عن القرافي وغيره فلا ينكر اعتماد الآلات إلا جاهل لا عبرة بقوله (المصدر نفسه: ١: ٢٢٣).

وهذا الشيخ السنوسي على جلالة قدره ومكانته في العلم والعمل جعل آلة الاسطرلاب منةً منَّ الله تعالى بها على المسلمين (المصدر نفسه: ١: ٢٢٨) [....].

ومعروف أن الاسطرلاب الذي أجاز الفقهاء استعماله ولم يذكروا كراهةً فيه آلة من مهامّها مع تحديد الوقت بيان سمت القبلة، ففي أبجد العلوم للقنوجي عند الكلام على الاسطرلاب: إنه علم يعرف منه كيفية استخراج الأعمال الفلكية من الاسطرلاب بطريق خاصة وهذا أيضاً علم نافع يستخرج منه كثير من الأعمال من معرفة ارتفاع الشمس ومعرفة المطالع والطوالع وأوقات الصلاة وسمت القبلة (أبجد العلوم: ٢: ٣٨٥).

وإذا كان علماؤنا الأقدمون تلقوا آلات عصرهم بالقبول كما قدمنا واعتبروها منةً من الله تعالى مع تواضع الإمكانيات العلمية المتاحة آنذاك فما بالك بعصر الطفرة العلمية والثورة التكنولوجية (من فتوى الأستاذ الشيخ عبد الله العلوي الشنقيطي: ص١-٣؛ ٢٣ جمادى الآخرة ١٤٢١/ ٢١ أيلول ٢٠٠٠؛ تريم، حضرموت).

p. 126. Muhammad al-Tawil: "(1) Regarding knowledge . . . :"
(١) بالنسبة لمعرفة أوقات الصلاة فإن الراجح في المذهب المالكي أن ذلك فرض كفاية فقط، ولا يلزم كل واحد أن يعرف بنفسه دخول الوقت لا بالآلات ولا بغيرها، ويكفيه تقليد من يعرفها بأية وسيلة تؤديه إلى التحقق من دخول الوقت الذي هو شرط في صحة الصلاة.

لكنهم اختلفوا في استعمال الآلات فقال ابن العربي: يكره استعمالها لأنها ليست من فعل السلف، وقال المازري: يكره الاسطرلاب واختلف في علة كراهته كما نقل ذلك الشيخ كنون في حاشيته على الرهوني ١: ٢٨٤.

لكن قال البرزلي: ظاهر المذهب عندنا قبول قول المؤذن العدل العارف مطلقاً إذا كان عارفاً بالأوقات بالآلات مثل الرمليات والمنقانات وغيرها، ونسبه لابن يونس وغيره.

وهذا هو الرأي المعول عليه في الفقه المالكي وبه العمل كما نص على ذلك غير واحد من المتأخرين الذين عرفوا تلك الآلات وخبروها وعرفوا ضبطها ودقتها وقدموها على غيرها من العلامات، نكتفي بتسجيل نصوص بعضهم:

قال الشيخ التاودي: إن الآلات لها أصل في الشريعة وهي مبينة لما جاء عن الشارع وموصلة له، لا شيء زائد عليها، وإذا اختلف العارف المستند في معرفته للآلات مع غيره في دخول الوقت كان قوله أحق والاستناد إليه أولى وأوثق. المعيار الجديد ١: ٢٢٣-٢٢٤.

وقال الحطاب بعد ذكره طريقة الفقهاء في معرفة الزوال بالظل: وهذا الطريق الذي يذكره الفقهاء لسهولته، واشتراك الناس في معرفته، ولو عرف الوقت بغير ذلك من الآلات كالربع والاسطرلاب وغيرهما لجاز كما ذكره المازري وغيره. المعيار الجديد ١: ٢٢٦.

وقال العلامة الغُرْفي: وحيث دخلت هذه الآلات من ربع واسطرلاب وغيرهما في الإسلام وعند أهله واختبرت فوجدت تفيد اليقين للعارف بها إذا أتقنت في نفسها وجب تقليد العارف بها لمن لا علم له بها والعمل على قوله مع أنه ينبغي له بعض الاحتياط عند غيم السماء والأفق وعليه عمل الناس في المشارق والمغارب كما نقله الحطاب عن القرافي وغيره فلا ينكر اعتماد الآلات إلا جاهل لا عبرة بقوله. المعيار الجديد ١: ٢٢٣.

(٢) وبالنسبة للاستدلال بآلات على معرفة القبلة فإني لم أقف على نص صريح يكره ذلك وإن كان تعليل ابن العربي السابق بأنها ليست من فعل السلف يمكن إجراؤه هنا في موضوع معرفة الأوقات.

لكن عبارة القرطبي قد تفيد الجواز حين يقول فيما تعرف به القبلة لغير من يعاين الكعبة: والآخر أن تكون الكعبة بحيث لا يراها فيلزمه التوجه نحوها وتلقاءها بالدلائل، وهي الشمس والقمر والنجوم والرياح وكل ما يمكن به معرفة جهتها ١٠/ ٩٢.

فقوله وكل ما يمكن به معرفة جهتها هكذا بصيغة العموم تشمل كل آلة تهدي إلى القبلة فيجوز استعمالها والاستدلال بها لأن دلائل القبلة مجرد وسائل وطرق لمعرفتها لا تعبّد في أعيانها كوسائل القتال لا يلزم الاقتصار

فقوله وكل ما يمكن به معرفة جهتها هكذا بصيغة العموم تشمل كل آلة
تهدي إلىٰ القبلة فيجوز استعمالها والاستدلال بها لأن دلائل القبلة مجرد
وسائل وطرق لمعرفتها لا تعبّد في أعيانها كوسائل القتال لا يلزم الاقتصار
علىٰ ما كان في عهده صلى الله عليه وسلم (من فتوىٰ الدكتور محمد التاويل:
ص١-٢؛ ٧ شعبان ٣/١٤٢١ تشرين الثاني ٢٠٠٠؛ فاس).

p. 128. Muhammad al-ʿAmrawi: "The only [additional] point . . . ."
والملاحظة الوحيدة التي يمكن لمخاطبكم إبداؤها هي الفرق العظيم بين علم
الهندسة قديماً وهذا العلم حديثاً . . فالأمور لم تعد كما كان يتصورها الإمام
ابن سراج رحمه الله ولا غيره ممن سبق الإمام الونشريسي في الزمن . وقد
تقدم هذا العلم كغيره من العلوم العقلية والتجريبية والطبيعية تقدماً هائلاً
يجعلنا نعلن الثقة بنتائجه ونطمئن في الاعتماد عليها في حسم بعض أمور
الاجتهاد (من فتوىٰ الأستاذ الشيخ محمد بن محمد العمراوي: ص١؛ ٢٥
ربيع الأول ٢٨/١٤٢١ حزيران ٢٠٠٠؛ فاس).

p. 128. ʿAbd al-Malik al-Saʿdi: "One's personal certitude . . . ."
اتجاه القبلة يكفي بها غالب الظن ولا يُشترط فيها اليقين أو القطع . إذا وجد
من أهل الاختصاص من يحدد موضعها وجهتها لا يحق له الاجتهاد لأن
تحديد المختص يدخل تحت عموم قبول أخبار العدل، فإذا وجد المهندس
أو الجغرافي أو من له أي تخصص بتحديد الجهات وهم عدول لا يصح
الاجتهاد مع تحديدهم ولا سيما في هذا العصر الذي ظهرت به أحدث
الوسائل العلمية التي تحدد الجهات والمواضع بشكل دقيق .

ما ذكره الفقهاء من علامات وأمارات للوصول إلىٰ غالب الظن للاتجاه
فإنها علامات ليست إلزامية بل هي الوسائل المتوافرة لديهم في تلك
العصور، فإذا وجد ما هو أدق في تحديدها فالمفروض اللجوء إليه وتركها
(من فتوىٰ الدكتور عبد الملك بن عبد الرحمٰن السعدي: ص٢؛ ٢١ رجب
٢٠/١٤٢١ تشرين الأول ٢٠٠٠؛ الرمادي بالعراق).

p. 129. Fatwa Council of Tarim: "It is permissible to rely . . . ."
يجوز الاعتماد في تحديد جهة القبلة علىٰ بيت الإبرة (البوصلة) كما صرح به

الإمام شمس الدين الرملي في نهاية المحتاج (٤٤٣:١) فقال: «ويجوز الاعتماد علىٰ بيت الإبرة في دخول الوقت والقبلة لإفادتها الظن بذلك كما يفيده الاجتهاد. أفتىٰ به الوالد رحمه الله تعالىٰ وهو ظاهر» اهـ. والمراد بوالده الإمام شيخ الإسلام شهاب الدين أحمد الرملي (من فتوىٰ مجلس الإفتاء بتريم: ص٣؛ ١٣ جمادىٰ الآخرة ١٢/١٤٢١ أيلول ٢٠٠٠؛ تريم حضرموت).

p. 131. Ghazali: "When the sun passes...."

فإذا زالت الشمس عن منتهىٰ الارتفاع أخذ الظل في الزيادة فمن حيث صارت الزيادة مدركة بالحس دخل وقت الظهر ويعلم قطعاً أن الزوال في علم الله سبحانه وقع قبله ولكن التكاليف لا ترتبط إلا بما يدخل تحت الحس (الإمام الغزالي: إحياء علوم الدين ١ ١٧٤:١).

p. 132. Allah Most High: "has not placed any hardship...."

﴿وما جعل عليكم في الدين من حرج﴾ (الحج: ٧٨).

p. 133. Hadith: "Everything between where the sun rises...."

[حدثنا الحسن بن أبي بكر المروزي حدثنا المعلىٰ بن منصور حدثنا عبد الله بن جعفر المخرمي عن عثمان بن محمد الأخنسي عن سعيد المقبري عن أبي هريرة] عن النبي صلى الله عليه وسلم قال: «ما بين المشرق والمغرب قبلة». [قال أبو عيسىٰ: هذا حديث حسن صحيح] (الترمذي: الجامع الصحيح ٢: ١٧٣ (٣٤٤)).

p. 134. Hassan al-Hindi: "In the matter of the qibla...."

لقد أحال الفقهاء الناس في أمر القبلة علىٰ علم الفلك والهندسة مع اعتقادهم أنها ظنية وقدموها علىٰ التحري فكيف بنا اليوم ونحن نرىٰ قوة هذه العلوم ودقة الإصابة فيها مما يجعل الخطأ فيها بنسبة صغيرة جداً.

ولا يقال إن الشرع لم يكلفنا هذه التقنية في تعيين القبلة فإنا نقول الشرع لم يكلفنا بها عند عدم وجودها وأما إذا كانت بين أيدينا متيسرة فمن الذي يقول لا يلزمنا الأخذ بها وقد ذكر العيني في عمدة القاري ج٤ ص١٢٦ وفي تعلم أدلة القبلة ثلاثة أوجه أحدها أنه فرض كفاية والثاني فرض عين ولا

204

يصح والثالث فرض كفاية إلا أن يريد سفراً فقد أوجب تعلم الأدلة علىٰ القبلة ومنها قواعد الفلك والهندسة (من فتوىٰ الشيخ حسان الهندي: ص٤؛ ١٨ ربيع الثاني ١٤٢١/ ٢٠ تموز ٢٠٠٠؛ دمشق).

p. 134. Muhammad Hisham al-Burhani: "It is not permissible . . . ."

المعاين للكعبة والمصلي إلىٰ جهة ثبتت بالنقل لا يجوز له الاجتهاد ويلحق بهما من تحددت قبلته بوسائل العلم الحديث الدقيقة.

ومن لم يكن في واحد من الأوضاع السابقة فله الاجتهاد ويكفيه غلبة الظن في إصابة الجهة.

ومن المقطوع به في هذا العصر وشواهده الواقعية اليومية في حركة الأسفار الجوية والأقمار الصناعية التي ملأت الفضاء وكل نقطة علىٰ وجه الأرض بل والكواكب والنجوم والأجرام السابحة في الفضاء يمكن أن يكون هدفاً وغاية محددة بدقة متناهية وموقع الكعبة المشرفة علىٰ الأرض التي تحولت بالعلم الحديث إلىٰ قرية صغيرة صار معروفاً ومحدداً بإحداثياته الدقيقة بل المتناهية في الدقة.

وبناءً عليه فقد صار الإنسان قادراً بلا ريب ولا تردد علىٰ معرفة موقعه بالنسبة إلىٰ الكعبة المشرفة، فيلزمه التوجه إلىٰ عين الكعبة ولا يكفي أن يصلي إلىٰ جهتها اللهم إلا إذا كان بعيداً عن واقع الحضارة ومعطياتها أو عاجزاً عن الوصول إلىٰ ذلك بعذر.

فإن العمل بالأصل هو الواجب تطبيقاً للقواعد والمبادىء العامة القائلة بأنه لا يعمل بالبدل إلا عند العجز عن الأصل كالتيمم لا يكون إلا عند فقد الماء حقيقة أو تقديراً، والاجتهاد لا يكون في مورد النص، ويطرح الشك عند مقابلة اليقين.

ولا ننسىٰ أن نشير أخيراً إلىٰ قضية مهمة، وهي أن من صلىٰ إلىٰ جهة وهو يعلم علم اليقين أنه منحرف فيها عن الجهة الصحيحة انحرافاً بيناً وترك ذلك قاصداً لا تصح صلاته إلا إذا ترك ذلك لعذر، نعم قال الحنفية بأن من صلىٰ باجتهاد ورأىٰ أنه قد صادف سمت القبلة يكفيه ذلك وتصح صلاته لكن السؤال المطروح لو انحرف عامداً عما رأىٰ أنه جهة الكعبة هل تصح صلاته؟ كل ظني أنها لا تصح والله تعالىٰ أعلم.

وبالختام أقول: القبلة في الولايات المتحدة الأمريكية وفي غيرها من البلاد حيثما يدل عليه خبراء العلم الذين يوجهون حركة الأسفار والتنقّل بين البلدان في العالم، ولا يلتفت إلىٰ ما يخالف ذلك والله تعالىٰ أعلم (من فتوىٰ الدكتور الشيخ محمد هشام البرهاني: ص٣؛ ٢٦ ربيع الأول ١٤٢١/ ٢٩ حزيران ٢٠٠٠؛ دمشق).

p. 136. Allah Most High: "Wherever you all may be . . . ."

﴿وحيث ما كنتم فولوا وجوهكم شطره﴾ (البقرة: ١٤٤).

II. THE EXACT DIRECTION

p. 137. Ibn Siraj: "As for the exact direction . . . ."

وأما السمت فلم يرد الشرع بمراعاته فلا يلتفت إليه (الإمام ابن سراج: نقله الونشريسي في المعيار المعرب ١٢٢:١).

p. 139. Hadith: "Everything between where the sun rises . . . ."

[حدثنا الحسن بن أبي بكر المروزي حدثنا المعلىٰ بن منصور حدثنا عبد الله بن جعفر المخرمي عن عثمان بن محمد الأخنسي عن سعيد المقبري عن أبي هريرة] عن النبي صلى الله عليه وسلم قال: «ما بين المشرق والمغرب قبلة». [قال أبو عيسى: هذا حديث حسن صحيح] (الترمذي: الجامع الصحيح ٢: ١٧٣ (٣٤٤)).

p. 139. Muhammad al-Rugi: "The *qibla* in its lexical sense . . . ."

القبلة في المعنىٰ اللغوي هي الجهة. وفي المعنىٰ الشرعي هي جهة معينة وهي الكعبة. والمعنىٰ الحسي (أقصر طريق) داخل في الشرعي. فإن لم يتيسر لك أن تجعل بينك وبينها (الكعبة) أقصر طريق فلا حرج عليك، لأن المقصود الشرعي هو تحري الاستقبال والتوجه نحو الكعبة وشطرها، وكلما دققنا في ذلك كان أقرب لتحصيل مقصود الشرع (من فتوىٰ الدكتور محمد الروكي: ص١؛ ٣ ذو الحجة ١٤٢١/ ١٠ آذار ٢٠٠٠؛ فاس).

p. 140. al-Haytami: "[one must be] 'in line ....'"

والمعتبر مسامتتُها عرفاً لا حقيقةً (الإمام ابن حجر الهيتمي: تحفة المحتاج ١ : ٤٨٤).

p. 140. al-Shirwani: "with certitude (yaqinan) ...."

يقيناً في القرب وظناً في البعد (الشيخ عبد الحميد الشرواني: حاشية علىٰ تحفة المحتاج للإمام ابن حجر الهيتمي: ١ : ٤٨٤).

p. 140. Ibn Siraj: "As for the exact direction ...."

وأما السمت فلم يرد الشرع بمراعاته فلا يلتفت إليه، لأن السمت عند أهل الآلات هو أن يقدر أن لو وضع خط مستقيم من مكان الإنسان لوقع مقابلاً للكعبة. والقائلون بطلب السمت من الفقهاء لا يضيقون هذا التضييق، وإنما يكفي عندهم المسامتة بالأبصار كما تسامت النجوم، وإن كانا يقربان من جهة المعنىٰ، ولكن فيما قال أهل الآلة من التضييق ما ليس في كلام الفقهاء (الإمام ابن سراج: نقله الونشريسي في المعيار المعرب ١ : ١٢٢).

p. 140. al-Azhar: "someone praying who can see ...."

المصلي الذي يعاين الكعبة عليه إصابة عينها، فإن كان بعيداً فيكفي أن يستقبل الجهة التي فيها الكعبة، ولا يلزمه أن يستقبل عينها (من فتوىٰ مجمع البحوث الإسلامية بالأزهر الشريف: ص١؛ ٢٨ شوال ١٤١٨/ ٢٥ شباط ١٩٩٨؛ القاهرة).

p. 141. al-Azhar: "The approximate direction ...."

اتجاه القبلة في بلدان أمريكا الشمالية عموماً إلىٰ شرق الشمال مع اختلاف في زاوية الانحراف من موقع إلىٰ آخر في تلك البلاد حسب خطوط الطول والعرض كما قرره الخبراء . . .

وأن المتجه إلىٰ الجنوب الشرقي في تلك البلاد يكون منحرفاً انحرافاً كبيراً يجعله علىٰ خطر عدم استقبال جهة الكعبة ولا يكون محققاً للشرط الشرعي في استقبال القبلة (من فتوىٰ مجمع البحوث الإسلامية بالأزهر الشريف: ص٢؛ ٢٨ شوال ١٤١٨/ ٢٥ شباط ١٩٩٨؛ القاهرة).

12. THE TRADITIONAL DIRECTION OF MOSQUES

p. 143. Ibn Siraj: "The imam should not turn aside . . . ."

لا ينبغي للإمام أن ينحرف الانحراف المسؤول عنه، لأن المحراب المنصوب بمصر كبير يعلم أن نصبه باجتماع كثير من الناس والعلماء، وذلك مما يدل علىٰ صحته ونصبه باجتهاد. وقد نص العلماء رضي الله عنهم أن المحاريب التي بالأقطار الكبار يصح تقليدها (الإمام ابن سراج: نقله الونشريسي في المعيار المعرب ١: ١١٧).

p. 143. Ibn Qudama al-Maqdisi: "And so too if one . . . ."

وكذلك لو كان في مصر أو قرية. ففرضه: التوجه إلىٰ محاريبهم وقبلتهم المنصوبة. لأن هذه القبل ينصبها أهل الخبرة والمعرفة. فجرىٰ ذلك مجرىٰ الخبر، فأغنىٰ عن الاجتهاد (الإمام موفق الدين ابن قدامة المقدسي: المغني ١: ٤٣٩).

p. 143. Ibn ʿAbidin: "The people of a city . . . ."

[. . .] وأهل البلد لهم علم بجهة القبلة المبنية علىٰ الأمارات الدالة عليها من النجوم وغيرها فكان فوق الثابت بالتحرّي وكذا إذا وجد المحاريب المنصوبة في البلدة (الإمام ابن عابدين: رد المحتار ١: ٤٣٩).

p. 143. Nawawi: "As for mihrabs . . . ."

أما المحراب فيجب اعتماده ولا يجوز معه الاجتهاد ونقل صاحب الشامل إجماع المسلمين علىٰ هذا واحتج له أصحابنا بأن المحاريب لا تنصب إلا بحضرة جماعة من أهل المعرفة بسمت الكواكب والأدلة فجرى ذلك مجرىٰ الخبر واعلم أن المحراب إنما يعتمد بشرط أن يكون في بلد كبير أو في قرية صغيرة يكثر المارون بها بحيث لا يقرونه علىٰ الخطأ فإن كان في قرية صغيرة لا يكثر المارون بها لم يجز اعتماده (الإمام النووي: المجموع ٣: ٢٠١).

p. 143. Fatwa Council of Tarim: "Mihrabs may be divided . . . ."

«تنقسم المحاريب إلىٰ ما ثبت أنه صلى الله عليه وسلم صلىٰ فيه [. . .] وإلىٰ ما لم يثبت أنه صلى الله عليه وسلم صلىٰ فيه.

«فإن كان بمحل نشأ به قرون من المسلمين أو كثر به المارون منهم بحيث لا يقرون علىٰ الخطأ وسلم من الطعن لم يجز الاجتهاد جهة وجاز يمنة ويسرة ولم يجب علىٰ المعتمد، فإن انتفىٰ شرط من ذلك وجب الاجتهاد مطلقاً، والمراد باليمنة وضدها أن لا يخرج عن الجهة التي فيها الكعبة كما مر» انتهىٰ [من بغية المسترشدين (ص٤٠) للإمام عبد الرحمٰن باعلوي].

وقوله: (قرون من المسلمين) قال الحافظ الجلال السيوطي في فتاويه: «ليس المراد بالقرون ثلاثمائة سنة بلا شك ولا مائة سنة ولا نصفها وإنما المراد جماعات من المسلمين صلوا إلىٰ هذا المحراب ولم ينقل عن أحد منهم أنه طعن فيه [. . .] فالمرجع إلىٰ كثرة الناس لا إلىٰ طول الزمن ويكفي الطعن من واحد إذا ذكر له مستنداً أو كان من أهل العلم بالميقات فذلك يخرجه عن رتبة اليقين الذي لا يجتهد معه» (من فتوىٰ مجلس الإفتاء بتريم: ص٣-٤؛ ١٣ جمادىٰ الآخرة ١٤٢١/ ٢١ أيلول ٢٠٠٠؛ تريم حضرموت).

p. 146. Hadith: "There shall be troubles . . . ."

[حدثني عمرو الناقد والحسن الحلواني وعبد بن حميد (قال عبد: أخبرني. وقال الآخران: حدّثنا: حدّثنا يعقوب ـ وهو ابن إبراهيم بن سعد ـ حدثنا أبي عن صالح عن ابن شهاب حدثني المسيب ابن المسيب وأبو سلمة بنُ عبد الرحمٰن أن أبا هريرةَ قال: قال رسول الله صلى الله عليه وسلم] «ستكون فتن القاعد فيها خير من القائم والقائم فيها خير من الماشي والماشي فيها خير من الساعي من تشرف لها تستشرفه، ومن وجد فيها ملجأ فليعذ به» (رواه مسلم بهذا اللفظ في صحيحه: ٤:٢٢١١-٢٢١٢ (٢٨٨٦)).

p. 146. Abul Hasan 'Ali al-Quryani: "he was prevented . . . ."

[لما أراد الحكم بن عبد الرحمٰن تحويل قبلة المسجد الجامع بقرطبة، وقد اتفق من لديه من أهل الحساب ـ وفيهم أئمة يُقتدىٰ بهم ـ علىٰ انحرافها إلىٰ جهة المغرب كثيراً] صُرِفَ عن ذلك لاستعظام عامة الناس مخالفة ما درج عليه أسلافهم (أبو الحسَن علي القرياني: نقله عنه الونشريسي في المعيار المعرب ١: ١١٨).

209

p. 146. Hadith: "Make things easy...."

[حدثنا عبيد الله بن معاذ العنبري حدثنا أبي حدثنا شعبة عن أبي التياح، عن
أنس. ح وحدثنا أبو بكر بن أبي شيبة حدثنا عبيد الله بن سعيد. ح وحدثنا
محمد بن الوليد حدثنا محمد بن جعفر كلاهما عن شعبة عن أبي التياح.
قال: سمعت] أنس بن مالك يقول: قال رسول الله صلى الله عليه وسلم:
«يسروا ولا تعسروا، وسكنوا ولا تنفروا» (رواه مسلم بهذا اللفظ في صحيحه:
٣:١٣٥٩ (١٧٣٤)).

p. 148. 'Abdullah al-'Alawi al-Shinqiti: "A tempest...."

ولقد عصفت بأكثر المسلمين اليوم الأهواء وفرقتهم المذاهب والنحل ولم يعد
يجمعهم إلا القبلة فإن تعددت الاتجاهات في المدينة الواحدة كان ذلك
مصيبة في الدين، وبالاجتهاد الجماعي والرجوع إلىٰ المختصين واستعمال
الأجهزة الدقيقة يمكن التغلب علىٰ هذه المشكلة فوحدة الصف مقصد شرعي
هام (من فتوىٰ الشيخ الأستاذ عبد الله العلوي الشنقيطي: ص٤؛ ٢٣ جمادىٰ
الآخرة ١٤٢١/ ٢١ أيلول ٢٠٠٠؛ تريم حضرموت).

13. THE FOUR DIRECTIONS OF THE WORLD

p. 150. al-Qarafi: "The direction of the Kaaba...."

[القاعدة الخامسة هي أن] جهة الكعبة تكون شرقاً في قطر وغرباً في قطر،
وكل نقطة تفرض بين المشرق والمغرب من جهة الشمال أو الجنوب فهي
جهة الكعبة لقوم، وعلىٰ ثلاثمائة وستين نقطة؛ وتحرير ذلك يحصل بالطرق
المتقدمة من الاستدلال (الإمام القرافي: الذخيرة ٢:١٣١).

p. 150. al-Qarafi: "[the] strongest [are] latitude and longitude...."

[وأصول الأدلة علىٰ الكعبة ستة:] العروض والأطوال مع الدائرة الهندسية أو
غيرها من الأشكال الهندسية علىٰ ما بُسط في علم المواقيت [والقطب
والكواكب والشمس والقمر، والرياح وهي أضعفها؛ كما أن] أقواها العروض
والأطوال [،ثم القطب] (الإمام القرافي: الذخيرة ٢:١٢٣-١٢٤).

p. 152. Ibn ʿAbd al-Barr: "whoever is out of sight of it . . . ."

أجمعوا أنّ على‌ من غابَ عنها بعد أو قرب أن يتوجه في صلاته نحوها بما قدر عليه من الاستدلال على‌ جهتها من النجوم والجبال والرياح وغيرها (الإمام ابن عبد البر: الاستذكار ٧: ٢١٥).

p. 153. Malik: "If a man prays turned somewhat away . . . ."

وقال مالك لو أن رجلاً صلى‌ فانحرف عن القبلة ولم يشرق ولم يغرب فعلم بذلك قبل أن يقضي صلاته قال ينحرف إلى‌ القبلة ويبني على‌ صلاته ولا يقطع صلاته (الإمام سحنون عن الإمام ابن قاسم: المدونة الكبرى‌ ١: ٩٢).

p. 153. Salih al-Abi: "If the mistakeness . . . ."

وإن تبين خطأ (في القبلة التي هو مستقبلها) بصلاة قطع غير أعمى ومنحرف يسيراً فيستقبلانها (أي القبلة ويبنيان على‌ ما صلياه إلى‌ غيرها. وإن لم يستقبلا وأتماها إلى‌ الجهة التي تبين خطؤها بطلت صلاة الأعمى المنحرف كثيراً، وصحّت صلاة المنحرف يسيراً، بصيراً كان أو أعمى‌ مع الحرمة عليهما) (الإمام خليل بن إسحاق الجندي؛ وبين الأقواس شرح الشيخ صالح بن عبد السميع الآبي: جواهر الإكليل شرح مختصر العلامة الشيخ خليل في مذهب الإمام مالك إمام دار التنزيل ١: ٤٥).

p. 156. Ghazali: "As for the proof . . . ."

وأما دليل صحة الصورة التي صورناها وهو حصر جهات العالم في أربع جهات فقوله عليه الصلاة والسلام في آداب قضاء الحاجة: «لا تستقبلوا بها القبلة ولا تستدبروها ولكن شرقوا أو غربوا» وقال هذا بالمدينة والمشرق على‌ يسار المستقبل بها والمغرب على‌ يمينه.

فنهى‌ عن جهتين ورخص في جهتين ومجموع ذلك أربع جهات ولم يخطر ببال أحد أن جهات العالم يمكن أن تفرض في ست أو سبع أو عشر وكيفما كان فما حكم الباقي!

بل الجهات تثبت في الاعتقادات بناء على‌ خلقة الإنسان وليس له إلا أربع جهات قدام وخلف ويمين وشمال فكانت الجهات بالإضافة إلى‌ الإنسان في

ظاهر النظر أربعاً والشرع لا يبني إلا على مثل هذه الاعتقادات فظهر أن المطلوب الجهة (الإمام الغزالي: إحياء علوم الدين ٢: ٢٣٤-٢٣٥).

14. PORT IN A STORM

p. 165. Hadith: "Adhere to the group . . . ."

[حدثنا أحمد بن منيع حدثنا النضر بن إسماعيل أبو المغيرة عن محمد بن سوقة عن عبد الله بن دينار عن ابن عمر قال: خطبنا عمر بالجابية فقال: يا أيها الناس إني قمت فيكم كمقام رسول الله صلى الله عليه وسلم فينا فقال: أوصيكم بأصحابي ثم الذين يلونهم ثم الذين يلونهم ثم يفشو الكذب حتى يحلف الرجل ولا يستحلف، ويشهد الشاهد ولا يُستشهد، ألا لا يخلون رجل بامرأة إلا كان ثالثهما الشيطان،] عليكم بالجماعة وإياكم والفرقة فإن الشيطان مع الواحد وهو من الإثنين أبعد، من أراد بحبوحة الجنة فيلزم الجماعة [من سرّه حسنته وساءته سيئته فذلك المؤمن. قال أبو عيسى: هذا حديث حسن صحيح غريب من هذا الوجه، وقد رواه ابن المبارك عن محمد بن سوقة، وقد روي هذا الحديث من غير وجه عن عمر عن النبي صلى الله عليه وسلم] (رواه الترمذي بهذا اللفظ في الجامع الصحيح: ٤: ٤٦٥-٤٦٦ (٢١٦٥)).

p. 165. al-Azhar: "All Muslims must cease discord . . . ."

على جميع المسلمين رفع النزاع والخلاف بينهم واعتبار ما استقر عليه رأي العلماء في هذا الشأن ملزماً لا يجوز مخالفته بحال من الأحوال (من فتوى مجمع البُحوث الإسلامية بالأزهر الشريف: ص٣؛ ٢٨ شوال ١٤١٨/ ٢٥ شباط ١٩٩٨؛ القاهرة).

p. 166. Allah Most High: "Wherever you all may be . . . ."

﴿وحيث ما كنتم فولوا وجوهكم شطره﴾ (البقرة: ١٤٤).

p. 167. Ibn Hamdun: "People fall into three categories . . . ."

الناس بالنظر للتوجه في الاستقبال على ثلاثة أقسام، الأول من فرضه في التوجه اليقين إما بمعاينة كالمصلي بحضرة الكعبة، وإما بغير معاينة وهم أهل

مكة الذين يصلون في بيوتهم لحصول اليقين لهم بالمسامتة بطول المدة .

وكلاهما لا يجوز له الاجتهاد قولاً واحداً لأنه رجوع من اليقين إلىٰ الظن
[. . .] .

وهذا الحكم يجري في محراب النبي صلى الله عليه وسلم بالمدينة لأنه متوجه
إلىٰ الكعبة بيقين مقطوع لإمامة جبريل له قاله في ك ونحوه سائر المساجد
التي صلىٰ فيها رسول الله صلى الله عليه وسلم (ابن حمدون: حاشية علىٰ
شرح ميارة لمنظومة المرشد المعين ١ : ١٤٩) .

p. 168. Ahmad al-Ghurfi: "Because these instruments . . . ."
وحيث دخلت هذه الآلات من ربع واسطرلاب وغيرهما في الإسلام وعند
أهله واختبرت فوجدت تفيد اليقين للعارف بها إذا أتقنت في نفسها وجب
تقليد العارف بها لمن لا علم له بها والعمل علىٰ قوله (العلامة أحمد بن
عبدالله الغُرفي: نقله عنه الوزاني في المعيار الجديد ١ : ٢٢٣) .

p. 169. Muhammad Hisham al-Burhani: "It is not permissible . . . ."
المعاين للكعبة والمصلي إلىٰ جهة ثبتت بالنقل لا يجوز له الاجتهاد ويلحق
بهما من تحددت قبلته بوسائل العلم الحديث الدقيقة .

ومن لم يكن في واحد من الأوضاع السابقة فله الاجتهاد أو يكفيه غلبة
الظن في إصابة الجهة .

ومن المقطوع به في هذا العصر وشواهده الواقعية اليومية في حركة
الأسفار الجوية والأقمار الصناعية التي ملأت الفضاء وكل نقطة علىٰ وجه
الأرض بل والكواكب والنجوم والأجرام السابحة في الفضاء يمكن أن يكون
هدفاً وغاية محددة بدقة متناهية، وموقع الكعبة المشرفة علىٰ الأرض التي
تحولت بالعلم الحديث إلىٰ قرية صغيرة صار معروفاً ومحدداً بإحداثياته
الدقيقة بل المتناهية في الدقة .

وبناء عليه فقد صار الإنسان قادراً بلا ريب ولا تردد علىٰ معرفة موقعه
بالنسبة إلىٰ الكعبة المشرفة، فيلزمه التوجه إلىٰ عين الكعبة ولا يكفي أن
يصلي إلىٰ جهتها، اللهم إلا إذا كان بعيداً عن واقع الحضارة ومعطياتها أو
عاجزاً عن الوصول إلىٰ ذلك بعذر .

فإن العمل بالأصل هو الواجب تطبيقاً للقواعد والمبادىء العامة القائلة بأن لا يُعمل بالبدل إلا عند العجز عن الأصل كالتيمم لا يكون إلا عند فقد الماء حقيقة أو تقديراً، والاجتهاد لا يكون في مورد النص، ويطرح الشك عند مقابلة اليقين (من فتوىٰ الدكتور الشيخ محمد هشام البرهاني: ص٣؛ ٢٦ ربيع الأول ١٤٢١/ ٢٩ حزيران ٢٠٠٠؛ دمشق).

p. 172. Ibn Hamdun: "The second category...."

الثاني: مَن فرضه الاجتهاد وهو من لم يكن مقيماً بالحرمين وكان عارفاً بأدلة القبلة أو له قدرة علىٰ معرفتها فيجب عليه الاجتهاد الموصل إلىٰ جهتها كما استظهر ابن رشد في باب الأقضية من المقدمات وأشار له خ بقوله أي أي بأن لم يكن بمكة جهتها اجتهاداً فالأظهر جهتها اجتهاداً كأن نقضت وبطلت إن خالفها وإن صادف ولا يقلد مجتهداً غيره ولا محراباً إلا لمصرٍ وإن أعمىٰ وسأل عن الأدلة ابن القصار.

والبلد العامر التي تتكرر فيها الصلوات ويعلم أن إمام المسلمين نصب محرابه أو اجتمع أهل البلد علىٰ نصبه فإن العالم والعامي يقلدونه [....].

ويستأنف المجتهد الاجتهاد لكل صلاة إذ لعله يتغير اجتهاده قاله ابن شاس وابن الحاجب وفي الطراز إذا كان الوقتان تختلف فيهما الأدلة اجتهد ثانياً وإلا فلا وهو أظهر مما قاله ابن شاس وابن الحاجب [...] (ابن حمدون: حاشية علىٰ شرح ميارة لمنظومة المرشد المعين ١: ١٤٩-١٥٠).

p. 173. Ibn Hamdun: "The third category...."

الثالث: مَن فرضه التقليد وهو من لا قدرة له علىٰ الاجتهاد بأن يكون ممن لا يعرف القبلة ولا يمكنه تعلم طرق الاجتهاد فيقلد مكلفاً عارفاً عدلاً أو محراباً ولو لغير مصر (ابن حمدون: حاشية علىٰ شرح ميارة لمنظومة المرشد المعين ١: ١٥٠).

p. 174. Allah Most High: "each faction exulting...."

﴿كل حزب بما لديهم فرحون﴾ (المؤمنون: ٥٣).

APPENDIX B

The Azhar Fatwa in Arabic

الأزهر
مجمع البحوث الإسلامية
إدارة شئون اللجان والأروقة

بسم الله الرحمٰن الرحيم

رأي مجمع البحوث الإسلامية في الاتجاه إلىٰ الكعبة
في الصلاة بأمريكا الشمالية

الحمد لله، والصلاة والسلام علىٰ سيدنا رسول الله وآله وصحبه. وبعد:

فقد ورد إلىٰ صاحب الفضيلة الإمام الأكبر شيخ الأزهر خطاب من إدارة
المجمع الفقهي بالأمانة العامة برابطة العالم الإسلامي بمكة المكرمة رقم
١٠/١٠١٨٨ بتاريخ ٣ من شوال ١٤١٥هـ يتضمن سؤال الأمين العام ونائب
رئيس مجلس المجمع الفقهي الإسلامي الدكتور/ أحمد محمد علي عن
الاتجاه الصحيح للقبلة في أمريكا الشمالية، فأحال فضيلته المسألة إلىٰ مجمع
البحوث الإسلامية فشكل لجنة من علماء الشريعة وخبراء الهندسة والفلك
لدراسة الموضوع، وبعد البحث المستفيض والنظر في كل ما ورد من
استفسارات ودراسات من الجهات المختلفة ومنها مركز بحوث الشريعة
الإسلامية والمجلس الفقهي التابع للاتحاد الإسلامي في أمريكا الشمالية
والجمعية الإسلامية لأورانج كاونتي كاليفورنيا والجمعية الإسلامية للخريجين
العرب بكندا وجمعية المشاريع الخيرية الإسلامية بأمريكا الشمالية والدكتور/
كمال الدين حسين والدكتور/ توفيق محمد شاهين والسيد/ محمد أمين
العوام والسيد/ محمد حمادي من مونتريال بكندا.

ولما كان استقبال القبلة من شروط صحة الصلاة لقوله تعالىٰ: ﴿فول وجهك شطر المسجد الحرام وحيثما كنتم فولوا وجوهكم شطره﴾ (البقرة: ١٤٤)، ولما رواه مسلم في صحيحه قال رسول الله صلى الله عليه وسلم: «إذا قمت إلىٰ الصلاة فأسبغ الوضوء ثم استقبل القبلة وكبر»، ولما انعقد عليه إجماع المسلمين من وجوب استقبال القبلة في الصلاة فقد قرر جمهور الفقهاء أن المصلي الذي يعاين الكعبة عليه إصابة عينها، فإن كان بعيداً فيكفي أن يستقبل الجهة التي فيها الكعبة، ولا يلزمه أن يستقبل عينها؛ لأن الشرط هو أن يكون جزء من سطح الوجه مقابلاً لجهة الكعبة.

وفيما يلي فتوىٰ دار الإفتاء المصرية بخصوص هذا الشأن:

« إن التوجه إلىٰ القبلة في الصلاة، ركن من أركانها لقوله تعالىٰ: ﴿قد نرىٰ تقلب وجهك في السماء فلنولينك قبلة ترضاها فول وجهك شطر المسجد الحرام وحيثما كنتم فولوا وجوهكم شطره﴾ (البقرة: ١٤٤).

«أما تحديد جهة القبلة بالنسبة لأي مكان في العالم، فالذي يتولاه هم السادة المتخصصون من المهندسين وهيئات المساحة ومصلحة الأرصاد وعلماء الجغرافيا وغيرهم من المتخصصين في هذا المجال.

« ودار الإفتاء المصرية ترجو من المسلمين المقيمين بأمريكا الشمالية، أن يتبعوا ما تقوله الهيئات العلمية المتخصصة في هذا الشأن، وأن يبتعدوا عن الخلافات التي تضر ولا تنفع.

« ودار الإفتاء المصرية توافق علىٰ تحديد القبلة بالنسبة لمسلمي أمريكا الشمالية، حسب ما يقوله الخبراء في هذا الشأن، امتثالاً لقوله تعالىٰ: ﴿فاسألوا أهل الذكر إن كنتم لا تعلمون﴾ (الأنبياء: ٧) ».

وأهل الذكر في مسألة تحديد القبلة هم المهندسون ومن يعاونهم من أهل الاختصاص كعلماء الفلك والجغرافيا وغيرهم.

وبعد هذا التحديد للقبلة من أهل الاختصاص علينا أن نذكر قول الله تعالىٰ: ﴿ولله المشرق والمغرب فأينما تولوا فثم وجه الله إن الله واسع عليم﴾ (البقرة: ١١٥).

وأهل الخبرة عندنا في مصر عندما استشرناهم في هذه المسألة قالوا لنا إن

القبلة في جميع بلدان أمريكا الشمالية تكون إلىٰ شرق الشمال مع اختلاف في زاوية الانحراف من موقع إلىٰ آخر حسب خطوط الطول والعرض بما لا يخل باتجاه الشمال الشرقي .

وهناك رأي واحد خرج علىٰ إجماع مجمع البحوث الإسلامية فقال : إن اتجاه القبلة بالنسبة لأمريكا الشمالية إلىٰ الجنوب الشرقي ، والغالبية المطلقة لمجمع البحوث الإسلامية يؤيدون الرأي الأول بأنها إلىٰ شرق الشمال في أمريكا الشمالية وكندا .

(ومرفق صورة مفسرة مما كتبه الخبراء من مصر وغيرها) .

وقد استقر رأي الخبراء الذين جمعهم مجمع البحوث الإسلامية علىٰ ما يلي :

أولاً : إن اتجاه القبلة في بلدان أمريكا الشمالية عموماً إلىٰ شرق الشمال مع اختلاف في زاوية الانحراف من موقع إلىٰ آخر في تلك البلاد حسب خطوط الطول والعرض كما قرره الخبراء .

وأن المتجه إلىٰ الجنوب الشرقي في تلك البلاد يكون منحرفاً انحرافاً كبيراً يجعله علىٰ خطر عدم استقبال جهة الكعبة ولا يكون محققاً للشرط الشرعي في استقبال القبلة .

ثانياً : المحاريب التي يراد إنشاؤها في المساجد الجديدة يجب أن تتوجه إلىٰ جهة شرق الشمال مع مراعاة اختلاف زاوية الانحراف حسب خطوط الطول والعرض من موقع لآخر ، وينبغي تصحيح المحاريب القائمة الآن المخالفة لهذا الاتجاه .

وصلاة من صلىٰ إلىٰ غير ذلك من الجهات عن اجتهاد منه صحيحة فيما مضىٰ قبل هذه الفتوىٰ .

ثالثاً : يستثنىٰ مما سبق أقصىٰ شرق قارة أمريكا الشمالية فاتجاه القبلة في وسط جرينلاند هو الشرق تماماً ، وإلىٰ الشرق من هذه المنطقة يصح الاتجاه إلىٰ جنوب الشرق ، أما أقصىٰ الغرب لقارة أمريكا الشمالية عند مدينة داسون في شمال غرب كندا فاتجاه القبلة فيه إلىٰ الشمال تماماً .

وأما غرب تلك المنطقة وهي منطقة ألاسكا فاتجاه القبلة منه إلىٰ غرب الشمال .

رابعاً : علىٰ جميع المسلمين رفع النزاع والخلاف بينهم واعتبار ما استقر عليه

رأي العلماء في هذا الشأن ملزماً لا يجوز مخالفته بحال من الأحوال .

ومجمع البحوث الإسلامية يرىٰ أن القبلة في البلد الواحد يجب أن تتجه إلىٰ جهة واحدة منعاً للاختلاف ودعوة إلىٰ الوحدة التي يجب أن يعيش في ظلها المسلمون .

والله ولي التوفيق .

الأمين العام	[تحرير] عزّ العرب
لمجمـــع البحـــوث الإســلاميـــة	
[توقيع]	تحريراً في : ٢٨/١/١٤١٨هـ.
(سامي محمد متولي الشعراوي)	٢٥/٢/١٩٩٨م.

[ختم]

[ختم]

___

لتحديد اتجاه القبلة علىٰ سطح الأرض يجب التسليم بالحقائق الآتية :

١ ـ إن الأرض كروية وليست مستوية فيجب التعامل معها بقوانين المثلثات الكروية وليست قوانين الهندسة المستوية .

٢ ـ استخدام الخرائط المستوية يؤدي إلىٰ أخطاء في تحديد اتجاه القبلة حيث إن الخرائط وخاصة خرائط مركيتور يكون فيها اتجاه الشمال متوازياً عند جميع الأماكن ولكن من المفروض أن تلتقي في نقطة واحدة وهي القطب كما هو الوضع الحقيقي علىٰ سطح الكرة الأرضية .

طريقة تحديد اتجاه القبلة في مكان ما علىٰ سطح الكرة الأرضية :

يلزم لتحديد اتجاه القبلة في مكان ما أن يمر مستوىً رأسي بثلاثة نقط هي مكان المصلي ومكة المكرمة ومركز الأرض وهذا المستوىٰ يحدد اتجاه القبلة

في مكان المصلي ، ويقطع هذا المستوىٰ سطح الكرة الأرضية في دائرة تعرف بالدائرة العظمىٰ، نصف قطرها مساوٍ لنصف قطر الأرض والخط المستقيم الواصل بين المصلي ومكة المكرمة هو المماس لهذه الدائرة العظمىٰ في موقع المصلي وهو الذي يحدد اتجاه القبلة . ثم يلزم تعيين اتجاه الشمال في موقع المصلي لاتخاذه مرجعاً لمعرفة انحراف القبلة، واتجاه الشمال في أي مكان هو اتجاه القطب الشمالي وهو أحد الأدلة الشرعية في تحديد اتجاه القبلة فلهذا يلزم مستوىً رأسي آخر يمر بموقع المصلي والقطب الشمالي ومركز الأرض فيقطع هذا المستوىٰ سطح الأرض في دائرة عظمىٰ تعرف بخط طول مكان المصلي، والزاوية بين المستويين السابق ذكرهما عند مكان المصلي تحدد زاوية انحراف القبلة عن الشمال .

وبناء علىٰ ما سبق فإن الاتجاه الصحيح للقبلة في جميع بلدان أمريكا الشمالية تكون إلىٰ الشمال الشرقي مع اختلاف في زاوية الانحراف من موقع إلىٰ آخر حسب خطوط الطول والعرض بما لا يخل باتجاه الشمال الشرقي .

وكذلك بتطبيق ما سبق علىٰ أستراليا وجد أن جميع أرجائها يكون اتجاه القبلة فيها إلىٰ الشمال الغربي مع اختلاف في زاوية الانحراف من موقع إلىٰ آخر حسب خطوط الطول والعرض بما لا يخل باتجاه الشمال الغربي .

بالاطّلاع علىٰ المكاتبات والأبحاث التي وردت إلىٰ أمانة مجمع البحوث الإسلامية بخصوص هذا الموضوع اتضح أن الغالبية العظمىٰ تؤيد اتجاه القبلة بأمريكا الشمالية إلىٰ الشمال الشرقي بالحقائق العلمية والحسابات ومنهم علىٰ سبيل المثال لا الحصر :

ــ المرحوم أ . د/ حسين كمال الدين (أستاذ سابق بكليات الهندسة بمصر وجامعة الإمام محمد بن سعود الإسلامية وجامعة الرياض بالسعودية) .

ــ أ . د/ أولاف سليمكر (أستاذ الجغرافيا بجامعة كولومبيا البريطانية بكندا) .

ــ أ . د/ جون كيمرانج (أستاذ الجغرافيا بجامعة ولاية أوريجون) .

ــ د/ محمد صلاح الصاوي (مدير مركز بحوث الشريعة الإسلامية بالأكاديمية الإسلامية للبحث العلمي) .

ــ عميد بحري/ محمد عبد العزيز سلام (بالجمعية العربية للملاحة البحرية) .

ــ د/ عرفات العشي (مدير مكتب رابطة العالم الإسلامي بكندا) .

ــ د/ أحمد محمد علي (أمين عام رابطة العالم الإسلامي بمكة المكرمة ونائب رئيس المجمع الفقهي) .

هذا وبالله التوفيق . .

﴿ربنا لا تزغ قلوبنا بعد إذ هديتنا وهب لنا من لدنك رحمة إنك أنت الوهاب﴾ .

والسلام عليكم ورحمة الله وبركاته .

أعضاء اللجنة

م/ محمد مسعد إبراهيم	أ. د/ أحمد إسماعيل خليفة
م/ حمدي الشعراوي	أ. د/ أنس إبراهيم عثمان
	د/ عبد العزيز بكري

بسم الله الرحمن الرحيم

رأى مجمع البحوث الإسلامية فى الاتجاه إلى الكعبة
فــى الصــلاة بأمريكــا الشماليــــة

الحمد لله ، والصلاة والسلام على سيدنا رسول الله وآله وصحبه ٠٠ وبعد :

فقد ورد إلى صاحب الفضيلة الإمام الأكبر شيخ الأزهر خطاب من إدارة المجمع الفقهى
بالأمانة العامة برابطة العالم الإسلامى بمكة المكرمة رقم ١٠١٨٨/١٠ بتاريخ ٣ من شوال
١٤١٥ هـ يتضمن سؤال الأمين العام ونائب رئيس مجلس المجمع الفقهى الإسلامى الدكتور/
أحمد محمد على عن الاتجاه الصحيح للقبلة فى أمريكا الشمالية ، فأحال فضيلته المسألة
إلى مجمع البحوث الإسلامية فشكل لجنة من علماء الشريعة وخبراء الهندسة والفلك لدراسة
الموضوع ، وبعد البحث المستفيض والنظر فى كل ما ورد من استفسارات ودراسات مــن
الجهات المختلفة ومنها مركز بحوث الشريعة الإسلامية والمجلس الفقهى التابع للاتحـــــاد
الإسلامى فى أمريكا الشمالية والجمعية الإسلامية لأوراج كاونتى كاليفورنيا والجمعيـــــة
الإسلامية للخريجين العرب بكندا وجمعية المشاريع الخيرية الإسلامية بأمريكا الشماليــــة
والدكتور/ كمال الدين حسين والدكتور/توفيق محمد شاهين والسيد / محمد أمين العوام
والسيد / محمد حمادى من مونتريال بكندا ٠٠

ولما كان استقبال القبلة من شروط صحة الصلاة لقوله تعالى :((فول وجهك شطـر
المسجد الحرام وحيثما كنتم فولوا وجوهكم شطره)) سورة البقرة آية ١٤٤ ، ولما رواه مسلم
فى صحيحه قال رسول الله ـ صلى الله عليه وسلم ـ:" إذا قمت إلى الصلاة فأسبـــغ
الوضوء ، ثم استقبل القبلة وكبر :" ، ولما انعقد عليه إجماع المسلمين من وجوب استقبــال
القبلة فى الصلاة فقد قرر جمهور الفقهاء أن المصلى الذى يعاين الكعبة عليه إصابـــة
عينها ، فإن كان بعيدا فيكفى أن يستقبل الجهة التى فيها الكعبة ، ولايلزمه أن يستقبل
عينها ، لأن الشرط هو أن يكون جزء من سطح الوجه مقابلا لجهة الكعبة ٠٠

وفيما يلى فتوى دار الإفتاء المصرية بخصوص هذا الشأن :ــ
(إن التوجه إلى القبلة فى الصلاة ، ركن من أركانها لقوله تعالى :" قد نـرى
تقلب وجهك فى السماء فلنولينك قبلة ترضاها فول وجهك شطر المسجــد
الحرام وحيثما كنتم فولوا وجوهكم شطره" ٠٠ سورة البقرة الآية ١٤٤ ٠٠

: أما تحديد جهة القبلة بالنسبة لأى مكان فى العالم ، فالذى يتـــولاه
هم السادة المتخصصون من المهندسين وهيئات المساحة ومصلحة الأرصـاد
وعلماء الجغرافيا وغيرهم من المتخصصين فى هذا المجال ٠٠

ودار الإفتاء المصرية ترجو من المسلمين المقيمين بأمريكا الشمالية ، أن

221

(٢)

يتبعوا ما تقوله الهيئات العلمية المتخصصة فى هذا الشأن ، وأن يبتعدوا
عن الخلافات التى تضر ولا تنفع ٠٠

ودار الإفتاء المصرية توافق على تحديد القبلة بالنسبة لمصلى أمريكا
الشمالية ، حسب ما يقوله الخبراء فى هذا الشأن ، امتثالا لقوله ــ تعالى ــ
" فاسألوا أهل الذكر إن كنتم لا تعلمون " ٠٠ سورة الأنبياء : الآية ٧ ٠٠

وأهل الذكر فى مسألة تحديد القبلة هم المهندسون ومن يعاونهـم
من أهل الاختصاص كعلماء الفلك والجغرافيا وغيرهم ٠٠

وبعد هذا التحديد للقبلة من أهل الاختصاص علينا أن نذكر قـول
الله ــ تعالى ــ : " ولله المشرق والمغرب فأينما تولوا فثم وجه اللـه إن
الله واسع عليم " ٠٠ سورة البقرة : الآية ١١٥ ٠٠)

وأهل الخبرة عندنا فى مصر عندما استشرناهم فى هذه المسألة قالوا لنا إن القبلـة
فى جميع بلدان أمريكا الشمالية تكون إلى شرق الشمـال مع اختلاف فى زاوية الانحراف
من موقع إلى آخر حسب خطوط الطول والعرض بما لايخل باتجاه الشمال الشرقى ٠٠

وهناك رأى واحد خرج على إجماع مجمع البحوث الإسلامية فقال : إن اتجاه القبلـــة
بالنسبة لأمريكا الشمالية إلى الجنوب الشرقى ، والغالبية المطلقة لمجمع البحوث الإسلاميــة
يؤيدون الرأى الأول بأنها إلى شرق الشمال فى أمريكا الشمالية وكذا٠٠
(ومرفق صورة مفسرة ما كتبه الخبراء من مصر وغيرها)٠٠

وقد استقر رأى الخبراء الذين جمعهم مجمع البحوث الإسلامية على ما يلى :ــ

أولا :
        إن اتجاه القبلة فى بلدان أمريكا الشمالية عموما إلى شرق الشمال مع اختلاف
فى زاوية الانحراف من موقع إلى آخر فى تلك البلاد حسب خطوط الطول والعرض
كما قرره الخبراء ٠٠

وأن التجه إلى الجنوب الشرقى فى تلك البلاد يكون منحرفا انحرافا كبيـرا
يجعله على خطر عدم استقبال جهة الكعبة ولايكون محققا للشرط الشرعى فـى
استقبال القبلة ٠

ثانيا :
        المحاريب التى يراد إنشاؤها فى المساجد الجديدة يجب أن تتوجه إلـى
جهة شرق الشمال مع مراعاة اختلاف زاوية الانحراف حسب خطوط الطول والعرض،
من موقع لآخر ، وينبغى تصحيح المحاريب القائمة الآن المخالفة لهذا الاتجاه ٠٠
وصلاة من صلى إلى غير ذلك من الجهات عن اجتهاد منه صحيحة فيمـا

(٣)

مضى قبل هذه الفتوى ٠

ثالثا : ـــــ يستثنى ما سبق أقصى شرق قارة أمريكا الشمالية فاتجاه القبلة فى وسط
جرينلاند هو الشرق تماما ، وإلى الشرق من هذه المنطقة يصح الاتجاه إلى
جنوب الشرق أما أقصى الغرب لقارة أمريكا الشمالية عند مدينة داسون فى شمال
غرب كندا فاتجاه القبلة فيه إلى الشمال تماما ٠٠

وأما غرب تلك المنطقة وهى منطقة ألاسكا فاتجاه القبلة منه إلى غرب الشمال ٠

رابعا : ـــــ على جميع المسلمين رفع النزاع والخلاف بينهم واعتبار ما استقر عليه رأى العلماء
فى هذا الشأن ملزما لايجوز مخالفته بحال من الأحوال ٠٠

ومجمع البحوث الإسلامية يرى أن القبلة فى البلد الواحد يجب أن تتجه إلى جهة
واحدة منعا للاختلاف ودعوة إلى الوحدة التى يجب أن يعيش فى ظلها المسلمون ٠٠
واللـــه ولى التوفيق ٠٠ه

الأمين العام
لجمـــع البحوث الإسلامية
( )
(أسامى محمد متولى الشعراوى)

تحريرا فى : ٢٨/١٠/١٤١٨هـ
          ٢٥/٢/١٩٦٨م

صورة طبق الأصل

رمضان ٠٠

223

لتحديد اتجاه القبله على سطح الأرض يجب التسليم بالحقائق الآتيه -

١- إن الأرض كرويه وليست مستويه فيجب التعامل معها بقوانين المثلثات الكرويه وليست قوانين الهندسة المستويه .

٢- استخدام الخرائط المستويه يؤدى إلى أخطاء فى تحديد اتجاه القبله . حيث إن الخرائط وخاصة خرائط مركيتور يكون فيها اتجاه الشمال متوازى عند جميع الأماكن ولكن من المفروض أن تلتقى فى نقطة واحـــدة وهى القطب كما هو الوضع الحقيقى على سطح الكرة الأرضيه .

طريقة تحديد اتجاه القبله فى مكان ما على سطح الكرة الأرضيه

يلزم لتحديد اتجاه القبلة فى مكان ما أن يمر مستوى رأس بثلاثـــة نقط هى مكان المصلى ومكة المكرمة ومركز الأرض وهذا المستوى يحدد اتجاه القبله فى مكان المصلى ويقطع هذا المستوى سطح الكرة الأرضية فى دائـــرة تعرف بالدائرة العظمى قطرها مساو لنصف قطر الأرض والخط المستقيم الواصل بين المصلى ومكة المكرمة هو المماس لهذه الدائرة العظمى فى موقع المصلى وهو الذى يحدد اتجاه القبلة . ثم يلزم تعيين اتجاه الشمال فى موقـــع المصلى لاتخاذه مرجعا لمعرفة انحراف القبله ، واتجاه الشمال فى أى مكان هو اتجاه القطب الشمالى وهو أحد الأدله الشرعية فى تحديد اتجاه القبله فلهذا يلزم مستوى رأس آخر يمر بموقع المصلى والقطب الشمالى ومركـــز الأرض فيقطع هذا المستوى سطح الأرض فى دائره عظمى تعرف بخط طول مكـان المصلى والزاوية بين المستويين السابق ذكرهما عند مكان المصلى تحدد زاوية انحراف القبله عن الشمال .

وبناء على ما سبق فإن الاتجاه الصحيح للقبله فى جميع بلدان أمريكـا الشماليه تكون إلى الشمال الشرقى مع اختلاف فى زاوية الانحراف من موقـــع إلى آخر حسب خطوط الطول والعرض بما لا يخل باتجاه الشمال الشرقى .

وكذلك بتطبيق ما سبق على استراليا وجد أن جميع أرجائها يكون اتجاه القبله إلى الشمال الغربى مع اختلاف فى زاوية الانحراف من موقع إلى آخر حسب خطوط الطول والعرض بما لايخل باتجاه الشمال الغربى .

(٢)

وبالاطلاع على المكاتبات والأبحاث التى وردت إلى أمانه مجمع البحوث
الإسلاميه بخصوص هذا الموضوع اتضح أن الغالبيه العظمى تؤيد اتجـــاه القبله بأمريكا
السماليه إلى الشمال الشرقى بالحقائق العلميه والحسابات ومنهم على سبيل المثـــال
لا الحصر : ـ

ـ المرحوم أ.د/ حسين كمال الدين (أستاذ سابق بكليات الهندسه بمصر
وجامعة إمام محمد بن سعود الإسلاميه وجامعة الرياض بالسعودية)٠

ـ أ.د/ أولاف سليمكر (أستاذ الجغرافيا بجامعة كولومبيا البريطانيه
بكندا)٠

ـ أ.د/ جون كيمرانج (أستاذ الجغرافيا بجامعة ولاية أوريجون)٠

ـ د/ محمد صلاح الصاوى (مدير مركز بحوث الشريعه الإسلاميه بالأكاديميـه
الإسلاميه للبحث العلمى)٠

ـ عميد بحرى / محمد عبد العزيز سلام (بالجمعيه العربيه للملاحـــه
البحريه)٠

ـ د/ عرفات العشى (مدير مكتب رابطة العالم الإسلامى بكندا)٠

ـ د/ أحمد محمد على (أمين عام رابطة العالم الإسلامى بمكة المكرمـه
وشائب رئيس المجمع الفقهى)٠

هذا وبالله التوفيـــق ٠٠

" ربنا لاتزغ قلوبنا بعد إذ هديتنا وهب لنا من لدنك رحمه إنك أنت
الوهاب "٠

والسلام عليكم ورحمه الله وبركاته ٠٠

أعضاء اللجنه

م / محمد مسعد ابراهيم
أ.د / احمد اسماعيل خليفه   م / حمدى الشعراوى
أ.د / انس ابراهيم عثمان ابن ابراهيم
د / عبد العزيز بكرى

APPENDIX C

Other Fatwa Questions

BESIDES the Azhar Fatwa, most of the fatwas of the ulema in the present volume were given in response to four questions originally addressed to the Mufti of Damascus Dr. 'Abd al-Fattah al-Bizm by the Hanafi student Ashraf Ahmed Muneeb, who wrote them after a visit to America. He showed a copy to the author, who felt that the text might profitably be sent to scholars of different schools, and with a few changes in the specifically Hanafi content, the letter was sent to most of the scholars we have quoted.

The questions and some of the scholars' answers were written before the author learned of the existence of the Azhar Fatwa, which turned out to be the best credentialed and most thoroughgoing in dealing with the main questions of the North American qibla, including one unasked by Ashraf, namely, "Which direction is the qibla from North America?" In view of the Azhar Fatwa's sufficiency, the present volume did not quote the ulema's answers to the following questions in their entirety, but only the parts of them that shed needed light upon related issues or difficulties.

Similarly, when working on chapter 10, "Instruments and Sacred Law," the author sent two additional questions to the Mauritanian Maliki sheikh 'Abdullah al-'Alawi al-Shinqiti, whom he had met earlier in the year in Yemen, and to three Maliki scholars in Fez, of the latter of whom one alone replied, Dr. Muhammad al-Tawil. The texts of Ashraf's and the author's questions have been translated into English as follows:

I. LETTER TO THE MUFTI OF DAMASCUS

I visited a certain foreign country in the summertime, in which some mosques had been built whose mihrabs were placed according to the principles of applied geometry (handasa, lit. "engineering") and mathematics. Certain distinguished scholars then visited those places, some of whom stated that the existing mihrabs were mistaken, and so far off as to lead to the invalidity of the prayer in that direction. When a discussion took place among scholars about how the qibla should be determined, they disagreed about the bases and principles upon which determination of the qibla should be made. The points of the disagreement have been summarized and put in the form of questions presented to your eminence, in hope that your eminence may honor us by answering them, to end the disagreement, and that the principles may be known upon which the qibla is to be determined according to the Hanafi school.

The First Question

Among the expressions used by Hanafi jurists in their books when they mention that facing the qibla is a condition for the validity of prayer is that "what is obligatory for someone who cannot see it is to face the direction (jiha) of the Kaaba."

What is the definition of direction? Does it mean the shortest path?

If the meaning of "direction" is the shortest path, is this definition legal, lexical, or physical? For the fuqaha have not mentioned in their books that the meaning of "direction" is the shortest path.

The Second Question

Ibn 'Abidin mentions in the commentary *Radd al-muhtar* that "the matter of the qibla is only to be ascertained by the principles of applied geometry (handasa) and mathematics, through knowing the distance of Mecca from the equator and from the west [i.e. its position latitudinally and longitudinally] as well as that of the city in question, it then being calculated according to these principles to ascertain the actual direction (samt) of the qibla."

Is the matter of determining the qibla to be left entirely to scholars of applied geometry (handasa), it not being permissible for the faqih to make a statement about the direction of the qibla unless he adduces its evidences, knows them, and knows how to draw conclusions from them?

227

If the matter of the qibla returns to those knowledgeable in applied geometry and mathematics, is the calculation of the direction of the qibla made on the basis of the earth being round or the earth being flat?

If you say [it should be made] on the basis of the earth being round, what is the proof of this, in view of the fact that the fuqaha do not mention in their books that the sphericality of the earth is a condition for calculating the direction of the qibla?

And if you say on the basis of the earth being flat, do his [Ibn 'Abidin's] words above "then it is calculated according to those rules" mean that we draw a straight line [on a flat map] between the place and Mecca, calculate the angle of its declination from north, and that is the direction of Mecca?

The Third Question

It is mentioned in the books of fiqh that "the fundamental evidences of the qibla are six, which are: (1) knowledge of the longitude and latitude of cities combined with the 'geometer's circle' or other geometrical forms; (2) the North Star; (3) the stars; (4) the sun; (5) the moon; and (6) the winds, which are the weakest evidence, for the strongest is the knowledge of longitude and latitude, then the North Star [, then the others]."[1]

Why have the stars been placed third among the fundamental evidences of the qibla, while Allah mentions in His Noble Book, 'And by the stars they are guided' [Qur'an 16:16].

Does "guided" in the noble verse mean finding out the cardinal directions of north, south, east, and west—or rather that one is guided by the stars to knowledge of the direction of the qibla, in a city where there are no old mihrabs, and the testimony of its people is unacceptable?

The Fourth Question

If a faqih goes to a city where there are mihrabs placed not by the prophetic Companions (Sahaba) or their followers, but rather

---

[1] The quotation is from *al-Dhakhira* (e66), 2.123–24, by the Maliki Imam al-Qarafi, which was cited in an article Ashraf found on qibla determination by the late Sheikh al-Azhar Jad al-Haqq.

according to the direction (samt) determined by trustworthy people possessing knowledge of applied geometry and mathematics, and he then personally checks for the qibla and prays towards the direction revealed by his checking, which contravenes the direction of the mosque qiblas—is his own checking for the direction valid, or must he face their mihrabs and established qiblas?

What position should ordinary Muslims adopt in such a case? Should they follow the ijtihad of the faqih, or follow those with knowledge of applied geometry and mathematics? Or are they free to choose between the two? And if it subsequently becomes known that the view of whomever they followed was mistaken, are they obliged to make up the prayers?

If there are differing mihrabs in a particular place (not established by the prophetic Companions or their followers) and each party claims to be certain that their determination of the direction of the qibla is correct, although 90 percent or more of the people pray in a particular direction, is this considered a legal consensus (ijma') on the correctness of the qibla in that direction? And is it obligatory for those who disagree to follow this direction, or not?

II. LETTER TO SHEIKH 'ABDULLAH AL-SHINQITI

May Allah continue to bless you with well-being and true faith. I hope that you are well, and that you remember my visiting you in the library of the [Shari'a] College [in Tarim] in the company of the Jordanian Amjad Rashid some five months ago. As I am working on a book on the subject of determining the qibla in North America, I asked you at that time about the view of Maliki scholars on the use of instruments for determining the qibla and prayer times, and whether there was any offensiveness (karaha) in it. You answered that there was no offensiveness therein according to the [Maliki] school.

The reason for the question was that some of those teaching Maliki fiqh in the United States and Britain have claimed that using a compass for the above-mentioned purpose is offensive, as is relying on a world globe instead of a flat map, since such a physical object resembles an instrument—all of which they ascribe to the school of Imam Malik (Allah be well pleased with him).

This position is perhaps lent support by the words of Imam Ibn Siraj which al-Wansharisi quotes in the *Mi'yar al-mu'rib* (1.122) "As for seeking the direction with instruments, it has not been conveyed from the pious early Muslims (Allah be well pleased with them), so they [instruments] are unnecessary to refer to, and may not be made the criterion governing the evidences of Sacred Law. It is sufficient for someone who uses instruments as evidence to merely establish the approximate direction (jiha), since it is known through inference that one can correctly ascertain the approximate direction by them."

They have also said that using clocks to know the time of the prayer is offensive, as well as seeking the assistance of the prayer-time calendars (produced, as is known, by specialists in this field), saying that the school of the Malikis entails that the legally responsible individual should rely only upon seeing his own shadow in determining the time of the prayer, not on clocks or calendars. To all of which, you replied at the time there was no offensiveness in it. We would like you to kindly provide a detailed written response of a page or two to the foregoing, to put in the above-mentioned work.

APPENDIX D

Map Projections

———

THIS APPENDIX has been added because "for him who has not travelled, his mother is the only cook," and someone unfamiliar with maps might think of the Mercator projection as the one "Map of the World." A glance through the maps below is meant to show not only that the Mercator is but one among many, but also that any reduction of our three-dimensional world to two dimensions entails distortion, from which the specific merits of each map are merely the exception. The examples are drawn from Snyder and Voxland's *An Album of Map Projections* (e83), in conformity with which we use the term *meridian* below for lines of longitude, and *parallel* for latitudes.

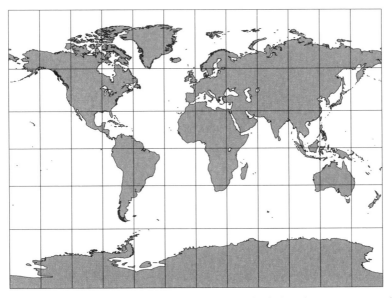

1. THE GALL PROJECTION. Drawn by James Gall of Edinburgh in 1855, it expands the degrees of latitude as it proceeds away from the equator, though not as fast as the Mercator, so there is less area-distortion at the poles.

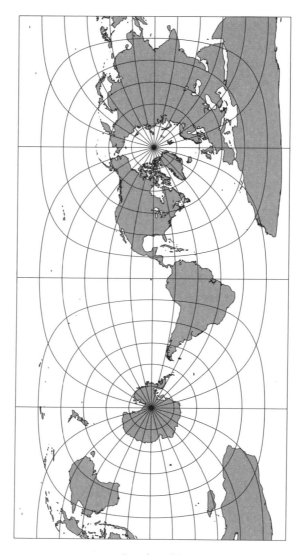

2. THE CASSINI PROJECTION. Developed by César François Cassini de Thury (1714–84) in the mid-18th century for the topographic mapping of France, the Cassini projection displays virtually no distortion along the central meridian, though both area-distortion and local shape distortion occur elsewhere, their intensity being a function of the distance from the central axis. The scale remains true along the central axis and along any of the straight lines perpendicular to it, which represent the equator and the meridians 90 degrees from the central axis.

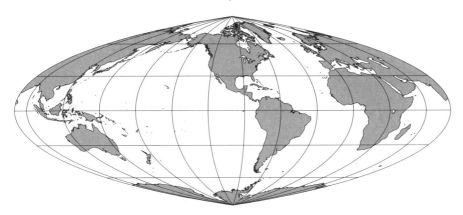

3. QUARTIC AUTHALIC PROJECTION. Drawn by Karl Siemon of Germany in 1937, the quartic authalic projection is true to scale along the equator. The scale is constant along any given parallel, and the same for the latitude of the opposite sign, north to south. In relation to the cartographic grid, the areas of all regions are shown in the same proportion to their true areas. Free of distortion at the equator, distortion is severe near the outer meridians at high latitudes.

4. HAMMER RETROAZIMUTHAL PROJECTION. First presented by H. H. Ernst von Hammer of Germany in 1910. Though extreme in distortion of area and shape, it was designed so that the direction from any point to the center of the map is the angle that a straight line connecting the two points makes with a vertical line. Its use is to determine the direction of the central point from any given location. Like other azimuthal projections, a different map must be drawn for each desired central point.

233

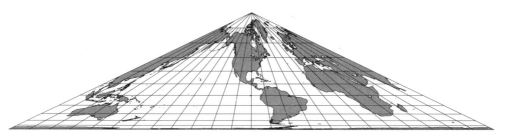

5. COLLIGNON PROJECTION. Produced by Édouard Collignon of France in 1865, the relative scale is constant along any give parallel, though different for each parallel. It is free of distortion only at 15° 51' North at the central north-south meridian and there is considerable shape-distortion elsewhere. Because it is an "equal-area projection," the areas shown are proportional to their true areas.

6. WERNER PROJECTION. Like the Collignon above, it is an equal-area projection, the areas shown being proportional to their counterparts in the real world in relation to the cartographic grid. It is free of distortion only along the central meridian, though it is true to scale along the central meridian and along each parallel. Known also as the "Stab-Werner projection," it was drawn by Johannes Stab of Vienna around 1500 and promoted by Johannes Werner of Nuremberg in 1514. It was frequently used for world and continental maps of the 16th and 17th centuries.

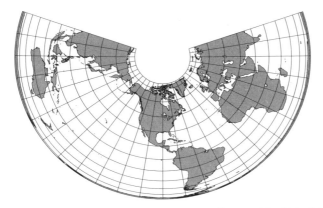

7. **ALBERS EQUAL-AREA CONIC PROJECTION.** Presented by Heinrich Christian Albers of Germany in 1805, it is conic, meaning resulting from the conceptual projection of the earth onto a tangent or secant cone, which is then cut lengthwise and laid flat. When the axis of the cone coincides with the polar axis of the earth, as it does here, all meridians are straight equidistant radii of concentric circular arcs representing the parallels. It is an "equal-area projection" showing the areas of all regions in the same proportion to their true areas.

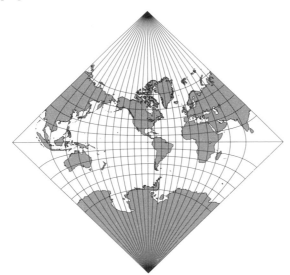

8. **ADAMS WORLD IN A SQUARE II.** Sometimes used for whole-world maps, it was drawn by Oscar Sherman Adams of the U.S. Coast and Geodetic Survey in 1925. It is conformal, meaning a projection in which all angles at each point are preserved. It has also been called an "orthomorphic projection." There is great area-distortion near the 180 meridians as well as at the higher latitudes.

235

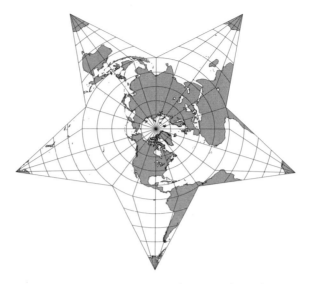

9. BERGHAUS STAR PROJECTION. Drawn by Heinrich Berghaus of Germany in 1879, its scale is constant along all great circle directions from the North Pole, and parallels are spaced in proportion to their true distance along each meridian. It is true to scale along meridians in the Northern Hemisphere and along the central meridians of the triangular points in the Southern Hemisphere.

10. VAN DER GRINTEN III PROJECTION. It was produced by Alphons J. van der Grinten of Chicago in 1904. The lines of latitude are depicted as straight lines, and it is true to scale along the equator, although the scale increases rapidly with distance from the equator, and there is great area-distortion near the poles.

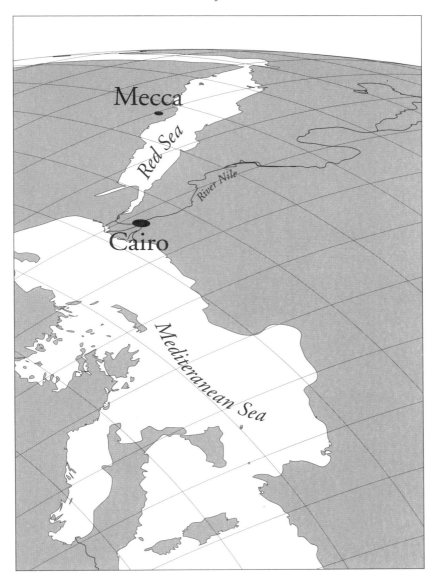

11. TILTED PERSPECTIVE PROJECTION. Developed primarily during the 20th century, it shows the earth geometrically as it would appear if photographed. While there is substantial distortion of shape, area, and scale if a large area is covered, it is used to provide pictorial views of the earth resembling those seen from space.

237

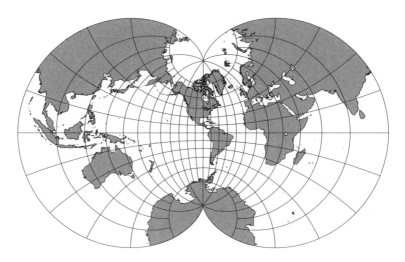

12. EISENLOHR PROJECTION. First drawn by Friedrich Eisenlohr of Germany in 1870, it is conformal, meaning a projection in which all angles are preserved at each point relative to the cartographic grid. Although there is great area distortion near the 180 meridians in comparison to the center because the scale increases rapidly as one proceeds away from it, the scale is constant around the boundary of a world map, so the Eisenlohr provides a minimal overall scale variation for a conformal map of the world.

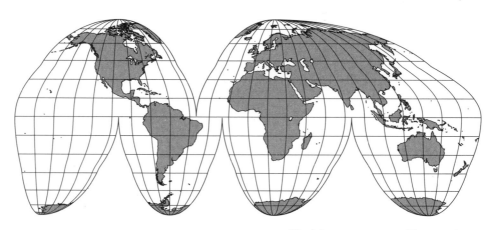

13. GOODE HOMOLOSINE PROJECTION. Used in numerous world maps, it was developed in 1923 by J. Paul Goode of the University of Chicago. It is an equal-area projection that is true to scale along every latitude between 40° 44' North and South and along the central meridian within the same latitudes.

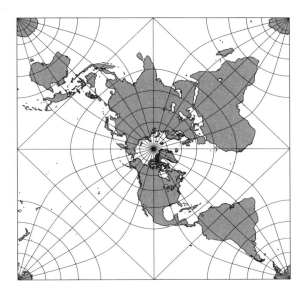

14. PEIRCE QUINCUNCIAL PROJECTION. Originated by the American scientist and philosopher Charles Sanders Peirce in 1879, it varies in scale considerably along each meridian and parallel, and there is great distortion of area, especially near each 90th meridian at the equator, although everywhere else it is conformal, preserving, relative to the cartographic grid, all angles as they actually are.

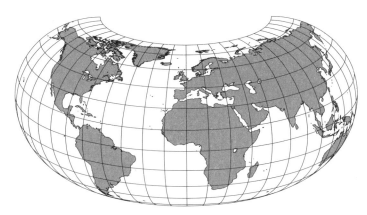

15. ARMADILLO PROJECTION. It is used in world maps, and is said to have more land area in proportion to sea that any other map of the world. Neither conformal nor equal-area, the map's distortion is moderate in central portions, though the scale gradually decreases with distance from the center. The Antarctic region cannot be shown. It was first drawn by Erwin J. Raisz of Harvard University in 1943.

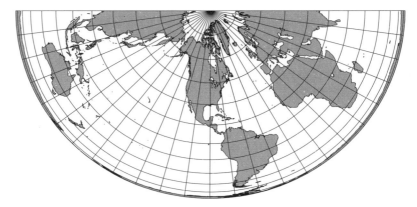

16. LAMBERT EQUAL-AREA CONIC PROJECTION. Presented by Johann Heinrich Lambert of Alsace in 1772, it is true to scale and free of angular distortion only along the chosen standard parallel, which in this example is the equator. There is severe stretching near each pole. Scale and angle distortion are constant along any given parallel, and being an equal-area projection, the areas it depicts are proportional to their actual areas.

17. WIECHEL PROJECTION. Normally only polar in aspect, it is an equal-area projection, like the Lambert above. While there is considerable distortion of shape at the map edge, it is true to scale along the meridians, and is classified as a modified azimuthal projection, showing the correct direction from any place to the central point relative to its cartographic grid. It was first drawn by H. Wiechel in 1879.

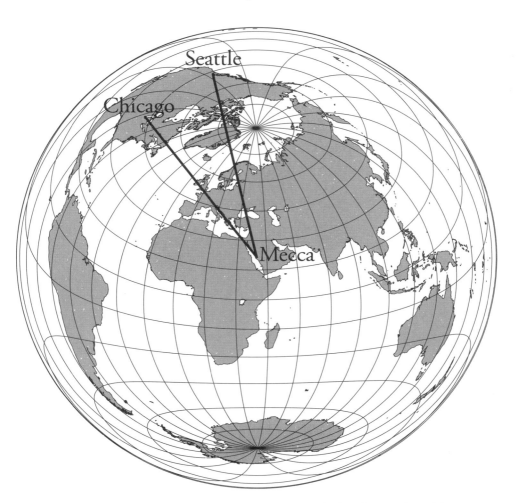

18. MECCAN AZIMUTHAL PROJECTION. A straight line from one's position on the map to the center reveals the true direction of Mecca from anywhere in the world relative to the cartographic grid. Other features of azimuthal projection maps have been discussed on pages 66 to 68 above. It has been reproduced here on a larger scale to facilitate photocopying for use in geographical qibla ijtihad by travellers.

APPENDIX E

Works and Documents Cited

━━━

e1   Abdali, S. Kamal. "The Correct Qibla." Internet article: http: // www.patriot.net/users/abdali/ftp/qibla. Washington D.C.: Abdali, 1997.

e2   'Abd al-Wahhab, Hasan. *Tarikh al-masajid al-athariyya fi al-Qahira.* 2 vols. Cairo: Maktaba al-Dar al-'Arabiyya li al-Kitab, 1413/ 1993.

e3   al-Abi, Salih ibn 'Abd al-Sami'. *Jawahir al-iklil sharh Mukhtasar al-'Allama Shaykh Khalil fi madhhab al-Imam Malik Imam Dar al-Tanzil* [an interlineal commentary on the *Mukhtasar* of Khalil ibn Ishaq al-Jundi]. 2 vols. Cairo n.d. Reprint. Beirut: 'Alam al-Kutub, n.d.

e4   Ahdab, Ahmad Talal, Ahson Ahmad, and Mostafa Azzam. Letter to author. 16 July 2000. Toronto. 1 page. Author's collection.

e5   al-'Alami, Idris Muhammad. *Fatwa.* 1 Dhul Hijja 1420/ 8 March 2000.[1] Fez. 2 pages. Author's collection.

e6   al-Amidi, 'Ali ibn Muhammad. *al-Ihkam fi usul al-ahkam.* Ed. 'Abd al-Razzaq 'Afifi. 4 vols. in 2. Beirut: al-Maktab al-Islami, 1402/1982.

e7   al-'Amrawi, Muhammad. *Fatwa.* 25 Rabi' I 1421/ 28 June 2000. Fez. 1 page. Author's collection.

e8   al-'Asqalani, Ibn Hajar, and Muhammad ibn Isma'il al-Bukhari. *Fath al-Bari bi sharh Sahih al-Bukhari* [a commentary by 'Asqalani on the hadiths of Bukhari's *al-Jami' al-sahih*]. Edited by Muhammad Fu'ad 'Abd al-Baqi and Muhibb al-Din al-Khatib. 14 vols. Cairo: al-Maktaba al-Salafiyya, 1390/1970.

---

[1] Some of the lunar hijra dates on the fatwas are based on local sightings of the moon, and so there is not complete consistency with the solar dates between countries. Fatwas undated by muftis were estimated or dated as received by the author.

e9 Ba-'Alawi, 'Abd al-Rahman. *Bughya al-mustarshidin fi talkhis fatawa ba'd al-a'imma min al-muta'akhkhirin.* Cairo: Mustafa al-Babi al-Halabi wa Akhuwahu, 1325/1907.

e10 Badran, Isma'il. *Fatwa.* 28 Safar 1421/ 1 June 2000. Duma, Syria. 1 page. Author's collection.

e11 al-Balisani, Ahmad. *Fatwa.* 14 Rajab 1421/ 12 October 2000. Baghdad. 2 pages. Author's collection.

e12 al-Bannuri, Muhammad Yusuf. *Bughya al-arib fi masa'il al-qibla wa al-maharib.* Cairo: Matba'a al-'Ulum, 1358/1939.

e13 Becker, Robert O. *Cross Currents: The Perils of Electropollution, the Promise of Electromedicine.* Los Angeles: Jeremy P. Tarcher, 1990.

e14 al-Biruni, Abu al-Rayhan. *Kitab al-tafhim li awa'il sina'a al-tanjim* [facing pages of Arabic text and an English translation entitled "The Book of Instruction in the Elements of the Art of Astrology"]. Tr. R. Ramsay Wright. London: Luzac, 1353/1934.

e15 ———. *Kitab tahdid nihayat al-amakin li tas-hih masafat al-masakin.* Ed. P. Boljakov and Imam Ibrahim Ahmad. Cairo: Ma'had al-Makhtutat al-'Arabiyya, 1416/1995.

e16 al-Bizm, 'Abd al-Fattah. *Fatwa.* 21 Jumada I 1421/ 21 August 2000. Damascus. 1 page. Author's collection.

e17 al-Buhuti, Mansur. *Kashshaf al-qina' 'an matn al-Iqna'.* 6 vols. Beirut: Dar al-Fikr, 1402/1982.

e18 al-Bukhari, Muhammad ibn Isma'il. *Sahih al-Bukhari.* 9 vols. Cairo 1313/1895. Reprint (9 vols. in 3). Beirut: Dar al-Jil, n.d.

e19 al-Burhani, Muhammad Hisham. *Fatwa.* 26 Rabi' I 1421/ 29 June 2000. Damascus. 3 pages. Author's collection.

e20 al-Buti, Muhammad Sa'id Ramadan. *Fatwa.* 1 Dhul Hijja 1420/ 7 March 2000. Damascus. 2 pages. Author's collection.

e21 al-Dardir, Ahmad. *al-Sharh al-saghir 'ala Aqrab al-masalik ila madhhab al-Imam Malik* [Dardir's interlineal commentary *al-Sharh al-saghir* on his own *Aqrab al-masalik ila madhhab al-Imam Malik* printed above Ahmad al-Sawi's interlineal commentary on both entitled *Bulgha al-salik li Aqrab al-masalik*]. 4 vols. Cairo: Dar al-Maʿarif, 1394/ 1974.

e22   al-Dusuqi, Muhammad ibn ʿArafa. *Hashiya al-Dusuqi ʿala al-Sharh al-kabir li al-Shaykh Abi al-Barakat Sayyidi Ahmad ibn Muhammad al-ʿAdawi al-shahir bi al-Dardir* [al-Dusuqi's interlineal commentary on al-Dardir's *Sharh al-kabir,* with notes by Muhammad ʿUlaysh]. Ed. Muhammad ʿAbdullah Shahin. 6 vols. Beirut: Dar al-Kutub al-ʿIlmiyya, 1417/1996.

e23   Encyclopædia Britannica Publishing Group. *The New Encyclopædia Britannica.* 32 vols. including Propædia and 2 index vols. Chicago: Encyclopædia Britannica Inc., 1994.

e24   al-Farra', Yahya ibn Ziyad. *Maʿani al-Qur'an.* 3 vols. N.p., n.d. Reprint. Beirut: ʿAlam al-Kutub, 1403/1983.

e25   al-Fayruzabadi, Majd al-Din. *al-Qamus al-muhit.* Ed. Muhammad Naʿim al-ʿIrqsusi. Beirut: Mu'assasa al-Risala, 1419/1998.

e26   al-Ghazali, Abu Hamid. *Ihya' ʿulum al-din* [with notes on its hadiths by Zayn al-Din al-ʿIraqi printed below it, and ʿUmar al-Suhrawardi's *ʿAwarif al-maʿarif* on its margins]. 4 vols. Cairo 1347/1929. Reprint. Beirut: ʿAlam al-Kutub, n.d.

e27   ————. *al-Mustasfa min ʿilm al-usul.* 2 vols. Cairo 1322/1904. Reprint. Beirut: Dar al-Kutub al-ʿIlmiyya, 1403/1983.

e28   al-Hadrami, ʿAbd al-Rahman ibn ʿAbdullah. *Jamiʿa al-Ashaʿir Zabid.* Sanʿa: al-Sharika al-Yamaniyya, 1394/1974.

e29   al-Hajri, Muhammad ibn Ahmad. *Majmuʿ buldan al-Yaman wa qaba'iliha.* Ed. Ismaʿil ibn ʿAli al-Akwaʿ. 2 vols. Sanʿa: Wizara al-Aʿlam wa al-Thaqafa. 1404/1984.

e30   ————. *Masajid Sanʿa'.* Sanʿa 1361/1942. Reprint. Beirut: Dar Ihya' al-Turath al-ʿArabi, 1398/1978.

e31   al-Hakim, Abu 'Abdullah. *al-Mustadrak 'ala al-Sahihayn*. 4 vols. Hyderabad, 1334/1916. Reprint (with index vol. 5). Beirut: Dar al-Ma'rifa, n.d.

e32   al-Hattab, Muhammad ibn Muhammad. *Mawahib al-Jalil li sharh Mukhtasar Khalil*. 6 vols. Cairo 1329/1911 [a commentary on the *Mukhtasar* of Khalil ibn Ishaq al-Jundi, printed interlineally with it, accompanied on its margin by another interlineal commentary on the *Mukhtasar* by Muhammad ibn Yusuf al-Mawwaq entitled *al-Taj wa al-iklil li Mukhtasar Khalil*]. Reprint. Beirut: Dar al-Fikr, 1412/1992.

e33   al-Haytami, Ahmad Ibn Hajar. *Tuhfa al-muhtaj bi sharh al-Minhaj*. 10 vols. Cairo 1315/1898 [a commentary on the *Minhaj al-talibin* of Imam Nawawi, printed interlineally with it on the margins of two supercommentaries on the *Tuhfa* by 'Abd al-Hamid al-Shirwani (above) and Ahmad ibn Qasim al-'Abbadi (below)]. Reprint. Beirut: Dar al-Fikr, n.d.

e34   al-Hindi, Hassan. *Fatwa*. 18 Rabi' II 1421/ 20 July 2000. Damascus. 8 pages. Author's collection.

e35   Ibn 'Abd al-Barr, Abu 'Umar. *al-Istidhkar al-jami' li madhahib fuqaha' al-amsar wa 'ulama' al-aqtar fi ma tadammanahu al-Muwatta' min ma'ani al-ray' wa al-athar wa sharh dhalika kullihi bi al-ijaz wa al-ikhtisar*. Ed. 'Abd al-Mu'ti Amin Qal'aji. 30 vols. Aleppo and Cairo: Dar al-Wa'y; and Damascus and Beirut: Dar Qutayba, 1414/1993.

e36   ———. *al-Kafi fi fiqh Ahl al-Madina al-Maliki*. Beirut: Dar al-Kutub al-'Ilmiyya, 1407/1987.

e37   Ibn 'Abidin, Muhammad Amin. *Radd al-muhtar 'ala al-Durr al-mukhtar*. 5 vols. Bulaq 1272/1855. Reprint. Beirut: Dar Ihya' al-Turath al-'Arabi, 1407/1987.

e38   Ibn Duqmaq, Ibrahim ibn Muhammad. *al-Intisar li wasita 'iqd al-amsar*. 4 vols. Bulaq: al-Matba'a al-Kubra al-Amiriyya, 1309/1892.

e39   Ibn al-Hajib, Jamal al-Din. *Jami' al-ummahat*. Ed. 'Abd al-Rahman al-Akhdar al-Akhdari. Beirut: al-Yamama li al-Tiba'a wa al-Nashr, 1408/1988.

e40   Ibn Hamdun, Muhammad al-Talib. *Hashiya Muhammad al-Talib ibn Hamdun al-Hajj 'ala Sharh Muhammad Ahmad al-shahir bi Mayyara li Manzuma al-Murshid al-mu'in li Ibn 'Ashir* [Mayyara's commentary on Ibn 'Ashir's *Murshid al-mu'in* printed interlineally with it on the margin of Ibn Hamdun's supercommentary]. 2 vols. Cairo 1355/1936. Reprint. Beirut: Dar al-Fikr, 1398/1978.

e41   Ibn Hazm, Abu Muhammad. *al-fisal fi al-milal wa al-ahwa' wa al-nihal.* Eds. 'Abd al-Rahman 'Amira and Muhammad Ibrahim Nasr. 5 vols. N.p., n.d. Beirut: Dar al-Jil, n.d.

e42   Ibn al-Manzur, Muhammad. *Lisan al-'Arab.* 15 vols. Beirut: Dar Sadir, 1410/1990.

e43   Ibn Qudama al-Maqdisi, Muwaffaq al-Din. *al-Mughni* [Ibn Qudama's interlineal commentary on the *Mukhtasar* of 'Umar al-Khiraqi]. 9 vols. Cairo n.d. Reprint (with index vols. 10 and 11). Beirut: Dar Ihya' al-Turath al-'Arabi, 1413/1993.

e44   Ibn Rushd, Abul Walid. *al-Bayan wa al-tahsil wa al-sharh wa al-tawjih wa al-ta'lil fi masa'il al-Mustakhraja.* 20 vols. Beirut: Dar al-Gharb al-Islami, 1404/1984.

e45   Ibn al-Shaykh Abu Bakr ibn Salem, (Habib) 'Alawi ibn (Habib) Ahmad, Astronomer. Article written at the request of Mahmoud Jastaniah bearing the title: *Ta'yin ittijahat al-Ka'ba al-Musharrafa min ayy makan 'ala sat-h al-ard* [Determining the direction of the Noble Kaaba from any place on the face of the earth], 22 July 2000. Mecca. 2 pages. Author's collection.

e46   al-Isfahani, al-Raghib. *Mufradat alfaz al-Qur'an.* Edited by Safwan 'Adnan Dawudi. Beirut: al-Dar al-Shamiyya, and Damascus: Dar al-Qalam, 1418/1998.

e47   Islamic Research Academy, al-Azhar. *Fatwa.* 28 Shawwal 1418/ 25 February 1998 Cairo. 3 pages (and enclosure of 2 pages). Certified copy: 6 Dhul Qa'da 1420/ 12 February 2000. al-Azhar, Cairo. Author's Collection.

e48   Jad al-Haqq, Jad al-Haqq 'Ali. *Buhuth wa fatawa Islamiyya fi qadaya mu'asira.* 5 vols. Cairo: al-Azhar al-Sharif, al-Amana al-'Amma li al-Lajna al-'Ulya li al-Da'wa al-Islamiyya, 1414/1994.

e49   Jastaniah, Mahmoud. Letter to author, 23 July 2000. Jedda. 1 page. Author's collection.

e50   al-Karmi, Muhammad Khalil. *Fatwa.* 12 Jumada II 1421/ 10 September 2000. Aleppo. 2 pages. Author's collection.

e51   Kennedy, H. S., and M. H. Kennedy. *Geographical Coordinates of Localities from Islamic Sources.* Frankfurt: Institut für Geschichte Wissenschaften an der Johann Wolfgang Goethe-Universität, 1987.

e52   al-Kharashi, Muhammad. *al-Kharashi 'ala Mukhtasar Sayyidi Khalil* [a commentary on the *Mukhtasar* of Khalil ibn Ishaq al-Jundi, printed interlineally with it, and accompanied on its margin by a supercommentary on al-Kharashi by 'Ali al-'Adawi entitled *Hashiya al-Shaykh 'Ali ibn Ahmad al-Sa'idi al-'Adawi 'ala Sharh al-Kharashi*]. 8 vols. Cairo 1318/1900. Reprint (8 vols. in 4). Beirut: Dar Sadir, n.d.

e53   King, David. *World Maps for finding the Direction and Distance to Mecca: Innovation and Tradition in Islamic Science.* Leiden: Brill, in association with Al-Furqan Islamic Heritage Foundation of London, 1999.

e54   Majlis al-Ifta' bi Tarim [al-Habib al-Sayyid Hasan ibn Mihsin al-Hamid al-Shaykh Abu Bakr, Sheikh Muhammad 'Ali Faraj Ba-'Udan, al-Habib 'Ali Mashhur ibn Muhammad ibn Salem ibn Hafidh, Sheikh Muhammad 'Ali al-Khatib, al-Habib 'Umar ibn Ahmad al-Mashhur, and al-Habib 'Abdullah ibn Muhammad ibn Shihab]. *Fatwa.* 13 Jumada II 1421/ 12 September 2000. Tarim, Wadi Hadramawt, Yemen. 5 pages. Author's collection.

e55   Malik ibn Anas. *al-Mudawwana al-kubra* [Malik's *Mudawwana* printed above Ibn Rushd's *Muqaddimat Ibn Rushd li bayan ma aqtadat-hu al-Mudawwana min al-ahkam*]. 4 vols. Cairo n.d. Reprint. Beirut: Dar al-Fikr, 1411/1991.

e56   al-Maliki, 'Abd al-Wahhab ibn 'Ali. *al-Ma'una 'ala madhhab 'Alim al-Madina.* 2 vols. Beirut: Dar al-Kutub al-'Ilmiyya, 1410/1988.

e57   al-Manufi, 'Ali ibn Nasir al-Din. *Kifaya al-talib al-rabbani bi Risala ibn Abi Zayd al-Qayrawani* [a commentary on the *Risala* of Imam Ibn Abi Zayd al-Qayrawani printed interlineally with it on the margins of the supercommentary of 'Ali al-'Adawi on al-Manufi's work entitled *Hashiya al-'Adawi 'ala Kifaya al-talib al-rabbani bi Risala Ibn Abi Zayd al-Qayrawani*]. Ed. Muhammad 'Abdullah Shahin. 2 vols. Beirut: Dar al-Kutub al-'Ilmiyya, 1418/1997.

e58   al-Maqrizi, Ahmad ibn 'Ali. *al-Mawa'iz wa al-i'tibar bi dhikr al-khitat wa al-athar.* 2 vols. Cairo: Maktaba al-Thaqafa al-Diniyya, 1409/1987.

e59   al-Maruni, Muhammad ibn 'Abd al-Malik. *al-Wajiz fi tarikh binaya masajid San'a' al-qadim wa al-jadid.* San'a: Matabi' al-Yaman al-'Asriyya, 1408/1988.

e60   al-Mazari, Muhammad. *Sharh al-Talqin li 'Abd al-Wahhab ibn 'Ali ibn Nasr al-Maliki.* Ed. Muhammad al-Mukhtar al-Sallami. 3 vols. Beirut: Dar al-Gharb al-Islami, 1418/1997.

e61   Mujahid ibn Jabr. *Tafsir al-Imam Mujahid ibn Jabr.* Ed. Muhammad 'Abd al-Salam Abu al-Nil. Cairo: Dar al-Fikr al-Islami al-Haditha, 1410/1989.

e62   Muslim ibn al-Hajjaj. *Sahih Muslim.* Ed. Muhammad Fu'ad 'Abd al-Baqi. 5 vols. Cairo 1376/1956. Reprint. Beirut: Dar al-Fikr, 1403/1983.

e63   al-Nawawi, Yahya ibn Sharaf, Abu Ishaq al-Shirazi, and Taqi al-Din al-Subki. *al-Majmu': sharh al-Muhadhdhab* [Shirazi's *Muhadhdhab* printed with Nawawi's interlineal commentary, which is completed by Subki's supplement (vols. 10–20) *Takmila al-Majmu'*]. 20 vols. Cairo n.d. Reprint. Medina: al-Maktaba al-Salafiyya, n.d.

e64   Newspaper Enterprise Association. *The World Almanac and Book of Facts 1986.* Ed. Hana Umlauf Lane. New York: Newspaper Enterprise Association, 1985.

e65   al-Qalqashandi, Ahmad ibn 'Ali. *Subh al-a'sha fi sina'a al-insha.* 3 vols. Beirut: Dar al-Kutub al-'Ilmiyya, 1407/1987.

e66   al-Qarafi, Ahmad ibn Idris. *al-Dhakhira.* Eds. Sa'id A'rab, Muhammad Bu-Khubza, and Muhammad Hajji. 14 vols. Beirut: Dar al-Gharb al-Islami, 1415/1994.

e67   al-Qastallani, Ahmad. *Irshad al-sari li sharh Sahih al-Bukhari.* 10 vols. Bulaq 1306/1888. Reprint. Beirut: Dar al-Fikr, 1410/1989.

e68   al-Qayrawani, Ibn Abi Zayd. *al-Nawadir wa al-ziyadat 'ala ma fi al-Mudawwana min ghayriha min al-ummahat.* Ed. 'Abd al-Fattah al-Halu. 15 vols. Beirut: Dar al-Gharb al-Islami, 1420/1999.

e69   al-Qinnawji, Siddiq Hasan Khan. *Abjad al-'ulum: al-Washy al-marqum fi bayan ahwal al-'ulum.* Damascus: Wizara al-Thaqafa wa al-Irshad al-Qawmi, 1407/1987.

e70   al-Qudah, Nuh 'Ali Salman. *Fatwa.* 7 Dhul Hijja 1420/ 13 March 2000. Tehran. 4 pages. Author's collection.

e71   al-Qurtubi, Muhammad ibn Ahmad. *al-Jami' li ahkam al-Qur'an.* Eds. Ahmad 'Abd al-'Alim al-Burduni, Bashandi Khalafa Allah, Ibrahim Itfaysh, and Muhammad Muhammad Hasanayn. 20 vols. Cairo 1387/1967. Reprint (20 vols. in 10). Beirut: Dar Ihya' al-Turath al-'Arabi, n.d.

e72   Ramadan, Muhammad. *Fatwa.* 12 Rajab 1420/ 10 October 2000. Baghdad. 1 page. Author's Collection.

e73   al-Ramli, Khayr al-Din. *al-Fatawa al-Khayriyya li naf' al-bariyya 'ala madhhab al-Imam al-A'zam Abi Hanifa al-Nu'man* [printed on the margins of Ibn 'Abidin's *al-'Uqud al-durriyya fi tanqih al-Fatawa al-Hamidiyya*]. 2 vols. Cairo: Matba'a al-Amiriyya, 1236/1821.

e74   al-Rassa', Muhammad. *Sharh Hudud Ibn 'Arafa: al-mawsum al-Hidaya al-kafiya li bayan haqa'iq al-Imam Ibn 'Arafa al-wafiya.* Eds. Muhammad Abu al-Ajfan and al-Tahir al-Ma'muri. 2 vols. Beirut: Dar al-Gharb al-Islami, 1414–15/1993.

e75   Razi, Fakhr al-Din. *al-Mahsul fi 'ilm al-usul.* Ed. Taha Jabir al-'Alwani. 6 vols. including final index volume. Beirut: Mu'assasa al-Risala, 1418/1998.

e76 ———. *Tafsir al-Fakhr al-Razi al-mushtahir bi al-Tafsir al-kabir wa Mafatih al-ghayb*. 32 vols. Beirut 1401/1981. Reprint (32 vols. in 16). Beirut: Dar al-Fikr, 1405/1985.

e77 al-Rugi, Muhammad. *Fatwa*. 3 Dhul Hijja 1420/ 10 March 2000. Fez. 3 pages. Author's collection.

e78 al-Sa'di, 'Abd al-Malik. *Fatwa*. 21 Rajab 1421/ 20 October 2000. Ramadi, Iraq. 3 pages. Author's collection.

e79 al-Saqqaf, 'Alawi ibn Ahmad. *Tarshih al-mustafidin bi tawshih Fath al-Mu'in* [al-Saqqaf's *Tarshih al-mustafidin* printed interlineally with the commentary *Fath al-Mu'in* of 'Abd al-'Aziz al-Mallibari on his own *Qurrat al-'Ayn,* accompanied on the lower half of the page by al-Saqqaf's additional comments upon (ziyadat) and clarifications of (taqrirat) his *Tarshih*]. Cairo: Dar Ihya al-Kutub al-'Arabiyya: 'Isa Babi al-Halabi wa Shuraka'uhu, n.d.

e80 al-Shafi'i, Muhammad ibn Idris. *Mawsu'a al-Imam al-Shafi'i: Kitab al-umm*. Ed. Ahmad Badr al-Din Hassun. 15 vols. in 10. Beirut: Dar Qutayba, 1416/1996.

e81 al-Shatibi, Abu Ishaq. *al-Muwafaqat fi usul al-shari'a*. Ed. Ibrahim Ramadan. 4 vols. in 2. Beirut: Dar al-Ma'rifa, 1420/1999.

e82 al-Shinqiti, 'Abdullah ibn Aslam al-'Alawi. *Fatwa*. 23 Jumada II 1421/ 21 September 2000. Tarim, Wadi Hadramawt, Yemen. 4 pages. Author's collection.

e83 Snyder, John P., and Philip M. Voxland. *An Album of Map Projections* [U.S. Geological Survey Professional Paper 1453]. Washington, D.C.: United States Government Printing Office, 1989.

e84 al-Subki, Taj al-Din. *Jam' al-jawami'* [printed with the interlineal commentary of Imam Jalal al-Din al-Mahalli, together with the super-commentary of al-Bannani below them, accompanied on its margins by the *Taqrir* of 'Abd al-Rahman al-Shirbini]. 2 vols. Cairo: Mustafa al-Babi al-Halabi wa Awladuhu, 1356/1937.

e85 al-Subki, Taj al-Din, and Taqi al-Din al-Subki. *al-Ibhaj fi sharh al-Minhaj:* [an interlineal commentary upon the *Minhaj al-wusul ila 'ilm al-usul* of al-Qadi al-Baydawi begun by Imam Taqi al-Din al-Subki, and completed from page 105 of the first volume to the end by his son Taj al-Din]. 3 vols. Beirut: Dar al-Kutub al-'Ilmiyya, 1404/1984.

e86 al-Subki, Taqi al-Din. *al-'Alam al-manshur fi ithbat al-shuhur.* Damascus 1328/1910. Ed. Muhammad Jamal al-Din al-Qasimi. Reprint. Riyad: Maktaba al-Imam al-Shafi'i, n.d.

e87 al-Subki, Taqi al-Din. *Fatawa al-Subki.* 2 vols. N.p., n.d. Reprint. Beirut: Dar al-Ma'rifa, n.d.

e88 al-Suyuti, Jalal al-Din, *Husn al-muhadara fi tarikh Misr wa al-Qahira.* Ed. Muhammad Abu al-Fadl Ibrahim. 2 vols. Cairo: Dar Ihya al-Kutub al-'Arabiyya: 'Isa al-Babi al-Halabi wa Shuraka'uhu, 1387/ 1967.

e89 al-Tabari, Ibn Jarir. *Jami' al-bayan 'an ta'wil ay al-Qur'an.* 30 vols. Cairo n.d. Reprint (30 vols. in 15). Beirut: Dar al-Fikr, 1405/1984.

e90 al-Tawil, Muhammad. *Fatwa.* 3 Dhul Hijja 1420/ 10 March 2000. Fez. 9 pages. Author's collection.

e91 ———. *Fatwa.* 7 Sha'ban 1421/ 3 November 2000. Fez. 2 pages. Author's collection.

e92 al-Tawil, Taha. *Islam in Iowa: The Islamic Center of Cedar Rapids, Iowa, U.S.A.* Cedar Rapids: Islamic Center and Mosque of Cedar Rapids, Iowa, n.d.

e93 al-Tirmidhi, Abu 'Isa. *Sunan al-Tirmidhi.* Ed. Muhammad Fu'ad 'Abd al-Baqi. 5 vols. Cairo n.d. Reprint. Beirut: Dar Ihya al-Turath al-'Arabi, n.d.

e94 al-Tusi, Nasir al-Din. *Kitab al-tadhkira fi 'ilm al-hay'a.* Ed. 'Abbas Sulayman. Kuwait: Dar Su'ad al-Sabah, 1413/1993.

e95 'Ulaysh, Muhammad. *Minah al-Jalil 'ala Mukhtasar Khalil* [a commentary on the *Mukhtasar* of Khalil ibn Ishaq al-Jundi, printed interlineally with it, and accompanied on its margin by a supercommentary on the *Minah* by 'Ulaysh entitled *Tas-hil Minah al-Jalil*]. 4 vols. Cairo 1294/1877. Reprint. Tripoli, Libya: Maktaba al-Najah, n.d.

e96   al-Wansharisi, Ahmad ibn Yahya. *al-Mi'yar al-mu'rib wa al-jami' al-mughrib 'an fatawi ahl Ifriqiya wa al-Andalus wa al-Maghrib.* 13 vols. Rabat and Beirut: Wizara al-Awqaf wa al-Shu'un al-Islamiyya li al-Mamlaka al-Maghribiyya and Dar al-Gharb al-Islami, 1401/1981.

e97   al-Wazzani, Muhammad al-Mahdi. *al-Nawazil al-jadida al-kubra fi ma li ahl Fas wa ghayrihim min al-badu wa al-qura, al-musamma bi al-Mi'yar al-jadid al-jami' al-mu'rib 'an fatawa al-muta'akhkhirin min 'ulama' al-Maghrib.* Ed. 'Umar Ibn 'Abbad. 8 vols. Rabat: Wizara al-Awqaf wa al-Shu'un al-Islamiyya li al-Mamlaka al-Maghribiyya, 1419/1998.

e98   Whitfield, Peter. *The Image of the World: 20 Centuries of World Maps.* San Francisco: Pomegranate Artbooks, in association with The British Library, 1994.

e99   al-Zajjaj, Abu Ishaq. *Ma'ani al-Qur'an.* Ed. 'Abd al-Jalil 'Abduh Shalabi. 5 vols. Cairo: Dar al-Hadith, 1414/1994.

e100   Zambouras, George J., Professional Engineer. Report to 'Imad al-Din Abu Hijleh, 28 May 2000. Beverly, Massachusetts. 1 page. Author's collection.

e101   Zarruq, Ahmad. *Sharh 'ala matn al-Risala li Ibn Abi Zayd al-Qayrawani* [a commentary on the *Risala* of Imam Ibn Abi Zayd al-Qayrawani, printed interlineally with it, accompanied on the bottom half of the page with another commentary on the *Risala* by Qasim ibn 'Isa al-Tanukhi entitled *Sharh Qasim ibn 'Isa ibn Naji al-Tanukhi*]. 2 vols. Cairo 1332/1914. Reprint (2 vols. in 1). Beirut: Dar al-Fikr, 1402/1982.

e102   al-Zuhayli, Wahbeh. *Fatwa.* 15 Dhul Hijja 1420/ 21 March 2000. Damascus. 2 pages. Author's collection.

Subject Index

253

Section Index

PORT IN A STORM

The principle text of this book is set in
11½ point Adobe Garamond, a typeface designed
for photocomposition by Robert Slimbach from the original
sixteenth-century face by Claude Garamond. The Arabic texts are set
in Abjad, a typeface designed by Muhammad al-Khatib. The cartography
was drawn with Geocart 2.6. The paper is vol. 16 White Antique Wove
made by Trekbrook Limited. It is of archival quality and acid-free.
The composition is by Sohail Nakhooda. Printing and binding
by Biddles Limited, Guildford and King's Lynn.
Designed by Nuh Ha Mim Keller.

اَلْعِلْمُ بَيْنَ أَهْلِ الْفَضْلِ وَالْعَقْلِ رَحِمٌ مُتَّصِلٌ

Learning, among the virtuous
and intelligent, is a strong family tie

IMAM SHAFI'I